CW00394417

Bo

990122318 0

Our sincere gratitude to the World Council of Churches for their generous financial support for this book project. We are particularly indebted to the Programme to Combat Racism (PCR) for the commitment of their staff and the organisational support they gave for the Harare seminar and the editorial work they provided for the manuscript of this book.

We are also grateful to the Oak Foundation for a research grant which enabled Lindy Wilson to conduct interviews with former BCM activists around the world and to write the biographical chapter on Steve Biko.

Thanks also to the Ford Foundation for their contribution to publication and distribution costs. We are grateful for the co-operation of all those who gave their time to be interviewed, particularly the Biko family members without whose assistance this book would have been impoverished.

Thanks to the participants of the Harare seminar which formed part of the process of producing this book. We would also like to express our appreciation to SAPES Trust for their assistance with the logistics of the seminar.

We would like to express our sincere gratitude to our publishers David Philip and Zed Press, particularly to the dedicated editors Russell Martin and John Daniel who gave so generously of their time to shape this book into its present form.

Above all, we salute all the heroes and heroines of the BC period, particularly those who paid the supreme sacrifice for the liberation of their country. This book is dedicated to all of them.

BOUNDS *of* POSSIBILITY

The Legacy of Steve Biko
& Black Consciousness

EDITED BY

N. Barney Pityana, Mamphela Ramphele,
Malusi Mpumlwana & Lindy Wilson

DAVID PHILIP: Cape Town
ZED BOOKS: London & New Jersey

Bounds of Possibility was first published in 1991 in
southern Africa by David Philip Publishers (Pty) Ltd,
208 Werdmuller Centre, Claremont 7700, South
Africa. First published in the Rest of the World by
Zed Books Ltd, 57 Caledonian Road, London
N1 9BU, UK, and 165 First Avenue, Atlantic
Highlands, New Jersey 07716, USA, in 1992.

Copyright © The editors (selection, arrangement and
Introduction); individual authors (for their particular
chapters), 1991.

Cover designed by Andrew Corbett.
Cover picture by courtesy of IDAF.
Printed and bound in the United Kingdom by
Biddles Ltd, Guildford and King's Lynn.

All rights reserved.

A catalogue record for this book is available from the
British Library.

ISBN 1 85649 047 5 Hb
ISBN 1 85649 048 3 Pb

GLOUCESTERSHIRE
CLASS
COPY
COUNTY LIBRARY

Contents

The Editors and Contributors

NEVILLE ALEXANDER is an educationist and secretary of the Health, Education and Welfare Society of South Africa.

GEOFF BUDLENDER, an attorney, is deputy national director of the Legal Resources Centre, Johannesburg

SIPHO BUTHELEZI is a senior lecturer in political economy and development studies at the Teacher Training College in Harare, Zimbabwe

C. R. D. HALISI is an assistant professor of political science at the University of Indiana

DWIGHT HOPKINS is an assistant professor of ethnic and religious studies at Santa Clara University, California

KEITH MOKOAPE is a senior member of Umkhonto we Sizwe

KOGILA MOODLEY is an associate professor of social and educational studies at the University of British Columbia, Vancouver

MALUSI MPUMLWANA is a minister involved in community work in Uitenhage, Eastern Cape

THENJIWE MTINTSO has been the ANC's ambassador to Uganda

MBULELO MZAMANE is a visiting professor in the department of comparative literature at the University of Georgia

WELILE NHLAPO works for the ANC

N. BARNEY PITYANA is director of the World Council of Churches' Programme to Combat Racism

MAMPHELA RAMPHELE is deputy vice-chancellor of the University of Cape Town and a research officer in the department of social anthropology

C. D. T. SIBISI is consultant psychiatrist at Dudley Hospital in the West Midlands, England

LINDY WILSON is an educationist and film-maker

Foreword

It was British Prime Minister Harold Macmillan who first challenged the minority rulers of South Africa with his speech about the 'winds of change'. That was in 1960, when the process of decolonisation was raging through the continent. There was much hope and a great deal of confidence about the future prospects for Africa. A new breed of African leaders was about to take centre-stage in world affairs. But just as these changes were occurring in the rest of Africa, South Africa, almost alone in the continent, was determined to resist them. Instead of hope, ominous clouds were gathering. 1960 is best remembered the world over less for Macmillan's prophetic words than for events associated with Sharpeville. It was Sharpeville which awakened the world community to the scale of the conflict which was about to engulf South Africa.

It was in such circumstances that my predecessor and founder General Secretary of the World Council of Churches, the late Dr W. Visser 't Hooft, called together a consultation of churches in South Africa to discuss what he called 'the race problem'. In his report to the Central Committee subsequent to what became known as the Cottesloe Consultation, Visser 't Hooft said: 'Our hope must be that through such a meeting of minds we will not only help to create more real ecumenical fellowship between the churches of all races in South Africa and between them and the World Council of Churches, but also and especially make a substantial contribution to the cause of justice and freedom for all races of mankind'.

That is the vision which has consistently guided the witness of the World Council of Churches regarding South Africa throughout the past three decades. It has at times seemed like a lonely pilgrimage and, more painfully, we were often at loggerheads with our member churches in South Africa, not just with the Dutch Reformed Churches.

Those in-between times need to be faithfully recorded. Apartheid seemed to be unstoppable and all our international efforts were too slow to show results. Meanwhile, within South Africa wave after wave of repression was gathering force. There were many momentous events in those dark years: the granting of 'independence' to the Bantustans, the Soweto revolt of 1976 and the emergence of the mass democratic movement in 1983. But the death of Bantu Stephen Biko in police custody in September 1977 outraged the world and set in motion a renewed determination to rid the world of apartheid. It seemed like the apartheid regime was out to crush any hope of an alternative society. The ideas associated with Biko and the Black Consciousness Movement bore all the hallmarks of a bright future for South Africa. After his death, his words were studied more closely, and only then did the scale of the tragedy for South Africa and the world strike us. At the World Council of Churches, the death of Steve Biko became an occasion for a renewed mobilisation and an opportunity to demonstrate the evil of apartheid.

Today, South Africa is at the threshold of a future that lies open ahead. There are many obstacles and stumbling-blocks as the tragedy of Inkatha-gate so graphically demonstrates. Our concern is that the people of South Africa should talk together about the future of their country. We owe it to Steve Biko, who taught the oppressed people of South Africa that there can be no freedom without sacrifice. Sacrifices are still being made in South Africa today.

Everyone now acknowledges that apartheid is the enemy of an open society. The key for the future is to devise constitutional mechanisms that guarantee human freedoms, civil rights and equal opportunities for all. That is the challenge which faces all South Africans today.

That is why I am delighted that the World Council of Churches has been associated with this project from its early stages. We saw it as a contribution to constructive dialogue among all South Africans about the present, the past and the future. It built upon the foundations of Cottesloe and, more recently, of Rustenburg. That is the South Africa which the ecumenical movement wishes to accompany on the journey to the promised land. I wish to add a personal word of gratitude to the editors for inviting me to write a Foreword to the book, *Bounds of Possibility*. Its appearance could not be more timely.

EMILIO CASTRO
Geneva
Feast of the Transfiguration, 1991

1

Introduction

N. BARNEY PITYANA, MAMPHELA RAMPHELE, MALUSI MPUMLWANA & LINDY WILSON

Without the search for meaning, the quest for vision, there can be no authentic movement towards liberation, no true identity or radical integration for an individual or a people. Above all, where there is no vision, we lose the sense of our great power to transcend history and create a new future for ourselves with others, and we perish utterly in hopelessness, mutual terror and despair. Therefore this quest is not a luxury; life itself demands it of us (Harding, 1983:xii).

Ideas about history, its meaning and how societies are shaped by historical processes are now undergoing radical revision. Events in Eastern Europe, the so-called end of the Cold War, and *glasnost* and *perestroika* in the Soviet Union, have brought into question the interpretations and analyses of history which formed the bedrock of the self-understanding and identity of Soviet and Communist states. Now, says V. Shostokovsky, a Party ideologue, 'It's a devastating thing for any society to discover that their greatest myths are based not on truth but on propaganda and fantasy. But that is what we are experiencing now in the case of Lenin and the revolution' (*International Herald Tribune*, 22 April 1991). This rereading of history strikes at the very roots of Soviet society. When not even the memory of Lenin is spared from this radical reassessment, then something fundamental is taking place. The necessity of historical revision applies as much to South Africa.

This introduction seeks to set, in a social and intellectual context, the place of both Steve Biko and the Black Consciousness Movement in the struggle for liberation in South Africa. We are mindful of the fact that this is being written within the bowels of changing times. We must accept that there is bound to be subjectivism. Understandably, many of our recollections and observations are coloured both by our experience since 1976 and by our intellectual development. In addition, we are committed to a process of imagination and deconstruction which will become evident in the pages that follow. Decoding and encoding take place at both conscious and unconscious levels, and some reinterpretations will be offered in the light of mature understanding and reflection. There are also instances where there may be a dispute about what is recollected. It will not surprise us if some readers put different nuances on the events and interpretations recorded here.

The essays in this volume, indeed the entire enterprise initiated by the editors, were not simply motivated by an ideological desire to develop the kind of liberatory history of Steve Biko and the Black Consciousness Movement which the Afro-American historian Vincent Harding proposes. We declare quite openly that we are all friends of the late Steve Biko and committed by our love for him and bitterness at the gruesome manner in which he was killed. Above that, however, we are political activists as committed to political change in our country as we were during the time of our participation in SASO and Black Consciousness in the 1970s. We are alive to the fact that after more than ten years, Biko and the memory of him are still very much with us. This volume also seeks to encourage debate about the quality of our society which we all have the privilege to participate in moulding. It is our belief that Black Consciousness has an important contribution to make to the debate.

This enterprise began out of our own experience of pain. The death of Steve Biko on 12 September 1977 shattered us emotionally, as it did countless others in South Africa. For us the feeling was not so much surprise that the regime was capable of such brutality. Other dear friends and comrades with whom we had shared bannings, detention without trial and various forms of torture had suffered the same fate: we were horrified by their deaths. But somehow Steve's murder struck nearer to home, close to the heart. We were for a time numbed but fearless, angry but impotent. We knew that part of ourselves had died with him. However, *a luta continua*. We all had lives to lead. We were thrust into the diaspora, and our lives even changed direction. But we always retained a close, though invisible and inexplicable bond. There was in our very being an insatiable need for fulfilment.

This Biko project was but part of that journey towards self-realisation. But it was 'the self' that was not solitude. The needful wrestling with ourselves, participation in our personal and political struggles, the therapeutic effect of reliving that past, the drawing together of many friends and comrades, talking seriously about political developments and changes in our own political understandings and commitments, the divergent political routes we have all taken – all these have never dimmed our bond, and through our writing we wanted to share our extraordinary experience with others.

Of course, in death Steve Biko soon became a phenomenon. Donald Woods wrote and spoke passionately about him, testifying to the impact he made on his life and that of his family. Biko's papers were published and widely distributed and translated. Sir Richard Attenborough directed and produced the film *Cry Freedom*, the story of the relationship between Donald Woods and Biko. Various television documentaries on the inquest into Steve's death appeared, and a stage production was performed in the West End of London. In 1987, the BBC Ebony programme produced a documentary to mark the tenth anniversary of Steve's death.

An initial idea of a major biography which we and a wider circle of friends first mooted never materialised because we felt that there was a need to allow time to create an historical distance so as to ensure an objective assessment of both Biko and Black Consciousness and their contribution to the liberation struggle in South Africa. No such definitive biography is available. But the task remains. The people who participated in Black Consciousness should speak for themselves. It is only when the historical subjects speak as agents of history that they shape the direction of society.

This volume is for us a tool and a method of understanding and evaluation. To bring out the manysidedness of Steve's contribution to the liberation struggle, we needed to bring together comrades and friends, social analysts, researchers and scholars from South Africa and abroad, and activists from across the political spectrum of the liberation movement. The goal was twofold: one, an analysis of Steve's life and political contributions in the context of the political developments in South Africa today; two, to demonstrate that Steve Biko's philosophy and the ideas of Black Consciousness have spread through the whole thought structure of liberatory politics in South Africa.

Some seventy participants attended a symposium in Harare in June 1990 on the theme, 'The Legacy of Bantu Stephen Biko'. The symposium brought together, some said for the first time, many who had been involved in the struggle with Biko but had since moved in diverse directions of political engagement within South Africa and in exile. There were some emotional reunions. Political differences were, for a moment, cast aside as stories of various pilgrimages were retold. Controversy emerged when the Harare-based Black Consciousness Movement of Azania (BCMA) and Azanian People's Organisation (AZAPO) from within South Africa decided to stay away. Many were deeply saddened by that. This, of course, did point to some of the cleavages among admirers of Biko and adherents of Black Consciousness which have made it no longer possible to share a common memory of a fallen comrade.

The symposium was co-sponsored by the World Council of Churches' Programme to Combat Racism, SAPES Trust in Harare and the University of Zimbabwe's Department of Political Studies. Unfortunately, it has not been possible to publish all the papers presented at Harare. We present here only a selection.

South Africa Today

The address by State President F. W. de Klerk to parliament on 2 February 1990 set South Africa on a path of transition. 'Reform' became part of the Nationalist vocabulary and 'negotiating a constitutional settlement' sprang into South Africa's political lexicon. What brought the apartheid regime to

that momentous point was a combination of factors, ranging from the persistent urban unrest, the growth and militancy of the trade unions, international isolation and economic sanctions. All these factors made it clear for
the government that the writing was on the wall. When P. W. Botha suffered a stroke in 1989, so low had the fortunes of the apartheid regime sunk
that there was a danger of paralysis setting in and the country going down
with him. Within the ruling National Party, it became apparent that new
strategies for survival were urgently required. De Klerk was the answer.

The process of transition from authoritarian rule which De Klerk set in
motion on 2 February 1990 has to be understood within an international
context. In the body of literature that has emerged over the last few years
documenting a number of case studies around the world (see O'Donnell
& Schmitter, 1986), the transition from authoritarian rule has been
defined as consisting of three phases: liberalisation, democratisation and
socialisation. The liberalisation phase is characterised by the opening up
of political space, allowing former opponents of the regime to operate
legally and without harassment from the government of the day. The
democratisation phase is marked by the holding of democratic elections
on the basis of an agreed constitution, while the socialisation phase
involves the creation and internalisation of a culture of participatory
democracy. South Africa is thus in the liberalisation phase at present.

What has been achieved, however, must be set against the backdrop of
the apartheid inheritance: a pervasive social crisis. The economy is stag-
nant and no significant new investment from overseas has been recorded
for years. Unemployment remains high because of public and private
sector mismanagement of the economy, and the priorities set by the
government. Flight from the hardships of rural poverty has resulted in
make-shift shanty towns (*favellas*) mushrooming on the peripheries of
most urban centres. Since the pass laws were lifted in 1986, enabling
freer movement to the cities, increasing population pressure has been
applied to the inadequate infrastructure of urban townships. Among
other things, the chronic lack of housing has grown daily.

Education has also suffered greatly. Since 1976, most children of school-
going age have hardly experienced a year of uninterrupted schooling.
Schools have been disrupted by legitimate protests and crippled by political opportunism. The combination of young people in the streets and sustained political protest in the townships has produced a generation of
streetwise children who have challenged the traditional social and political
structures of authority and control. Family life is being disrupted, and
social cohesion can no longer be taken for granted. Alongside efforts at
political reform and liberalisation, therefore, there remains a litany of crises
which the De Klerk government has failed so far to address. The dangerous
combination of social disintegration and economic bankruptcy is a recipe
for a disaster of catastrophic proportions. No policies have yet emerged to
address such a deep-seated crisis at all levels of society. It is not enough
merely to open up political space. Constraints on socio-economic develop-

ment need to be urgently reviewed as an essential part of the proc
political transition. The rising expectations of those previously excl
from the resources of this country are being frustrated, with alarm
implications for the future.

The South African crisis must also be seen in the context of the changes
now engulfing large parts of the world. Worthy of special note is the
crisis of confidence in the policies and programmes of social management
which are being rapidly abandoned. In Eastern Europe, Africa and Latin
America dictatorial regimes have been discredited. There have been too
many civil wars and too much political instability in Africa. Though
much of it was generated and sustained by Cold War interests, the
responsibility must remain attributable to bad government. Throughout
Africa there is a growing popular movement for human rights and participatory democracy.

This movement, far from buying into George Bush's 'New World Order',
can be said to represent a new search for sustainable values, social mores
and standards of order determined not so much by super-power interests
as by the refusal of many countries to become pawns in the game of super-
power politics. The demise of socialism should not be seen as authentica-
tion of the capitalist order. While the values attached to each individual in
the liberal democratic models have merit, any attempt to elevate self-
interest, individualism and achievement above care for the vulnerable and
opening up of opportunity for all, has to be resisted. True change requires
new values, new principles of participation and sustainability.

Emerging Trends

Violence

A dominant feature of South Africa since the epoch-making changes
were announced in February 1990 has been the unleashing of a spiral of
violence in the black communities. Black townships have been turned into
killing fields, whirlpools of violent confrontation between opposing political forces. Though no serious opposition to President De Klerk's reforms
can be detected from the majority of the white electorate, it seems that elements within the security forces are bent on trying to shipwreck De Klerk's
initiatives by fomenting violence and operating as a 'third force'.

Violence has become endemic in South Africa. Thousands of people have
died. Even before the De Klerk reforms, Natal was plunged into civil war
between members of Inkatha and the UDF. As ANC leaders returned home
from prison or exile, and began to organise politically, so the contest for
political space increased. Inkatha claimed and demanded total allegiance
from the people of Natal, whom for too long it claimed to represent in their
millions. The inroads being made by the ANC could not be allowed.
Warlords soon took the stage and unleashed untold death and destruction
on people in the villages around Pietermaritzburg. As the contest took root,

the conflagration became unstoppable.

In the years and months immediately preceding 2 February 1990, Inkatha had set itself up as a competitor for power in relation to the ANC. The contradiction between Inkatha rhetoric of non-violence and its involvement in violence in both Natal and on the Reef is a matter of concern for many South Africans. Competition between the ANC and Inkatha was also heightened by the latter's shedding of its Zulu character to become the Inkatha Freedom Party at the beginning of 1990. Inkatha was thus asserting itself as a national political force. Violence escalated country-wide as the contest for political turf increased. Revelations made in July 1991 of government funding of Inkatha confirmed suspicions long held that the government was attempting to weaken the ANC's position.

A recent (May 1991) report by CASE (the Community Agency for Social Enquiry) on violence in the Reef area reveals that 66 per cent of all acts of violence was attributable to Inkatha, 21 per cent to security forces and vigilantes and 6 per cent to elements associated with the ANC. The same report states that 1 805 people had died as a result of political violence in the Reef townships over a nine-month period, averaging seven people per day. These are by any account shocking figures.

The Reef violence centred mainly upon the notorious single men's hostels. Armed men killed indiscriminately, making attacks on the suburban trains and railway stations, against shack dwellers and wherever people gathered. Allegations were now made not just of connivance in the violence by some members of the police and security forces, but that men were known to be trained to kill in camps related to South Africa's security forces under the guise of training as security guards. Then the unthinkable began to happen: African traditions of mourning and respect for the dead were cast aside and massacres took place during funeral vigils. It was with exasperation that Archbishop Desmond Tutu spoke to the hearts of people in his Easter 1991 sermon at St George's Cathedral, Cape Town. He asked, more in pain than in anger, what had gone wrong with African people, their values and their sense of self-respect and national pride?

Violence is, however, not limited to Inkatha and the ANC. There are reported incidents of violence between the ANC and the PAC, between ANC and AZAPO, and other factions in many parts of South Africa. Bekkersdal on the West Rand is an example of a whole community engulfed by violence perpetrated by young people, where retribution and counter-retribution assumed frightening proportions towards the end of 1990.

Archbishop Tutu's question about what is wrong with the black community challenges one to see violence as a symptom of a sick society. The culture of violence has become part of the political and social landscape of South Africa. Several causes account for this. Firstly, domination of the majority by a minority requires violence, both institutional and physical, to enforce it. This process of repression, oppression and resistance has brutalised both the oppressor and the oppressed. Secondly, South Africa as a society has no experience of a culture of tolerance and democratic decision-making. The settlement of disputes and differences in viewpoints has tended to follow the route of violence rather than rational discussion. Thirdly, the social evil of the migrant labour system, as well as the related institution of migrant hostels in urban townships, needs to be addressed as a matter of urgency. Many of the migrant labour hostels are organised along tribal lines, which creates a serious potential for ethnic conflict. The immersion of hostel dwellers in filth and their lack of privacy 'kills a man's pride', as Matshoba (see Hodge, 1987) has so eloquently expressed it. Despised by township residents, among whom they live, hostel dwellers have responded with hostility. Such mutual antipathy is fertile ground for violence.[1]

Finally, the significant involvement of youth in the violence, as victims and perpetrators, across the political spectrum has serious implications. Both black and white youth in South Africa have been 'conscripted into the civil war' which has ravaged our society in recent years. Society is now paying the price of having in its midst young people whose only real skills are in the area of conflict and violence. Experiences in other parts of the world, notably the Middle East, point to the danger of violence becoming 'a beast which devours its children' (*Weekly Mail*, 14–20 June 1991).

Post-Honeymoon Blues

The general euphoria following the opening up of political space in February 1990 has since given way to greater realism. The romanticisation of political heroes and the formerly banned organisations that obtained after their release and unbanning has been replaced by a realistic assessment of their performance since their re-entry into the political arena. As the recently unbanned political organisations returned to assert their authority and leadership in the transition process, uncertainty at first characterised the mood amongst local political activists. Thereafter, competition for significant positions within liberation movement groupings has intensified.

In the more sober mood of today there is greater recognition of the real differences in the nature and conduct of the struggle against apartheid as waged by those outside and inside the country over the last two decades. These differences emerged as a logical consequence of the historical circumstances which shaped the strategies adopted by those inside the country as distinct from those outside. Firstly, exile politics of all kinds were led

1 J. Qwelane, in a column in the *Weekend Argus*, points to a systematic process of labelling and derogatory remarks about hostel dwellers as being part of township culture. They have also been subject to exclusion from township organisations and decision-making processes, even in matters affecting them, such as consumer boycotts. It is only very recently that in areas such as Alexandra, attempts have been made to include them. The Western Cape is a notable exception because of the work of the Western Cape Hostel Dwellers Association.

primarily by people strongly steeped in the Congress tradition of the 1950s. Their style of leadership, approaches to participation by ordinary members in decision-making and their vision of a liberated South Africa were all products of that particular tradition. It is thus not surprising to find amongst them a predominance of elderly men.

In contrast, political activists inside the country are mostly shaped by the political revival of the 1970s which the Black Consciousness Movement brought about in the aftermath of the massive repression of the early 1960s. Some had been imprisoned in the clampdown following the Soweto uprising of 1976, and had joined one or other (banned) organisation during that period. The youngest amongst these activists are products of the post-1976 era and the militant politics of the 1980s, when internal politics were characterised by a rhetoric of democratic participation, which was in practice achieved in large measure within the trade-union movement and, to a lesser extent, in civic association politics.

The restructuring of unbanned organisations has generated tensions between the two different traditions, which the South African press has tended to reduce to personalities. Anton Harber correctly pointed to the tension within the ANC between the tendency of returning exiles to hold on to jobs they had had over the years, and thus the control this gave them over policy, and the frustration of former UDF and MDM leaders whose skills and knowledge of the local political terrain remain underutilised (*Weekly Mail*, 21–27 September 1990).

Graduates at 'our university' (Robben Island) also bring a different perspective to the political arena. The youngest amongst them share an amalgam of the BCM heritage of the 1970s and Congress politics, forged in the chill prison climate. Their present frustrations are in some cases directed at both the MDM and the old guard. They are impatient with the lack of discipline amongst the youth, but also resentful of the non-democratic leadership style of the older generation.

The engagement of young people in the frontline of resistance politics has also upset traditional authority structures at many levels: the family, the school and wider society. Conservative black families, weakened by years of poverty and the disruption of the migrant labour system, and constrained by traditional patriarchal approaches to parenting, have been unable to respond adequately to the challenges posed by politicised youth. While the rebellious nature of youths has found political legitimacy, political organisations steeped in traditional leadership and authority structures are having difficulties responding creatively to the youth in their midst.

The Polluting Impact of Transitional Politics

The process of transition is similar to a birth experience. Anxiety, frustration, pain and joyful anticipation all find meaning in the context of the birth process. But the process is also not a clean or tidy one. Those participating in such a process end up with a measure of dirt on their person. The very process of agreeing to negotiate signals a preparedness to take risks, including that of being polluted by the legacy of the past as well as by the problems of the present.

Points of disagreement between the government and the ANC since 2 February 1990 have in some cases been exacerbated by the legitimate concern on the part of the ANC to minimise the risks of pollution. Distrust about the position of the government as both player and referee in the process of negotiation is also a major bone of contention. Calls for an interim government and a constituent assembly, which have the support of the PAC and AZAPO, are attempts to address both the problem of pollution and the issue of player–referee. International experience points to similar tensions in other countries which have followed a similar path of transition (see O'Donnell & Schmitter, 1986). Interim government arrangements are difficult to negotiate because of the constitutional hiatus they are necessarily inserted into. South Africans will have to find their own compromise solution to this problem.

Biko and Black Consciousness: A Defiant Legacy

Attempts to appropriate Biko and Black Consciousness by persons and organisations seeing themselves as the natural heirs of that legacy have added further confusion to our complex political environment. Conversely, those who have sought to deny Biko and Black Consciousness a significant place in the history of the struggle for liberation in South Africa have failed.

The impact of Black Consciousness as articulated by Biko and his comrades in the late sixties and seventies goes beyond the organisations forged to propagate and live out that philosophical approach to liberation. It is indeed 'a way of life', as its proponents were often heard to say, and not just political rhetoric. It posed a challenge to all those traditionally excluded from full citizenship in South Africa to realise that liberation was central to consciousness of self, 'for we cannot be conscious of ourselves and yet remain in bondage' (Biko, 1988:63).

Blacks in all walks of life were affected by the message of Black Consciousness. For the first time in their lives, they were able to walk tall and not feel they were sub-humans or negatives of a greater humanity represented by whiteness. The profound psychological impact of this realisation is indescribable. Mongane Wally Serote (1990) expressed it in this way:

> Black Consciousness transformed the word 'black' and made it synonymous with the word 'freedom'. This definition, which imbued the followers of Black Consciousness with spiritual power which is otherwise absent among the apathetic, while transforming objects into initiators, inferior beings into equals among peoples and claiming a country and a right to be in the world, was also an effective manner of raising one of the most crucial issues of the liberating process and freedom – the national question... The Black Consciousness philoso-

phy and its slogans claimed the past for black people, a country and the right of its people to its wealth and land.

White South Africans were also liberated by Black Consciousness from their superiority complex which entrapped even the best amongst them. White liberals had to find a new reason for opposing the political dispensation in South Africa, beyond their mission of speaking on behalf of mute victims.

An important part of the legacy of Black Consciousness is the demand it made on blacks to acknowledge their active agency in history. Practical manifestations of Black Consciousness took the form of preparing blacks to organise themselves effectively and to learn how to govern. It is thus not surprising that many important political activists and public figures of today, who are in their forties and thirties, are products of the leadership training programmes of that period: Cyril Ramaphosa, Terror Lekota, Aubrey Mokoena, Diliza Mji, Strini Moodley, Saths Cooper, Thenjiwe Mtintso, to name but a few.

The paralysing image of the victim was replaced by that of an active agent of history in all spheres of life. Black Consciousness made an effective contribution to the struggle for liberation by, in the words of Mongane Serote (1990), 'giving to the ANC oxygen and new life, which the movement desperately needed – youth of the South African people, tempered in defiance in action'. The same can be said about other liberation movements.

But what about the claims by AZAPO and the BCMA of being the only true heirs to this legacy? Both organisations have adopted the Black Consciousness philosophy and have articulated their *raison d'être* as that of carrying forward the struggle for liberation on the basis of their reinterpreting its analytical framework in the current political climate. Both organisations have adopted scientific socialism in recognition of the shortcomings of the Black Consciousness Movement of the seventies. Their political choice is their prerogative.

It is, however, regrettable, though understandable in terms of competition for symbolic resources, that some officials of both AZAPO and BCMA have attempted to appropriate the legacy of Black Consciousness for themselves. The controversy around the Harare symposium referred to above is part of the attempt at appropriation. Such attempts indicate a fundamental failure to understand that 'a way of life' cannot be appropriated. The legacy of Black Consciousness spans the whole political spectrum: ANC, PAC, Unity Movement, and many individuals not aligned to any particular political organisation.

Attempts to deny the significance of the impact of Black Consciousness in South Africa are equally futile. An interesting example of this was a review article on the fortieth anniversary of the birth of NUSAS, which was carried by *South African Outlook*. There was little reference in that article to the role of SASO and Black Consciousness in shaping the NUSAS of today. Such a denial of historical fact is also part of the myths South Africans have to jettison in their re-examination of history.

Biko and Black Consciousness have left South Africa a legacy of defiance which defies attempts to distort it. As Biko in life defied attempts to pigeon-hole him, so he continues to do so many years after his death. The legacy of defiance in action has infused the liberation movement as a whole with a new energy.

It is regrettable that other aspects of this legacy have been weakened in recent years. Firstly, the victim mentality has crept back into the anti-apartheid rhetoric, which sought to make political capital out of the iniquity of the apartheid system. The agency of blacks in maintaining this system was underplayed. 'Victims of apartheid' were paraded at international forums and many rewards came with this label. South Africa will pay dearly for the disempowering effect this label has had on many blacks.

Secondly, self-respect and pride in oneself have largely disappeared in the struggle for political turf. The intolerance which blacks display towards other blacks is shocking. In many instances the willingness to embrace and forgive whites who have committed crimes against blacks stands in sharp relief to the vengeance shown towards blacks in similar circumstances. The gruesome acts committed in the violence engulfing the black community are indicative of a people who have lost their self-respect. The message of Black Consciousness is as relevant today as it was in the seventies.

Thirdly, political tolerance, which was an important feature of the BCM era of the seventies, has been thrown overboard as the struggle for political turf intensifies. Johan Degenaar, in a thought-provoking article on the concept of violence, reminds us that 'where violence rules, man [sic] is forced to silence' (Degenaar, 1990:84). Black Consciousness broke the silence imposed by the violence of apartheid in the late sixties by enabling blacks to articulate their aspirations and to engage in forging a democratic future. 'If violence is mute,' says Degenaar, 'then one way of holding it off is to keep reason and democracy alive' (Degenaar, 1990:85). South Africans are in danger of failing to create a legacy of reason.

Overview of Contributions

This book focusses on Steve Biko and the Black Consciousness Movement up to the bannings of 1977. Each contributor has also attempted to examine the legacy of that period in the light of contemporary political realities in South Africa. It has been particularly difficult to capture the essence of who Steve Biko really was in a single chapter, but we believe that Lindy Wilson's chapter forms a basis for further biographical work which will have to be done in the future. We present him as we saw him and interacted with him.

A large section of the book is devoted to an historical documentation of that period by participant observers of the time. The limitations of an inadequate data base are considerable, but through discussion and sharing of information and memories, we have been able to piece together as authentic an historical account as we could under the circumstances.

The chapter on the armed struggle is, for obvious reasons, but a sketch of this sensitive issue in South African history. Firstly, those intimately involved in the armed struggle who are qualified to reflect on their disillusionment with the BCM's lack of a programme of action that included this aspect, are not yet free to do so more fully. Secondly, the armed struggle remains a contested issue in the transitional phase we are in. There are different interpretations even of the same events within and amongst liberation movements. There are also still too many sensitivities to take cognisance of in an academic analysis of this subject. A fuller exposition will have to await greater historical distance.

The last part of the book comprises several critiques of the Black Consciousness period. Most of the contributors were outsiders who bring in a particular perspective. Of particular significance is Neville Alexander's critique, which was written in the 1970s from the peculiar perspective of the Western Cape. We believe that it presents an authentic position of a particular ideological tendency, without the intrusion of hindsight, and believe it could make a contribution to the building of a capacity among South Africans to look back honestly and learn from their experiences.

We offer this book as a perspective on an important part of our history, hoping that it will add to the debate about the future of South Africa.

PART ONE

BANTU STEPHEN BIKO

"I am not a potentiality of something:
I am wholly what I am" – Frantz Fanon

2

Bantu Stephen Biko: A Life
LINDY WILSON

'September '77
In Port Elizabeth weather fine
It was business as usual
In Police Room 619'
(*from* 'Biko', a song by Peter Gabriel)

On 12 September 1977 'business as usual' for the South African Police
claimed the life of Bantu Stephen Biko, the twenty-first person to die in a
South African prison within a period of twelve months.

As yet, the only story of Biko's death and the days preceding it comes
from the perpetrators themselves and their associates, given as evidence at
the inquest into his death. The truth is still shrouded but the words remind
us of the time and climate of Biko's short life. He was 30 years old.

On 2 September 1977 Biko was reported to be physically sound when
visited by a magistrate at the Walmer police cells in Port Elizabeth. He did,
however, make some requests for 'water and soap to wash himself and a
washcloth and a comb', and added: 'I want to be allowed to buy food. I live
on bread only here. Is it compulsory that I have to be naked? I have been
naked since I came here' (Woods, 1987:237).

On 6 September, an investigative team under the leadership of Major
Harold Snyman, appointed to interrogate 'the Black Power detainees', took
Biko to Room 619 of the Sanlam Building, where, according to Snyman, his
interrogation began at 10.30 a.m. and lasted to 6 p.m. when he was left,
chained, in the offices overnight (Woods, 1987:238).[1] Before 7 a.m. the next
morning Biko had sustained head injuries amounting to five brain lesions,
which led to his death (Woods, 1987:347). Although Snyman's superior, Lt.-
Col. P. J. Goosen, Officer Commanding, Eastern Cape Security Branch,
spoke at the inquest about his suspicion at the time that Biko had 'suffered
a stroke' and said he had called in a doctor, 'business as usual' meant

---

1 The detail of the style of this particular team at work is described later in the chapter by Peter Jones, who had been arrested at the same time.

leaving Biko shackled in leg-irons and handcuffs for two more days, at which point he was found lying, helpless, in urine-wet trousers on a mat. After that, Biko, as is well known, was sent, naked, in the back of a Landrover hundreds of miles to Pretoria, where he died (Woods, 1987:344).

The details of Biko's death horrified the world.

It is not his death, however, but his life – Steve Biko's life-giving force – that concerns us. Biko had a vitality that drew people to him, not only for his counsel but his exuberance, not only for his extraordinary clarity of thought but his love of life, his political insight, his capacity to listen, his capacity to learn, his ability to keep placing himself within a circle of people and not up-front – a practice contradicted by his undeniable 'presence'. His gift of leadership was not of the kind that people got to know him and followed him in a slavish kind of way but that, suddenly, and to their great surprise, they got to know *themselves* and thus empowered their own resources.

Biko was by no means a paragon of virtue. He could hold his drink but he often drank too much and earned himself the reputation of being a 'womaniser'. He was not always the best judge of people nor could he always judge for himself his own emotional and psychological capacity. Like everybody else, he was human. But he was also exceptional. Young as he was he saw, early on, that a whole new psychological climate had to be created if the liberation of his country was to continue. He recognised the collusion of the oppressed with the oppressor, and expressed what he saw as the bitter truth: that of black people 'bearing the yoke of oppression with sheepish timidity' (Biko, 1988:43). What seemed of prime importance to Biko was described by his colleague Malusi Mpumlwana. It was 'to awaken the people as to whom they are by getting them to state their identity. He thought that if you could do that then there was no stopping them from revolution' (MM to LW, 1990).

This consciousness towards a common identity was actively lived and led to renewed political commitment, not only during his lifetime but after his death; not only in the movement that carries the name he and others coined, the Black Consciousness Movement, but also in the liberation movements of the African National Congress (ANC) and the Pan-Africanist Congress (PAC), in the trade unions, in basic grassroots community movements; not only as politicians and soldiers but as lawyers, doctors, priests, poets, community workers, mothers and fathers.

This brief biography of Bantu Stephen Biko is grounded in the relevant published literature but also draws substantially from interviews. A few of them were done with Biko himself, particularly near the end of his life. Twenty-six were conducted in 1989 and 1990, specifically for this study, with people who knew him best. Interviews, of course, have weaknesses as historical sources. They are subjective and also rely on memory, often blurred and distorted by time and perspective. Further, describing another's life is often a projection of one's own. However, those who worked with him, loved him, argued and debated with him, who disagreed with him and recognised his faults, are the key witnesses to his life.

In South Africa, where much written evidence has been lost or delibe-rately destroyed or carefully not recorded – fearing reprisals in a fearful age – biography may well emerge as one of the most important clues to its recent history. As the psychologist N. C. Manganyi puts it, 'writing about an individual then becomes equivalent to writing about a community' (Couve, 1984:34).

Biko's life expressed only in words diminishes him considerably. His arrival in the doorway, his physical presence relaxed into a chair, were, more than for most people, a very powerful part of who he was; the sound of his laughter and his visible capacity both to listen quietly and yet to be so vitally present, are what are so glaringly missing here. Nevertheless, the Biko who does emerge is not easily placed in any immediately definable category. At the same time, he cannot really be excluded from many of them. He strongly criticised the institutional Church yet he believed in God and had insight into Christ's teachings. He was not a Marxist – indeed he was criticised for rejecting Marx's relevance for most of his life, preferring to identify the oppressed as a classless solidarity – yet he believed in the importance of the future role of the black working class, and in the redistri-bution of the land and wealth. He was more at home in African Socialism than in socio-political examples from Europe. Although he set out to study medicine he never became a doctor, and though he never set out to become a martyr, this was what he became. Although he never had time to com-plete his law studies, he donned the mantle of a lawyer of considerable skill when summoned to give evidence in defence of some of the leaders of two of the organisations he helped establish. Perhaps the thing he least set out to do was to convert white liberals, yet the Black Consciousness Movement changed the political direction of a whole generation of white students, and he converted one of the leading liberal editors in South Africa without apparent effort. Above all, although he advocated a philosophy called 'Black Consciousness', Steve Biko was not a racist.

This brief narrative of his life traces some of the origins of Biko's political thinking and the role he played in the growth of Black Consciousness. At the same time it also reveals his curiosity and fascination with the human condition, with humanity, with what being human truly is.

Biko the Boy

Bantu Stephen Biko was born on 18 December 1946 in Tarkastad, in the Eastern Cape, the third child of Mzingaye and Alice Duna 'Mamcete' Biko. His birth, in his grandmother's home, included the traditional smearing and burying of the umbilical cord into the floor of the room where he was born.

Mzingaye chose to name him Bantu Stephen Biko. 'Bantu' literally means 'people'. Later Biko called himself 'son of man'. Although this was done often with tongue in cheek, Malusi Mpumlwana interprets Biko as understanding his name to mean that he was a person for other people, or more precisely, *umntu ngumtu ngabanye abantu*, 'a person is a person by means of other people'.

The name 'Stephen' was prophetic in the manner of his death. It connects with that of his biblical namesake, Stephen, who was stoned to death. Stephen accused the Jews of being false to their vocation, of being stubborn, like their forebears, in refusing to acknowledge that 'Jesus was actually the path of the Truth, which is very much in line with what the whole vocation of Israel was about. Even as he died he challenged them in the face of their anger' (MM to LW, 1990). Stephen Biko challenged people to recognise their humanity and acknowledge it. This included the authorities and those who persecuted him. But as they could not see him as a human being nor recognise who he was, they, too, were bound to kill him.

Biko grew up in a Christian family. His parents met and married in Whittlesea when Mzingaye was sent to work with Mamcete's father, both of them policemen. The Bikos were later transferred to Queenstown, then to Port Elizabeth, to Fort Cox and finally King William's Town, where they lived in a house in Ginsberg location. In 1950, when Mzingaye was studying for a law degree by correspondence through the University of South Africa, he fell ill. After being admitted to St Matthew's Hospital in Keiskammahoek, he died. Biko (who was called Bantu by his family) was 4 years old. The first-born, his sister Bukelwa, had been delegated by her father to look after him, while Khaya, an elder brother, was delegated to look after his younger sister, Nobandile. The children kept asking where their father was but Mamcete could not at first bring herself to tell them he had died. Because he was often away, she said he had gone to Cape Town for work and an aeroplane would bring him back. While playing with a group of other children they saw an aeroplane and shouted: 'Aeroplane, come back with our father!' But the other children said: 'No, your father died!'

As a widow with four young children, Mamcete earned a meagre income for the next twenty-three years as a domestic worker. She remembers her first employer, the superintendent of Ginsberg, as a helpful and 'good man', who welcomed her children to play with his, included them at Christmas time and was generally generous. After he left, however, she had to take a job as a cook in the much tougher environment of Grey Hospital in King William's Town, the white town across the railway line from Ginsberg location (MB to LW, 1989).

In spite of her slender means, her two-roomed house, though simple, was by no means destitute, and with her quiet and singular dignity she welcomed the community around her to share it.

The Ginsberg of Steve Biko's childhood was a closely knit community of about eight-hundred families, every four families sharing communal taps and toilets. 'Everybody knew the next person,' his younger sister remembers. 'It was common, then, if you didn't have food you'd go to your neighbours and they'd give you samp, beans, mealie-meal, sugar in dishes, and when you had [eaten] you'd just return the dishes!' Steve and Nobandile grew up side by side in the small township, where the languages of English, Afrikaans and Xhosa intermingled. At the age of 6 or 7 he took Nobandile, aged 4, to the crèche each day on his way to Charles Morgan Primary School and collected her on his way home. Young Biko would avoid doing things that bored him: errands for aunts or feeding the chickens before school, when he would deliberately get up late. He loved experiments and, like most boys, used his younger sister as guinea-pig and partner in them. From a young age he made people laugh, not only by tomfoolery and clowning but by the way he engaged in conversation. If he had been too busy playing soccer in the streets and had missed a meal, he would demand it with the next one! Nobandile enjoyed 'every minute' of that shared childhood with him and, on reflection, remembers that 'We never regarded ourselves as poor but when I look back I realise that, in fact, we were poor' (NB to LW, 1990).

Bantu Biko grew tall and slender and went to secondary school at Forbes Grant. His mother began to notice that when other children had parties he refused to have clothes bought for him and would say: 'I know we don't have a father. We can't afford these new clothes' (MB to LW, 1989). She would tell him not to worry about such things. The fact is that he worried about his mother all his life and was deeply committed to her well-being. It made a profound impression on him that she had to do such unrewarding jobs, toiling all day for little pay.

Mamcete wanted her children to be educated. Young Biko was doing so well that the Ginsberg community gave him a bursary to go to Lovedale Institution in nearby Alice. It was, in fact, money they had collected to build two senior classrooms, which had not materialised. His elder brother, Khaya, was already there at boarding school. Steve was 16. Within the first three months of his arrival, Khaya was arrested, suspected of PAC sympathies. Steve was also arrested: 'They took us to the police camp, decided I was the younger of the two and sent me in for sort of heavy grilling, seven people around me. It didn't take long for them to discover that I didn't know a single thing about it. They were talking about "friends" of mine who had been arrested; I didn't know these people. They were talking about things I was *doing* with "friends"; I didn't know about this. This was how I got a glimpse into what was going to happen to my brother. I never saw him thereafter. He just disappeared. I saw him ten months later. It was a very bitter experience. I was terribly young.' Khaya was convicted but acquitted on appeal. When Biko returned to school, however, he was immediately expelled although he was entirely innocent. 'I began to develop an attitude which was much more directed at authority than at anything else. I hated authority like hell' (SB to GG, 1972).

In 1964, having missed a full year of studies after his dismissal from Lovedale, Biko went to boarding school at St Francis' College in Mariannhill, Natal. He had just turned 18. It was run by Catholic nuns and priests, and he later described an atmosphere free of government intervention. 'I think it helped a lot in the formulation of ideas in a slow sense. We saw the principal and all the authorities [as] obviously not representative of the system but, all the same, they had an approach to us which was sort of provocative and challenging. That's where one began to see, in a sense, the totality of white power. These were liberals, presumably, who were enunciating a solution for us.' Biko was not loth to question anybody and did so: 'I personally had many wars with those guys, most of them non-political wars in a sense, but again this kind of authority problem' (SB to GG, 1972).

Biko began to question 'all sorts of [practices] within the Church, within the authority structure within the school' (MR to LW, 1989). He befriended a Catholic nun, who gave him a good deal of her time discussing such issues as the position of nuns within the church, for example, and why it was necessary to have the institution anyway, which apart from other things imposed strictly disciplined relationships between nuns and monks. And, doubtless, he was curious about celibacy. He also sought answers to these questions by initiating a correspondence with Father Aelred Stubbs, of the Anglican Community of the Resurrection, who was principal of St Peter's College at the Federal Theological Seminary in Alice, near King William's Town. Father Stubbs had, in his normal round of duty, come across the Biko family at the time of the two boys' arrest. It was the start of an important and long-term relationship between spiritual 'father' and 'son'.

As we will see later when Biko befriended a challenging Anglican priest, David Russell, he would continue to pursue with interest questions of faith, his understanding of religion and his disappointment in the Church. Consciously, however, these questions were not central to his life. Already, at school in Mariannhill, he sought information of an increasingly political nature and he recalled how the pupils found intellectual debates very valuable, particularly about Africa's independence, which was under way: 'We were great listeners to news services,' Biko recalled, 'and at that time Banda and a whole host of other African leaders were coming up.' Several of them became 'heroes', particularly Algeria's Ahmed Ben Bella, while Biko himself identified particularly with Oginga Odinga, one of Kenya's national leaders. Their ideas and stances were hotly debated while the whole question of coups was carefully discussed. Biko remembered, however, that all of them agreed on the ideas of a common society. 'I don't know to what extent Christian principles played a part here,' he mused, 'but I was always sold on the idea of a common society.' He added that nobody was to enunciate the method or approach or design on his behalf but that, talking of himself as an 'oppressed person', he would do so for himself (SB to GG, 1972).

Biko was full of zest and youthful confidence whenever he came home. He would arrive at the door in high spirits, hardly pausing before describing his journey home and whom he had met: 'He was like a father who comes home. We would hug and kiss and there would be laughter', and then he and Nobandile might go off next day and visit some of the older, more lonely people in the township, or they would sit on the verandah until late at night singing Kente songs (NB to LW, 1990).

It was partly this zest for life, combined with incorrigible optimism and excitement at Africa's increasing independence, that drew him towards the future rather than the pessimism of the immediate past. He had been only a boy of 13 when the massacre at Sharpeville took place in 1960 and both the major black political movements, the African National Congress and the Pan-Africanist Congress, were banned and went underground. Spurred by the police action, which killed 69 people in that non-violent protest against the pass laws, there was strong opinion in both organisations that the door was finally closed on passive resistance and that some form of insurgency was necessary for fundamental change in South Africa. Biko was 14 when Nelson Mandela proposed in June 1961 the formation of the military wing of the ANC, Umkhonto we Sizwe, in the development of which the banned South African Communist Party made an important contribution. He was 15 when Mandela was arrested on his return from an illegal visit overseas and sentenced to five years' imprisonment, and 16 when most of the Umkhonto (MK) national high command were arrested at Lilliesleaf Farm in Johannesburg and were sentenced to life imprisonment after the Rivonia Trial in 1964.

Running alongside the ANC's 'controlled sabotage' programme was the PAC's militant group, known as Poqo. (It was with this organisation that his brother Khaya had been suspected of having connections.) The PAC did not accept white membership nor was it sympathetic towards Communist ideology. It also believed informers should be severely dealt with and implemented that. It had particularly strong support in the Vereeniging district (which included Sharpeville), in Pretoria and in the Western Cape. There was also activity in the Eastern Cape, notably Port Elizabeth, East London, Grahamstown and King William's Town (Lodge, 1983:246). Biko talks of the only 'politicos' in his family being PAC and how 'at a very young age I listened to a whole host of their debates'. In spite of his admiration for their courage and their 'terribly good organisation', however, he was not convinced by what he saw as an exclusive Africanism (SB to GG, 1972). Just as the ANC's 'Operation Mayibuye' never came into operation, neither did Potlako Leballo's PAC proposal for a planned uprising take place from Maseru in April 1963. Infiltration and indiscretion in leaking the plan too early to the press led to the arrest of three thousand people that same month (Lodge, 1983:247).

When Steve Biko matriculated from school in 1965, aged 19, all this history had only very recently come to pass. As far as the government was concerned, the black opposition was neatly rolled up into the jails and under lock and key, with many people having fled into exile. To what extent all these events were known or in what way they affected the emergent ideas of the young Biko is difficult to judge. Whatever the case, Biko was optimistic and expressed his distaste at what he saw as 'this sort of appalling silence on the part of Africans and this tendency to play kids and hide behind the skirts of white liberals who were speaking for them' (SB to GG, 1972). Excited about the future, Biko believed that blacks should be playing a far greater role in politics. Presumably influenced by his Catholic school background, he believed in what was then known as the non-racial approach – that already established institutions should be opened up to a far greater participation by blacks – thinking that it was a matter of recruitment and greater representation that would transform institutions from being predominantly white to becoming more representative.

Biko wanted to do law at university but there was a popular mentality in the Eastern Cape that equated law with political activism, and that, under the circumstances, was to be discouraged. Medicine was the safe alternative for a good profession, and Biko won a scholarship to study it. There was also a pattern at the time that bright black students with good matric results should automatically go to medical school at the University of Natal (Non-European Section: UNNE).[2] This may well be the reason why so many intelligent and remarkable young people found themselves together there as a core group, with a measure of freedom which did not exist in any other long-established liberal university, where blacks were always a small minority. In 1966 Biko went to UNNE at Wentworth to study medicine.

Steve as Student: 1966–1972

Biko entered the university keen for debate and participation in student politics. He went as an observer in his first year to the July congress of the National Union of South African Students (NUSAS), in spite of the many black student groups who disagreed with him and his view of the non-racial approach.[3] In the following year, 1967, when he went as a delegate to the congress, which was held at Rhodes University in Grahamstown, Biko challenged NUSAS to take an active stance against the segregated residential facilities which Rhodes University had imposed on the congress. The university discriminated against black delegates: 'Indians' and 'Coloureds' had to stay in town while Africans were required to stay some distance away in a church hall in the location; whites, on the other hand, could stay in the university residences (SB to GG, 1972). At the outset of the conference the executive of NUSAS dealt with this by bringing in a resolution condemning the Rhodes University Council for not allowing blacks in the residences. Biko then moved a private motion proposing that the conference adjourn until they could get a 'non-racist venue' (Woods, 1987:153). He later remembered that it was during the subsequent debate which lasted throughout the night that a lot of ideas became clear to him: 'I

2 This became known as the University of Natal Black Section (UNB) after SASO requested the name to be officially changed in 1970.
3 The Cape Peninsula Students' Union (CPSU), who were Trotskyite-orientated; the African Students' Association (ASA), who were ANC-orientated; the African Students' Union of South Africa (ASUSA), who were PAC-orientated; and the Durban Students' Union, who were NEUM-orientated (SB to GG, 1972).

realised that for a long time I had been holding onto the whole dogma of non-racism almost like a religion, feeling that it was sacrilegious to question it, and therefore not accommodating the attacks I was getting from other students. I began to feel there was a lot lacking in the proponents of the non-racist idea, that much as they were adhering to this impressive idea they were in fact subject to their own experience back home. They had this problem, you know, of superiority, and they tended to take us for granted and wanted us to accept things that were second-class' (Woods, 1987:153–4).

Further, there was the assumption that all affairs were automatically conducted in English. This gave an immediate advantage to those for whom English was their mother tongue. It was an extraordinary experience for blacks to listen to their own lives being articulated by whites, who had had an infinitely superior education, yet had had no experience of the reality. Biko recalls the effect: 'You are forced into a subservient role of having to say "yes" to what they are saying because you cannot express it so well. This in a sense [also] inculcates a sense of inadequacy. You tend to think it is not just a matter of language. You tend to tie it up also with intelligence. You tend to feel that that guy is better equipped than you mentally' (Woods, 1987:168). Biko thus identified, at first hand, the mental process that led to an inferiority complex among blacks, and he was certainly not going to be part of that.

There stirred within his own consciousness the germ of an idea. This was to flower into a student movement which conscientised blacks to analyse their socio-political condition by recognising that they could be their own liberators through resisting their oppression with a different mental attitude. It was this attitude that became known as 'Black Consciousness'. Amongst other things it debunked long-standing myths whites had woven about Africa generally and South Africa in particular, myths present in school and university textbooks: the inherent inferiority of blacks, their skin-deep savagery, the simplistic quality of their faith and beliefs, the inferiority of Africa's oral tradition as opposed to written history, the 'primitive' nature of its culture, and so forth. Blacks would be conscientised into discovering their true identity by refusing to live the lie. In the spirit of the 1960s world-wide, with the end to colonial rule in Africa, the emergence of Black Power in the United States, and the student revolts in Europe, the Black Consciousness Movement emerged to transform the minds of black South African students, thereby generating a lifestyle which eventually resisted oppression on a massive scale.

On leaving the NUSAS meeting Biko went immediately to New Brighton, in Port Elizabeth, to talk to Barney Pityana, who remembers how 'We literally sat in my room for probably the whole night and he was talking through his annoyance and what I was saying to myself was: "Why did you go? You must have known before you went that it would be like that, that nothing is really different and if you did go you were naive to have expected anything different!"' (BP to LW, 1989)

Pityana had also been been dismissed from Lovedale following a student strike in 1964. He was now one of the leading students in the Anglican Student Society, the English Dramatic Society and the Law Society at the University College of Fort Hare. He was not a person easily convinced. He tested and questioned ideas in a legal manner: Why this? Why not the other? Not so much a devil's advocate, he was a person whose intelligence was to be thoroughly trusted and whose questions often brought in aspects not yet thought of. In this instance Biko and Pityana were at one and thus began to work as a convincing team together. Pityana found Biko's idealism attractive: 'There was something about him that was really prepared to experiment with ideas, to really get going, could really take you away from the ordinary humdrum things and say there are other possibilities. He had the capacity to challenge and to make it a reality' (BP to LW, 1989).

In July 1968, Pityana and Biko attended a student meeting of the University Christian Movement (UCM) in Stutterheim. Under a provision of the Group Areas Act, blacks were only allowed to be in any urban area for 72 hours without a permit. The black participants met to discuss what to do about this. They presented a motion refusing to obey the rule. White delegates expressed displeasure at being left out of this, and a compromise motion was adopted whereby the whole conference was to march to the borders of the magisterial district. The black caucus also took a formal decision 'to work towards a conference in December to deal with the specific issue of a black student organisation as such' (Woods, 1987:155).

Pityana was not convinced about an on-going black caucus. In a country dominated by segregation, it might easily be seen as a group of students 'taken over by government-orientated thinking'. Shortly afterwards, he invited Biko to speak at Fort Hare at a UCM student discussion to put his point of view. When Biko told students that their responsibility was to the whole university, 'including the people that are working, underpaid, and treated like slaves', Pityana was convinced and saw the potential of the idea as 'a real link between student responsibility and the social concerns of the country' (BP to LW, 1989).

Pityana played a leading student role at Fort Hare and, at that time, was determined no Student Representative Council (SRC) should be formed that would be seen to collaborate with the government structures now ruling the university. In 1968 he was expelled during a strike. As regional director of the UCM, which was not allowed to operate on the Fort Hare campus, Pityana travelled to the Western Cape, and Biko, as president of the newly formed South African Students' Organisation, went to Natal and the Transvaal. 'We actually never sat down to agree about what we would say', but it was, more or less, that 'it's about time that black people up and down the country began to speak together in one voice'. 'Black' meant the oppressed, which included all people classified 'Coloured', 'Indian' or 'Asian' as well as 'Bantu'. This new definition had a liberating effect on many, freeing them from the categories defined by apartheid, while others were extremely dubious of something that sounded as though it smacked of racism. It took time to sow the seed. Biko and Pityana were in constant contact, travelling and writing each other long letters to keep in touch: 'he was a political writer and was very good at throwing out ideas'. Biko displayed another quality too, 'an eye to discern people and human nature in a very penetrating way without having to get into great discussions about things' (BP to LW, 1989). Biko and Pityana spent most of the early months of 1969 doing the rounds of the campuses in the country.

The result of all this energy and enthusiasm and growing conviction amongst the black student youth was the founding of the South African Students' Organisation (SASO) in July 1969 at one of the government's own tribalised universities, Turfloop (the University of the North). Biko was its first president. The first SASO communiqué has a breathless quality about it:

1. At a time when events are moving so fast in the country, it is not advisable to show any form of division amongst students' ranks – especially now that students appear to be a power to be reckoned with in this country.

2. Any move that tends to divide the student population into separate laagers on the basis of colour is in a way tacit submission to having been defeated and apparently seems in agreement with apartheid.

3. In a racially sensitive country like ours, provisions for racially exclusive bodies tend to build up resentment and to widen the gap that exists between the races, and the student community should resist all attempts to fall into this temptation.

4. Any formation of a purely non-white body shall be subject to a lot of scrutiny and so the chances of the organisations lasting are very little' (Biko, 1988:25–26).

Coincidentally, NUSAS itself underwent some radical changes as it came under the presidency of Neville Curtis in 1969, an 'outsider' who was not definable in the NUSAS liberal tradition. Curtis and Biko met at conferences on several occasions. They both wanted to find a way of working on black and white campuses alike that was fresh and innovative and not just defensive, that would 'enable us to mobilise students, that allowed us to *raise* issues, not just react to issues' (NC to GG, 1990). Their tasks were different but both had a breadth of vision that acknowledged the usefulness, at that point, of the continued existence of both organisations, co-operating but not coming under one umbrella.

SASO 'could have wrecked NUSAS' but instead it passed a resolution recognising it as the national student body. By keeping this contact with Curtis, Biko picked up some of NUSAS's most useful procedures, particularly the idea of training, which in SASO became known as formation schools. They concentrated on leadership training, which at the same time ensured that layers of leadership would persist. This was not only as a precaution in case people were 'knocked off' by the government but as a principle to avoid hierarchy. Both organisations were in a situation where neither might survive. NUSAS and the UCM had the universities and the church to draw on. SASO had neither. 'It was an extremely brave venture in organisational terms,' Neville Curtis recalls (NC to GG, 1990).

Biko built up different groups of people with whom he debated and discussed: 'I had a caucus on my campus, a caucus of two or three people and for the sake of balance I had two other caucuses: a "non-racial" caucus of NUSAS orientation and an Africanist caucus of PAC orientation, the two balancing across the central caucus,' he explained (SB to GG, 1972). In February 1970 he wrote a letter to the presidents of all the Student Representative Councils of the English and Afrikaans-speaking universities, to national student organisations and others (including overseas organisations), giving the historical background, the structure, policy and aims of SASO. In this letter the word 'non-white' was still used but this was to be short-lived.

'Non-white' was a negation of being. It still indicated a desire to become white eventually in the sense that 'whiteness' was the norm to which one attached other people who could not be defined in their own terms. It was soon removed from SASO's vocabulary and replaced by the word 'black', which gave identity to all the oppressed. Mpumlwana elaborates: 'Over time, blacks had been made to see themselves as just a mass, one of a mass without any sense of responsibility about who you are, your destiny and your society. Just "non-whites", non-something. Everything that you are has been taken away from you. You're a non-person. In order to be a person you have got to claim your identity. You name yourself. And we named ourselves "black"' (MM to LW, 1990).

In July 1970, Pityana became second president of SASO, and Biko editor of the *SASO Newsletter*. From August Biko began his column 'I Write What I Like' and signed it 'Frank Talk'.[4] Throughout the following two years it enabled the evolution of the philosophy of Black Consciousness to be recorded and expressed, ideas sounded out with colleagues and friends, tried and tested in the SASO style of consensus politics.

In January 1971 Pityana and Biko delivered two separate papers to an Abe Bailey conference[5] in Cape Town, statements that were 'a major refinement of what we were doing'. Barney recalls how incredible it was that neither of them had read each other's paper in advance. As they had dealt with the far more ideological question of whether or not they should participate, it was quite clear to both of them, in the papers presented, 'that there was a lot there between us that was actually a result of conversations and writing and sharing and thinking through precisely how you present in a hostile, in an ambiguous and uncertain climate, something positive and, in our view, certain. We felt certain about the capacity of black people

4 Several of these columns were put together in a book under the same title, edited by Aelred Stubbs, who included his own essay, 'Martyr of Hope', in 1978. The 1988 Penguin edition has a new introduction by Barney Pityana.
5 The idea of the Abe Bailey conference was to bring all students together: the Afrikaanse Studentebond, NUSAS, etc.

to participate in their own struggle but that it needed to be said in a challenging and in a critical way' (BP to LW, 1989).

There grew into being a particular style of leadership which recognised the enormous advantage of widespread consultation. This did not only mean consultation to win over a proposal but the creation of an atmosphere where individual opinions were considered and taken seriously. They were valued equally. It was time-consuming and costly in energy but it ensured true development and growth, both politically and in terms of human advance, so that people became more efficient and confident. This style was unique to Black Consciousness and developed at the height of the most oppressive and confident years of apartheid. It is worth exploring once again now when the future of the country is being negotiated so that the discussions involved in the process are truly representative of all the people of South Africa.

Style of Leadership

The concept of Black Consciousness drew intellectual and political inspiration and dialogue from the civil rights and Black Power movements in the United States, and from Négritude and other forms of post-colonial thinking in Africa. It concerned itself with the religious movements of Ethiopianism and African religious political prophecy (Biko, 1988:9), and some of its practices were confirmed and strengthened through the methods of Paulo Freire's pedagogy. All this was, however, fervently debated in a growing consciousness that was rooted in the South African situation. The impact was that, under the very gaze of a severely oppressive regime, people began to live lives actively aware of a growing identity and fearlessness. The aim of Black Consciousness was that this style of life should filter into the lives of all the oppressed, the vast majority of South Africans. It sought to use the greatest potential of each person, any person, within its ranks, never considering anyone incapable of contributing. Initiated in SASO, this was to become the hallmark of the Black Consciousness Movement as a whole. It is embodied today in those who were once versed in it. Because it was a lived experience, recognition of a new identity became an integral part of its proponents. In so far as was possible, leadership was rendered invisible. This was not only in preparation for the inevitable moment when the state would single people out to be banned, banished or arrested, but also an acknowledgment that multiple skills are the most productive.

Biko's personality had a large part to play in living and nurturing this style. His presence ensured that people would be heard and their opinion considered. He engendered trust and freed people to use their potential. To him it was clear that to obtain the common goal of a true humanity, the game of power politics would have no place (Biko, 1988:106). He recognised and enabled participation in such a way that the sum of the whole was richer, more useful and politically more powerful when thoroughly worked through than that of individual leadership and domination. Time was needed for a group to identify the skills in one another and then to trust those skills so that delegation could take place with the urgency and speed that was often necessary. Pityana describes Biko as 'the person who brought ideas. He was the fundamentalist, if you like, the person who brought the basic ideas which were being bandied about and thrown around. He was actually quite stubborn in some ways because he was very keen to push his point and his ideas to the limit' (BP to LW, 1989). Thus the very opposite of consensus politics might have been expected from a person like Biko. This was not so. He was also challenged by equally vocal and questioning people. And although he talked a lot he also really listened. He did not dominate and he had the capacity to be delighted by counter-argument.

SASO became a sub-culture of the university. Biko's room in the old army barracks of the medical student residence, Alan Taylor, doubled up as the SASO office, and it was there, Mpumlwana recalls, when he first came to UNNE, that you 'expected to find people in some conversation or another; very friendly people, warm and accommodating, non-hierarchical and always involved in debates, conversations, always something exciting with a new angle to develop' (MM to LW, 1990).

Everybody read books outside their university subjects. These provided the essence of the debates, and the discussion that made the future have some kind of meaningful possibility. Many people were involved, people who later became psychologists, doctors, poets, writers, politicians and trade-unionists. Among them were Charles Sibisi, who was considered the 'international expert', while Mamphela Ramphele and Malusi Mpumlwana worked on practical community programmes; Mandla Langa had started writing poetry and was getting it published in journals by small publishing houses in Johannesburg; Strini and Sam Moodley, Asha Rambally and Saths Cooper were founding members of the Theatre Council of Natal (TECON), a group that was concerned with creating 'relevant theatre' (*Black Review*, 1973:106–108) and produced plays and poetry readings at student conferences.

One of the main forces that kept writers and musicians active were the many meetings, teach-ins and seminars held throughout the country, and the General Student Councils (GSCs). To write and perform became an intrinsic part of these: 'you would find yourself with a certain captive audience, people who would criticise you or encourage you but who would be there to read your stuff and try and make sense out of it. Students were extremely instrumental in making sure that one continued writing' (ML to LW, 1989). This included writers like Mafika Gwala, Mongane Wally Serote, Njabulo Ndebele, Strini Moodley, and Saths Cooper, who, working alongside musicians and forming theatre groups, interpreted with anger, depth and humour 'the thrust of that time'. The very nature of being 'travelling players' gave them a consciousness and a 'global understanding' of the problems in the country (MWS to LW, 1990). In political and theological matters Biko and Pityana led the field. Langa remembers how 'we started sharing libraries, sharing books and also going to all these bookshops which had all these expensive books which we needed and, you know, finding a way of appropriating them. We started really widening our vistas and our minds by reading books which the regime never possibly thought we'd lay our hands on, anything from the African Writers Series to, well, we read Marcuse, we read the existential philosophers such as Jean-Paul Sartre. There was Mphahlele and maybe some hidden copies by Alex La Guma, Lewis Nkosi, Can Themba, Nat Nakasa, Bloke Modisane. We read all that' (ML to LW, 1989).

Biko discovered many of the books and authors. One of the most significant writers he read and passed on was Frantz Fanon. It seemed coincidental that Fanon's work was published in English for the first time in 1968. Born in Martinique, Fanon had studied medicine in France and practised psychiatry in the Antilles, where he wrote *Black Skin, White Masks*, a psychological and philosophical analysis of the state of being black, and *The Wretched of the Earth*, a book which included theory on the colonising of the mind, experience of which he gained when working in Algeria during the French–Algerian colonial war. Another important writer was James Cone, the black American theologian, while Malcolm X, the 'Black Consciousness' counterpart to Martin Luther King's liberal integrationist stance, had published his autobiography in 1965. The SASO group had twelve records of his speeches: 'Compared to Martin Luther King, we felt that Malcolm's preachings were much more gutsy, much more in tandem with what we were thinking and feeling. They were also very very influential in some of the plays which we wrote and performed.' Mandla Langa recalls that there was also a resonance with the kind of cultural awakening expressed by the Black Panthers and 'consciously or unconsciously there was a lot of borrowing, which is why you find the poetry of that time became very derivative really' (ML to LW, 1989). The Black Panthers would present a situation to an audience, which could have several endings, and then they would call upon the audience to debate the end and then act it out for them.

One of the main sources for information about relevant books was from the South African *Government Gazette* itself, which regularly listed all 'objectionable' books. Quite obviously these were the very books that became required reading. Pityana also recalls how a man in the United States consulate made much of the relevant American literature available while another source was a Lutheran bookshop which unobtrusively sold banned books.

Thorough discussion took place as a constant backdrop to student activity. In preparation for the 1971 General Student Council (GSC) – for the leadership-training aspect – Biko began to make an extensive study of South African political movements, concentrating on the early so-called religious breakaways of the 1890s; the Ethiopian movement; the foundation of the ANC; the history of the Industrial and Commercial Workers' Union (ICU), its operation, its growth and death, and so forth (SB to GG, 1972).

John Mbiti's book _Introduction to African Religions_ was also an important influence at the time. Pityana recalls much of this as a 'subconscious act of transcending the visions of the past without denying the authenticity of that'. At the same time there was a clear recognition that 'we could no longer proceed on the same basis [to] capture the imagination of our people, still bring people to a coherent unity and vision' (BP to LW, 1989).

And so the ball began to roll across the country. Without making him stand out too much there is no question that much of the setting in motion of that rolling spirit was initiated by Biko, or affirmed by Biko. Once moving, once in motion, he stepped back and others took over, and they, in turn, did the same. He was always of the belief that nobody should become cast in a mould, that diversity was educative, that people had different skills. No SASO president, for example, was in office for more than a year, a precedent set by Biko. This capacity to stand back, to put others forward, to initiate new ideas, get something going and make it practical, meant that although Biko was present, he managed not to be dominant. It was an infusion of ideas which he encouraged, resulting in a newly found energy that began to perpetuate itself country-wide.

He travelled extensively with different people. Not having a driving licence at this stage he always let others drive. 'It didn't matter where we were in South Africa, whether in rural areas, in townships, in town, in the suburbs, we always knew where to go, which shebeen to go to. We would arrive in a place, sometimes at three in the morning, when usually everything is shut. We would knock, the person would say "no", but as soon as they heard it was us they would open and we would get six boxes of beer, two quarts of whiskey and a gumba started,' Mongane Wally Serote recalls. 'We would all be tired and I would fall asleep and I would wake up and Steve would still be on his chair, talking and drinking. And the thing that struck you was his great joy at being among people. This seemed to inspire him, this seemed to give him the energy and even the willingness to challenge, you know. I think the gumba situation at that time was a very very important forum for us. Under a relaxed atmosphere we were able, then, to explore a whole lot of very complex issues, informally, of course always with Steve presiding' (MWS to LW, 1990).

In Johannesburg, as elsewhere, socialising took on a new form with the arrival of SASO. There had been a considerable 'crossing of the colour bar' as it was called, which mostly took place in white liberal and Communist homes. In the former, artists, writers and musicians often found each other and relaxed in a somewhat formal manner. Bokwe Mafuna remembers being introduced to Biko by Stanley Sabelo Ntwasa, the UCM roving representative, at a 'garden party' (_sic_). Mafuna, then working for the _Rand Daily Mail_,[6] remembers the ambivalence he and others often felt in performing the role of 'interpreters' of the black townships and the black world at these

6 At the time he made headlines with his story of the removals at Evaton, reminiscent of his childhood in Mafeking and his youth in Sophiatown.

parties. When SASO began to be active around that time, as Serote says, a new forum was established, often at the informal parties. Mafuna recalls that 'they were neither the quiet, intellectual discourse, sitting and drinking in the white suburbs nor were they getting drunk in the shebeen. They were social events which had a lot of political significance, where people met one another from all over the country, where you could speak out, pour out your souls to one another', a place where things raised in that informal atmosphere would be transformed into resolutions for later conferences (BM to LW, 1989).

Mafuna recalls how he had never been in such an environment before. He had been a worker since school-going age and a member of trade unions before he became a photographer and journalist. 'I had grown up in an environment of conflict all my life and here, for once, I was with people with whom I could be at ease, among whom I could start believing in myself. I found myself writing a book with other people, I found myself organising trade unions throughout the country. We went to Port Elizabeth, Cape Town, Durban, Johannesburg, all over. We were organising youth. We were organising women. All these things I had never believed I could do and we were getting other people to do them with us.' He later joined SASO's Black Workers' Project and spent many intimate moments with Biko travelling all over the country, with the resultant hours of long discussions which ensue on long journeys across the vast landscape. Mafuna talks of Biko's ease with all kinds of people. 'Steve respected people and he made people respect each other. His whole attitude and his whole experience was a working-class attitude and experience. He had extraordinary gifts of knowing how to relate to people and be able to inspire confidence in people and trust' (BM to LW, 1989).

Biko's style of leadership was similar when tensions arose in student or political meetings. With his various caucuses he had usually worked through his ideas in advance. He stuck to them but also had the flexibility of recognising a majority voice. An example of this capacity was remembered by many from the General Student Council of SASO in July 1972.

At that time hundreds of black students were boycotting the universities after the dismissal of Onkgopotse Ramothibi Tiro, a student leader at Turfloop (the University of the North), who had made a scathing attack on black education at his graduation in April 1972 (*Black Review*, 1972:175). Many of them came to the SASO General Student Council for discussion and strategising (BP to AS, 1978). SASO's president, Temba Sono, having failed to arrive at the executive meeting always held before the GSC, did not ensure the executive reached consensus before he delivered his address. The sum of what he subsequently said was that 'it was no use saying we were going to work against government institutions because they were part of our lives; and for SASO to exist it was necessary to work with government institutions' (BP to AS, 1978).

After he spoke Biko immediately called for an extraordinary session of the GSC. There he moved that 'the House censure the president strongly for his speech as it was against policy'. Biko behaved in a very mild, diplomatic way and drew up the statement to be issued to the press. On the whole, people were not satisfied that this was enough, but accepted it 'because it was Steve'. Next day, however, somebody from the floor asked the president to stand down. (Biko wasn't even there. He was still asleep!) Sono finally left the conference altogether. Biko later indicated to Pityana that 'he didn't think that was the right thing to do' but if it was what 'you guys' felt then he accepted it. 'Steve took an extremely mild stand. Steve is a diplomat. He liked to view all aspects of things, feeling we still couldn't afford, at that stage, to be seen to be divided. Rebuke was enough' (BP to AS, 1978).

A very serious debate then ensued regarding boycott strategy, the main speakers being Biko and Keith Mokoape. Mokoape proposed a motion that SASO should withdraw from the campuses, and all black students be urged not to attend Bantu Education institutions. He felt that the stage was set for confrontation, and being part of these institutions compromised that. 'He spoke very sound, emotional, politically liberated language' (BP to AS, 1978).

Biko raised four questions. As SASO, *were* they, in fact, operating within government institutions? Was there much to be achieved by students if they were not registered with universities? Would SASO be able to sustain political activity with a large number of students outside the campuses? What would happen to the remainder of students still at these universities?

Biko was of the opinion that liberation was still at a preparatory stage and that 'we should continue, for our sakes and for our children's sakes, to make our presence at these universities worthwhile, supplement deficiencies so that we can have more resources and a function of leadership there. As long as there are black students there would be a reason to be there. No black student was dispensable to be just thrown away' (BP to AS, 1978). If the armed struggle was the answer, then students needed to have time to prepare for this, not just make a beeline for the border. This question consistently recurred throughout the next two decades but at that GSC Mokoape's motion was defeated.[7]

This somewhat detailed account is a record of Biko at work. At the 1972 GSC he was there not as president but leading the UNB delegation. In spite of considerable disagreement, he was able to carry the initial motion about Sono. He was not actually in the hall next day when his milder motion was defeated. He then accepted that majority decision, even though it was harsher than he felt was required. In opposing Mokoape's motion it is clear that he was looking at the long-term, wider picture, continuing to take responsibility for all students and not getting caught up in the emotion of the moment; he had a vision of the potential impotence of students who, if they were no longer *students* in the struggle, would cease to have a base

---

7 Mokoape did, in fact, leave the university and go into exile and later joined Umkhonto we Sizwe (MK).

from which to operate, for then who would they be? There is evidence of his capacity to allow things to happen without needing or trying to 'control' but, rather, taking leadership when he saw possibilities of division or short-term misunderstanding.

Father Aelred Stubbs speaks of Biko as having 'this deep-rooted profound intuition of togetherness. He wanted to be in the background. He couldn't be in the background in any ultimate sort of way. He wanted other people to take the lead. I think it was his intuition of what real leadership involves' (AS to LW, 1989).

Youth and Identity: To Love and to Work

'Freud was once asked what he thought a normal person should be able to do well,' Erik Erikson tells us. And Freud had replied: *'Lieben und arbeiten'*, to love and to work. Erikson goes on to say that 'it pays to ponder on this simple formula; it grows deeper as you think about it. For when Freud said "love", he meant the generosity of intimacy as well as genital love; when he said "love and work", he meant a general work productiveness which would not preoccupy the individual to the extent that he might lose his right or capacity to be a sexual and loving being' (Erikson, 1968:136).

Capacity to Work

Biko's work was to awaken the people: first, from their own psychological oppression through recognising their inferiority complex; secondly, from the physical oppression accruing out of living in a white racist society (SASO resolution, quoted in Woods, 1987:161).

Biko explained: 'I had a man working on one of our projects in the Eastern Cape on electricity ... a white man with a black assistant. He had to be above the ceiling and the black man was under the ceiling and they were working together pushing up wires and pushing through the rods in which the wires are and so on, and all the time there was insult, insult, insult from the white man. "Push this, you fool." That sort of talk. And of course this touched me. I knew the white man very well, he spoke well to me, so at tea-time we invited them to tea and I asked him: "Why do you speak like this to this man?" And he said to me in front of the guy: "This is the only language he understands, he is a lazy bugger." And the black man smiled. I asked him if it was true and he said: "I am used to him." This sickened me. I thought for a moment that I did not understand black society. After some two hours I came back to this black guy and said to him: "Did you really mean it?" The man changed. He became very bitter. He was telling me how he wanted to leave his job, but what could he do? He did not have any skills, he had no assurances of another job, his job was to him some form of security, he had no reserves. If he did not work today he could not live tomorrow, he had to work, he had to take it. And as he had to take it he dared not show any form of what is called insolence to his boss' (Woods, 1987:163).

What mattered to Biko was what work he needed to do in order for this person to be himself all the time (MM to LW, 1990). He further understood that self-realisation and identity also depended on seizing the necessary tools to function in a technological world, tools deliberately denied blacks by the Bantu Education Act. As Dr H. F. Verwoerd, Minister of Native Affairs at the time, had explained in parliament, when speaking about the new laws of segregated education: 'There is no place for [the Bantu] in the European [white] community above the level of certain forms of labour... For that reason it is of no avail for him to receive a training which has as its aim absorption in the European community above the level of certain forms of labour... Up till now he has been subjected to a school system which drew him away from his own community and partially misled him by showing him the green pastures of the European but still did not allow him to graze there' (Wilson & Thompson, 1971:225).

Demanding those denied tools – at the same time recognising that the green pastures of white education were not so green after all – led to widespread disruption in the education system, which was sustained by black students for a whole generation over the next two decades. In 1972, although reluctant to believe he could not manage both studying and political work, Biko chose the more difficult political road. This was formally affirmed by his dismissal from medical school in June 1972, having only officially passed three years out of six. What was more painful was that he would also have to disappoint his family's ambitions for him and those of virtually the whole Ginsberg community (Biko, 1988:4). The choice he made was one that thousands of black students would come to face: the choice of either becoming a political activist or taking the time to gain some sort of qualification towards a professional life, whatever the compromise, under apartheid. Biko thus sacrificed his chance of becoming a professional doctor. For the time being, his work lay elsewhere.

Two months later, in August 1972, he joined Bennie A. Khoapa as a staff member of the Black Community Programmes (BCP), whose offices, at 86 Beatrice Street, Durban, were on the same premises as SASO.[8] This programme was concerned to develop skills in the black community – 'issues of empowerment; the development of the ability to decide; the ability to be critical' were some of these – as well as to create practical programmes to meet sheer need. Biko's brief was primarily to coordinate youth leadership training and thereby 'expand the thrust of conscientising to youth beyond the schools' (BK to LW, 1989). He worked closely with Harry Ranwedzi Nengwekhulu. Youth groups already existed, country-wide, and many of them were well defined. They consisted not only of pupils in school but also those who had had to drop out of school early, for economic reasons, most of them now on the streets but some young workers in industry.

8 BCP was linked to the Special Project for Christian Action in Society or SPROCAS, a programme of the South African Council of Churches and the Christian Institute.

In this regard Biko recognised the importance of the educational methodology of Paulo Freire. He had read his book *Pedagogy of the Oppressed*, and
in July had sought out Anne Hope[9] who was running training courses on
Freire's educational method in Johannesburg and Swaziland. Biko assured
her that it was a methodology 'we really want to understand properly and
use' (AH to LW, 1991). Fifteen people enrolled, including Pityana, Mafuna,
Cooper, Moodley, Johnny Issel, Mthuli Shezi, Jerry Modisane, Deborah
Matshoba and others. They attended workshops over four months. Each
month's session consisted of five days of intensive training, after which
they returned to their local communities for three weeks of research and
practice. Key to Freire's methodology is the recognition that teaching
should be a political act, directly related to production, health, social conditions, to the regular system of instruction, and to the overall plan for the
society still to be realised in the future (Freire, 1978:13). The act of teaching
should not be separated from the act of learning. The trainees, therefore,
needed to be able to submerge themselves in the context of the learners,
primarily to be able to listen while encouraging learners to unveil and
'unpackage' their lives and experiences and problems. Listening did not
only mean literally hearing but listening in order to build a curriculum or a
meaningful training programme for people out of what they disclosed. This
training influenced Biko considerably and dovetailed with his style of leadership.

In the meantime BCP had applied to the Ford Foundation for funds to
produce a state-of-the-black-nation annual review, similar to the annual
survey of the Institute of Race Relations but written, researched and produced by blacks. Ford favoured Race Relations. Undeterred, Biko set about
organising the first issue of the *Black Review*. Khoapa says this was virtually
paid for out of the petty cash of the Black Community Programmes and, as
Biko explained, could be realised with 'the help of some boys who are
being chucked out of school and are not going back to university, like
Welile Nhlapo and Tomeka Mafole'.[10] Biko assured Khoapa that 'All they
need is some food and transport. I'm sure they'll be glad to do the paper,
the coordination and so on' (BK to LW, 1989). Biko was the editor.
However, by the time it was printed in 1973 Biko had been banned and
prevented from preparing any material for publication, and so *Black Review*
came out under Khoapa's name and was dedicated to Biko and Mafuna –
who was also banned.

Early in that new year Biko enrolled for a law degree through the correspondence university, UNISA – the degree his father had also aspired to. In
this and in his decision to continue with his political work, he selected the
career from which his relatives had sought to protect him and pursued his
vision: a vision that projected him beyond short-term historical processes
(PJ to LW, 1990).

9 A member of the Grail, a lay Catholic sisterhood, and coordinator of group work
at the Christian Institute, also serving on one of the SPROCAS commissions.
10 Mafole later became ANC observer at the United Nations.

Generosity of Intimacy

At a remarkably young age, Biko was capable of having very warm and strong ties with people. The effect of these ties was not to subordinate them but to support them in their own right, thus freeing them to develop, to recognise their potential and to grow. 'He was best at helping you be who *you* are best,' Mpumlwana explains (MM to LW, 1990). Most people who knew Biko well, felt an intimacy of their very own in relation to him, whether it was a friend, fellow student, lover, spiritual father, teacher or someone in authority. This intimacy did not engender rivalry. And this was part of his generosity in the sense that he spent a great deal of his time giving each person his undivided attention.

Neville Curtis, NUSAS president, describes him in those student days as 'an incredibly attractive human being. He was good-looking and articulate. He was a sparkler, a vivid person, a wonderful person. He could hardly ever talk to you without putting his arm around you. And also this "no bullshit" thing.' At the same time 'he was far from a perfect personality, a perfect human being. He was apt to over-indulge, but he was living life to the full and doing it with vividness and style' (NC to LW, 1990).

This generosity of intimacy naturally grew in complexity when it involved women, a complexity he largely chose to ignore. In those early travelling days there was an exploitativeness towards women which certainly bordered on chauvinism (WMS to LW, 1990). With his 'vivid style', Biko gained the reputation of being a 'womaniser'. His view of himself was that he was always open and people could take it or leave it. There was a certain defiance in his attitude reminiscent of his defiance against authority. Sexism, as a similar form of oppression to the one all too familiar to him, did not enter his head. Even when it was pointed out to him by women in the groups he worked in, it tended to be set aside. Doubtless, like many others in liberation movements in Africa and other parts of the world, he possibly believed that Black Consciousness would liberate everything at once. What it did do was to raise questions regarding sexism, among those women who worked within the movement. However, Dimza Pityana affirms that women were involved in Black Consciousness as blacks but not as black *women* (DP to LW, 1989).

Basically, Biko was insatiably curious and loved people. He found exploring relationships constantly fascinating, and though his exploration might lead to complications, which he sometimes did not know how to handle, he was someone seldom without love and respect. In the genre of the time, he accepted, without much thought, women's attention and did not hesitate to have relationships with many of them. Being the person he was, he was much sought after. Pityana, on looking back, feels that Biko had not yet come 'to judge for himself how much you could have a fulfilled relationship with a woman without all the sexual overtones'. At the same time, in the circles that emerged, it was also true that 'many of the women [themselves] did not accept that there could be an authentic relationship with a man without that relationship becoming sexually loaded' (BP to LW, 1989). At another level he treated all people the same. Serote observed that 'When you looked at the women around Steve, whom you knew he had personal relationships with, somehow the relationship between them had made something bloom – put lots of energy into every one of them. Even in relations like that he would continuously discuss these very complex issues, so many of the women had no choice but to continuously be conscientised and politicised!' (MWS to LW, 1990)

There is no denying that women are often drawn to men who exhibit a combination of both power and human understanding – Martin Luther King and John F. Kennedy immediately spring to mind. In Biko's case, he was still a young man and not in the kind of political limelight of international figures. Nevertheless, he had a similar ease of manner and charisma that was magnetic. He was not, however, always a good judge of his own emotional and psychological capacity. Sometimes, too, he did not correctly assess the emotional impact of his behaviour on others, and there were certainly times when he got himself into relationships he had not bargained for. He accepted people, all people, without prejudice. Even the security police he knew were human and, initially, he appealed to that. If that humanity continued to hide itself he virtually demanded it by his action and behaviour. It was only when he finally gave up on somebody that he sometimes became very angry. He accepted people first and then challenged them and, in risking his generosity of intimacy, usually had a profound effect on them. There was certainly no apparent seeking of power. Aelred Stubbs had the sense that Biko was somewhat wary of this potential power within him and that his saving grace was his recognition of his own vulnerability. This enabled him to be open to people. One of the reasons that so many people wanted to be associated with him was this very capacity to 'radiate joy and confidence, which gave people a sense of ease and of love' (BP to LW, 1989).

This kind of challenge, these relationships, not only enriched him personally but were the way he chose to become informed about his country. The parties and shebeening, apart from being an important antidote to his intense lifestyle, also provided the forum, the access to a variety of people he might otherwise never have met. Although he read and digested many materials and books immediate to his task, it was people who became the library of his life.

Love and Marriage

Freud, by his own definition, would have found Bantu Stephen Biko 'normal': Biko certainly knew how to work, and yet work was never without a circle or group of others, without consultation with colleagues and the trust of friends. His 'love' seemed bound to set people free. Later he exhibited a fearlessness and a powerful reasonableness that demanded respect even from the security police. Biko never lost 'his capacity to be a sexual and loving being'. Indeed, as we have seen, this capacity led to some complexity in his relationships. Few of these, however, had significant bearing on the two basic relationships which were of paramount importance to him. These attachments were different and deeply personal. They ran parallel, each one seeming to fulfil different aspects and needs in his life. He never found it possible to give up one for the other. One was with Ntsiki Mashalaba, who became his wife, and the other, Mamphela Ramphele, his colleague at medical school, who grew visibly in his presence and who became the doctor of the first BCP clinic, Zanempilo, near King William's Town, where she put into action much of the theory of Black Consciousness.

By 1969 Ramphele had known Biko casually for about a year, and had met him regularly in the SASO circle as she became part of it. She remembers a sense of deep attraction for him then, which she dutifully ignored as she was engaged to be married to 'home-boy' Dick Mmabane at the end of the year. In early 1970 she returned to medical school, married, and excitedly displaying wedding photographs and rings. It was only later that she discovered that Biko had written her a letter, which she never received, encouraging her to delay her marriage. Ramphele was 22. Biko meantime met Nontsikelelo (Ntsiki) Mashalaba and they were married at the end of 1970. They were both 23.

Ntsiki was training as a midwife at King Edward VIII Hospital in Durban. On their marrying, Biko's mother gave her the name Nosizwe – meaning 'Mother of the Nation' – warning her that 'your husband's name is Bantu and you are Nosizwe and you must know you are going to have lots of people around you' (NB to LW, 1990). Later Steve and Barney found a four-roomed house in Durban. Nosidima (Dimza) Pityana, Barney's wife, joined them. The relationship between the two women was warm and easy as they became good friends. During those few years they played a more or less accepted traditional role, sharing their first two babies, Nkosinati (Biko) and Loyiso (Pityana), who were virtually the same age. They also had the nursing profession in common, Ntsiki having finished her midwifery by the time she got married, Dimza still completing hers.

Nontsikelelo Biko, small and dark with large soft eyes, describes herself then as quiet. 'I was very quiet indeed,' she explained, particularly when she went to medical school and listened to the discussions, seldom participating but learning a great deal. She was a private person, owning herself but creating a sense of ease and welcome around her: 'You feel very safe with Ntsiki,' Dimza explains, 'and very comfortable. She was a non-threatening person.' 'Still waters,' says Malusi Mpumlwana.

The house was always full of people. They would arrive with or without Biko, at any time of the day or night. The main room more often than not contained sleeping bodies in the mornings: people from SASO, students from different universities throughout the country, and others. 'The money was short, short! But because we were working together with Barney at least we managed to have good meals,' Ntsiki recalls (NtB to LW, 1990).

'Sometimes we cooked meat, meat which would have been enough for the whole month!' Biko expected everybody to be fed as they had been in his mother's house, even when they were very poor. Although Biko led such a politically demanding life, Ntsiki chose not to get involved in that side in a superficial way, but to play a deeper, politically supportive role (DP & AS to LW, 1989). Biko, on his side, believed in his commitment to his family, loved Ntsiki, and, whenever he was there, nurtured his children. They loved being with him, the huge father with strength and humour. Later, in King William's Town, he sometimes took Samora (his younger son) to the office, forgetting to bring clean nappies to change him, to the infuriation of his co-worker and secretary Nohle Mohapi! Given his lifestyle, Biko was often away from home but 'I accepted him as he was,' says Ntsiki, 'a husband deeply involved in his politics. I very much accepted him.' He used to say when he brought his friends over: 'This is my wife, she's the people's wife, but we mustn't share her!' (NtB to LW, 1990)

And yet he expected her to share him. This type of expectation, this particular attitude towards his wife, highlights the ambivalence that existed within Biko. Whilst he questioned just about everything else, he accepted, without question, a traditional view of the role of a wife, and this included her total loyalty under all circumstances. His mother, to whom he was dedicated all his life, was, herself, a powerful model, a woman whose home and personality had enabled the community of Ginsberg to be welcomed, to be accepted in the true sense of community. And Ntsiki complied, as wives do, not knowing what great demands would be made on her in her marriage to Steve Biko, demands which, ironically, set her questioning and led her later to claim her own self-image with dignity and independence. Biko's expectations required what amounted to an inordinate degree of tolerance and forbearing. Deep down he wished and hoped to make a real go with his family and children but he soon realised – as with his medical studies – that this would not be possible (BP to LW, 1989). As his political commitment grew, things which he had expected to stay in place were submerged in its wake.

Biko was often obliged to work late at night and would sometimes remain in medical residence, where the SASO office still flourished. Amongst many others, he found himself working regularly alongside Mamphela Ramphele. She remembers how, in 1971, she got more and more involved with his thinking in the writing of the 'Frank Talk' articles. 'He would lie on his back and talk loudly about what he wanted to say, kind of dictating to me and I would take down the thoughts.' She would then have to respond because 'he was never the kind of person who would say, "Look, this is what happened." You just had to pick things up' (MR to LW, 1989). A dynamic, exciting, symbiotic relationship grew up between them, their skills complementing one another in many ways. A new energy was born. Being alongside Biko, Ramphele admits that she learnt a great deal about how to relate to people. On the other hand Ramphele's capacity to transform ideas into practical action made her presence strengthening and critically relevant to him. Apart from her obvious intelligence, she was disciplined and totally reliable. They were two powerfully attractive people and their relationship rapidly grew in depth, both politically and personally.

Soon after Steve married Ntsiki, Ramphele separated from her husband. She was very upset but, once back at medical school and into the swing of things, she increasingly became her own person, her inhibitions disappeared and, as her colleague Jay Pillaye says, she 'became very very energetic'. She removed her wig – another Black Consciousness abhorrence was the practice of black women using skin-lightening creams – and was more and more conscious of being proud of being black, sometimes expressing it with anger and verve.

Biko became bound into two relationships. In most cases, under these circumstances, choices and sacrifices eventually have to be made. But, until he died at the age of 30, Biko did not make them. All three people lived with another's shadow cast over them, sometimes more encompassing than at other times. Changing circumstances constantly affected their lives and equilibrium, but the complexity of this triangular relationship remained. Both Ntsiki and Mamphela bore two of Steve's children. Ntsiki had two boys: Nkosinati (1971) and Samora Mzontsundu (1975). Mamphela had a girl, Lerato (1974), who died at two months, and a boy, Hlumelo (1978), born after Biko's death.

It would be too bald to leave it at that. Biko was deeply sensitive and agonised over many things. This situation often moved into bright focus, demanding some resolution, especially when his relationship with Mamphela became more open and public, moving beyond a student affection into a powerful force. It was difficult to contain it without exposing its dynamic, and a vow they made early on, when it had begun to grow, not to hurt Ntsiki, was not sustained. She was deeply hurt by this relationship.

It is difficult to know whether (and, if so, when) Biko felt a real need to face these circumstances. The fact that he never *acted* to change them indicates that for a long while either he did not know how to or they were more acceptable to him as they were, unchanged. Aelred Stubbs raised the matter in 1974 just as he was leaving the Zanempilo clinic after a visit. Whether it was a shock coming from his 'dear priest' or whether he felt it to be a slight on his judgment, Biko was hurt and reacted with uncharacteristic anger: 'I regard topics of this nature as being extremely private. I am in many instances aware of the complexity that can be introduced by a willingness to accommodate the feelings of friends in a matter that is essentially private between two – or in this case three – parties. I have never found it necessary to reflect on my friends' private activities except in so far as I thought they affected at any one stage their political standing and their performance. Similarly I could never wish to ask you about your love life, your sexual life, etc. because I regard that as strictly speaking your business...'

He went on to make a more general observation: 'There is a profound difference in the way Westerners basically believe in character analysis to that adopted by us here. In many discussions I used to have with David [Russell] I agreed with him in comparing our attitude on the whole to that of the European working-class approach to life. When you guys talk about a person you tear him apart, analyse the way he speaks, looks at someone, thinks; you find a motive for everything he does; you categorise him politically, socially, etc. In short you are not satisfied until you have really torn him apart and have really parcelled off each and every aspect of his general behaviour and labelled it' (Biko, 1988:194, quoting letter to AS, late August 1974).

He admits, in the same letter, that in the political sphere, however, he had learnt to do this himself. Did he feel, then, that it was all right, and maybe useful, to subject politics to what he describes as a 'Western' analysis, but that his personal decisions were fiercely and culturally his own, in spite of affecting friends and colleagues around him? In Xhosa culture the cautioning of a young man by an older man would be acceptable; moreover, Steve had been brought up as a Christian. The puzzle was too great and too sensitive for rational answers. In someone who seldom failed to look at problems head-on and act on them in order to solve them, Biko in this instance was defiant, not yet ready for the solution. He obviously decided to live with these circumstances the way they were, in some ways refusing to see the implications in his usual clear, rational and human way. And then, there was the daily reality and, thereby, the rationale, of never giving it sufficient time. It was only in prison, in 1976, during a forced four months of solitary confinement, that he indicated he had begun to ponder this side of his life more fully and seriously

Bantu, Son of Man: 1973–1977

In October 1972, Biko was interviewed by Gail Gerhart, an American scholar and archivist.[11] He summed up the potential for the Nationalist government's stance, that if they were intelligent, they could 'create a capitalist black society', that South Africa was the one country in Africa where blacks might compete favourably with whites in industry, commerce and other professions. If they created this, 'South Africa could succeed [in putting across] to the world a pretty convincing, integrated picture with still 70 per cent of the population being underdogs!' However, whites were terribly afraid of this and, instead, were creating 'the best economic system for revolution'. The way they were going about it made communication among blacks easier, made the 'communication of ideas' possible through a shared, common stimulus as no physical or intellectual distance existed. 'In this whole conscientising programme, this is what makes ideas easily flow amongst people; this common ghetto experience blacks are subjected to.'

11 Author of *Black Power in South Africa* (1979).

In talking of the government's reaction to Black Consciousness, he predicted that it was obvious they would become more vigilant and take more definite action against the movement. 'But,' he went on to say, 'it's too late in a sense. We don't need an organisation to push the kind of ideology we are pushing. It's there. It's already been planted. It's in the people. We've got a very broad front, which is completely unintimidated. This constant change in leadership in SASO is partly to accommodate a very quick gradation of people to a certain level' (SB to GG, 1972).

When the first bannings came in March 1973, the movement was determined to treat it as a kind of hiccup. The state order immediately scattered eight of the leadership to different parts of the country, to whatever was their designated magisterial district: Pityana to Port Elizabeth, Mafuna to Johannesburg, Biko to King William's Town, and so forth. They removed some of the current SASO office-bearers – Jerry Modisane, then president, and Harry Nengwekhulu, permanent organiser; they took out two of the founding members of the Theatre Council of Natal (TECON) – Strini Moodley (also editor of the *SASO Newsletter*) and Saths Cooper (public relations officer for the Black People's Convention) – and Drake Koka, a founding member of BPC and general secretary of the Black Allied Workers' Union.[12]

The address given in the banning order to Biko was that of his mother's house in Ginsberg. There he returned, empty-handed, as it were, to the community that had funded an important part of his education. His mother remembers saying to him: 'Bantu, things are now hard for you. You are at home. You are doing nothing. When I was educating you I thought that by now I would be able to rest. Now, I am not resting. I cannot rest. You are imprisoned forever.'

Biko responded to her in the paradigm she best understood and asked her what Christ's mission on earth had been, and she had replied, 'To save the oppressed.' Then he said: 'I too have a mission.' She remembers looking at him standing in the doorway of her house and realising that 'there was something deep in this child and I had an understanding of what was going on'. Very soon Mamcete overcame her disappointment and, like the Mother in Bertholt Brecht's play of that name, became an ally who developed an expertise in dealing with the security police herself. Her open home now became home to all the young people who came to work in King William's Town. Although she never said so, she lived in fear of Biko's life night and day, and often lay awake until the early hours of the morning until she would hear his car return, the door open and she'd know he was safe (MB to LW, 1989).

Very soon after his arrival Biko located the Anglican priest, David Russell, who had broken the news of his banning to his mother. Russell lived in a small house in the grounds of the church of St Chad's in the heart of King William's Town's white residential area: no. 15a Leopold Street.

12 For details of others banned during the year, see *Black Review*, 1973:93-103.

The church had not been used for a year because of the collapse of the roof and the subsequent move of the congregation to the local townships of Zwelitsha and Ginsberg. When Russell approached the priest-in-charge, James Gawe, they agreed it should be used as an office for SASO and BCP. Very shortly all three organisations were functioning, the BPC existing through the facilities of the other two with no official status of its own, and a new committed community began to form.

Russell was not part of Black Consciousness but had his own agenda, which was well under way when Biko arrived. Speaking fluent Xhosa, he had taken up the cause of people removed from farms and towns like Middelburg and Burgersdorp, to an area in his parish called Dimbaza. This was one of many ill-prepared resettlement places in the homelands where blacks were forced to go, where there was no form of subsistence, no proper housing on arrival, where old people died of shock and infants of malnutrition. The state pensions were R5 a month, and for widows with children, about R3 a month plus rations. Russell had first fasted on the steps of the Cathedral in Cape Town to draw attention to this, and then himself lived on R5 per month, for six months, writing a letter each month to the Minister responsible.

Biko was undoubtedly drawn to Russell as a kindred spirit – not only intellectually but also finding him helpful and trusting him as a friend and confidant. Russell also knew about local conditions, including the security police. Biko trusted Russell's political antennae and would enjoy dropping in on him at different times of the day or night to relax, letting slip his own political persona to discuss all kinds of issues – one of which was Russell's own stance and the nature of his commitment. When Russell explained that, as a priest, he was called to poverty, chastity and obedience, which included leading a celibate life, Biko was curious enough to test himself against these in the light of *his* own commitment and wrote a rare six-page document, which he and Russell discussed at length (see Biko, 1988:230–236).

'Does God exist? I have never had problems with this question. I am sufficiently convinced of the inadequacy of man and the rest of creation to believe that a greater force than mortals is responsible for creation, maintenance and continuation of life. I am also sufficiently religious to believe that man's internal insecurity can only be alleviated by an almost enigmatic and supernatural force to which we ascribe all power, all wisdom and love... God has laid for man certain basic laws that must govern interactior between man and man, man and nature at large. These laws I see as inscribed in the ultimate conscience of each living mortal.' He goes on to say that 'Obedience to God in the sense that I have accepted it is in fact at the heart of the conviction of most selfless revolutionaries. It is a call to men of conscience to offer themselves and sometimes their lives for the eradication of evil.'

Biko was a religious person in the broad sense of the word. He also knew that anybody who would attempt to try and influence the black population politically and de-emphasise religion would not succeed (BK to LW, 1990). In the document to Russell, Biko is at pains to be honest and grapple with the Christian faith, not only because he is talking to a Christian but also because he is exploring his own self in relation to the way he has absorbed some of that faith. Choosing the word 'revolutionary' distances him from the practice of the Church and seems to enable him the freedom to pursue obedience to conscience (what he calls 'ultimate conscience' as opposed to a person's own conscience) without the cloying aspects of an institution.

'To the revolutionary the Church is anti-progress and therefore anti God's wishes because long ago it decided not to obey God but to obey man; long ago the Church introduced segregated worship and segregated seminaries.' Further, the 'Churches have tended to complicate religion and theology' and 'to drive away the common man by immersing themselves in bureaucracy and institutionalisation.' Christ 'is so conservatively interpreted at times that I find him foreign to me. On the other hand if I accept him and ascribe to him the characteristics that flow logically from my contemplation about him and his work, then I must reject the Church almost completely.'

In Biko's definition, the Church as an institution was not so distant from other institutions like segregated schools and universities, which in turn were not distinct from the law and the state. In Biko's view all these were the antithesis of God's basic laws, and in working towards obedience to God as he saw it – the exploration towards his own 'ultimate conscience' – he fulfilled his definition of a selfless revolutionary by knowing before he died that he, too, would have to give his life for 'the eradication of evil'. Early on, as we have seen, he had an intense dislike for mindless and destructive authority, and a healthy distaste for institutions that became ossified and limited and behaved accordingly.

In the confined enclosure of apartheid he refused to be reactive to its system. Instead he ignored its desired psychological stranglehold and used its racism to forge a common cause with many others, a community dedicated to creative and practical action. He recognised that beneath the layered levels of anxiety and fears was a deep seam with which to work. He was convinced that the ground rules that made for human communication and interaction lay in coming to know this consciousness. This involved demanding in others an encounter with what was ultimately humane in them, a quality he sought and often brought forth. His life now turned him face-to-face with the law and the state in the form of both the security police and the courts. In this formidable encounter he was to put to the test his faith and the essence of who he was and what he understood, knowing that the revolutionary's task includes 'liberation not only of the oppressed but also of the oppressor'.

Banning and the Culture of Fearlessness

Banning was intended as a drastic form of restriction. Its conditions put banned people in charge of their own imprisonment. It confined any movement out of the specified magisterial district – this was often the district where one was born – and could mean losing one's job if one worked elsewhere. It prevented one from entering any place of learning; from preparing anything for publication; from attending a gathering of any kind; from talking to the press. It prohibited a person from being with more than one other person at a time, and in some 'house-arrested' cases banned people had to report to the police once a week and were confined to their homes between the hours of 6 p.m. and 6 a.m., as if under a private curfew.

'Banning orders have a strong tendency to turn a person into a social leper', wrote David Russell, in the *Daily Dispatch* of 1 September 1973. 'The banned are legally innocent citizens incarcerated in an inhuman twilight existence. It is no exaggeration to say that banning is a form of violence; violence to justice, violence to family, violence to persons. [There is] no means of appeal or recourse to a just hearing. If he [Biko] has a meal with friends he can be dragged before the courts and smeared as a common criminal. He can be found guilty and sentenced to imprisonment for anything between one and ten years.'

Biko was not in the worst position. Father Aelred Stubbs, who regularly visited the banned, estimated that King William's Town was preferable to, say, Kimberley, and Kimberley preferable to Port Elizabeth (AS to LW, 1989).

As people were banned they were very closely watched by the system. The security police did everything to catch them out. Even if a person was meticulous, it was virtually impossible to live within the confines of the banning order. If one did try one found oneself being one's own jailer, which was just the psychological condition desired by the government, because that began to make one despise oneself, an unacceptable state for anyone involved in Black Consciousness. So it became a cat and mouse game.

The suppression came in waves. No sooner had the leadership of SASO, BPC and BCP, which was banned in March 1973, been replaced than they, in turn, were banned in August; those who replaced the August people were banned in October, and so on. Harassment by the security police was relentless, and charges were consistently laid in a further attempt to secure impotence and a sense of despair.

How did the movement respond to the banning order? In King William's Town, to begin with, people were afraid of being seen with Biko. 'I mean, we had the police actually driving bumper to bumper behind us 24 hours a day, and that scared people,' Mpumlwana recalls. The basic principle was not to ban yourself but to let the police do all the work: to monitor the system, to have to trail around following people night and day, to be made to work hard to ensure that what they had implemented was their responsibility. 'So we didn't recognise the banning order in a sense. We put good locks on our doors. To all intents and purposes, if you're indoors the police have got no power.' There could be a party in one's house but they would have to prove one was part of it. Mpumlwana laughed at the irony: 'You can't be held responsible for being in your house where the party is being held!' (MM to LW, 1990) The banning order was studied, the loopholes found, and those banned began to interpret it for the police. For example, 'We told them that if you are in a car the principle of [being in] a group doesn't apply in the same way as it applies in a house because you've got passengers, because you could be a bus-driver or a taxi-driver. The fact that you are with people doesn't mean you are in a group. They accepted that interpretation all along and we drove happily all over the town!' (MM to LW, 1990)

They also held to the principle of not being reckless, not giving the police the opportunity to have them in court. At the same time, Mpumlwana explained how 'we learnt not to trust lawyers' opinions on things. We found that they were very conservative legally, and so it was important, if you wanted to break the law, to make your own rules. If you happen to be wrong they will have to defend you but don't ask them what is right!' (MM to LW, 1990) This, in turn, led to a strategy of *using* the courts as a public forum. It was not new for South Africans, accused of political opposition, to use the dock for defence speeches, thus keeping alive historic political statements and realities, which could be quoted and put to use by the media and opposition world-wide. However, Black Consciousness was not banned as such, only individuals were, and it was realised that the courts could be used to their purpose as much as everything else, part of the defiance of every day. On the occasions when Biko, for example, was taken to court for infringement or violation of his banning order he displayed his new-found legal skills, having thought ahead before he broke the conditions as to what new legal point he could appeal to or what interpretation had not yet been tested. He was never jailed on that account. This helped strengthen the resistance of other banned people, who were isolated or particularly harassed by police vigilance, and of those in prison.

As banning persisted and detention without trial increased, the Black Consciousness style of leadership, passed on to many groups in formation schools and workshops, came into good effect. An indefinable community, country-wide, with no easily identifiable leadership was already in existence. And those banished by the state were never considered separate from the others. Rather, they were considered to have been 'relocated' and it was assumed they would become effective working in these areas. They were part of decision-making, part of a circuit, and were consulted. Just as in the early days Biko had visited the banned as a matter of course, this was extended to a wider community network created out of trust and regular interaction. Those people who could be, were constantly on the move. Pityana, who was banned in the tough Port Elizabeth district, remembers the extraordinary way in which each person, no matter where he or she was staying, would be considered. Nobody was allowed to feel abandoned, however remote and however harassed. Enormous risks were taken at times in order to assure that this happened. Thenjiwe Mtintso, a Fort Hare student, who came to work in King William's Town, says that those around Biko often forgot he was restricted and admits that it was only later, when she herself was banned to Johannesburg, that she became aware of how Biko had 'given so much to us, politically and otherwise, done so much and lived under such pressure. The guy was restricted and we could move. I don't think I spent even one little worried day thinking about "Oh, shame, Steve can't move!" Steve was not all that old but we expected him to have all the answers' (TM to LW, 1990). Biko was 26 when he was restricted.

It was necessary to become fearless, to conquer fear – the kind of quality that grows through exercise (AS to LW, 1989). 'They weren't polite, they were tough,' recalls David Russell, 'but they knew the kind of parameters of how tough you could be without overplaying your cards and so the [Security] Branch was scared of them. They didn't know how to handle them.' Russell recalls one incident when they raided Biko's home in Ginsberg at night. Biko asked them what they wanted. They usually said they had come to see if somebody was there or that they were looking for banned literature, or some such pretext. They wanted to go into rooms where people were asleep. 'Biko said, "Well, let me tell you now that you are not going into *that* room because that is where my mother sleeps and you're not going into *that* room," [indicating] where his brother-in-law was with his wife. But they *did* go in there. And he said: "You see what you are doing with yourselves, you are opening people's doors and looking at people sleeping in bed with their wives at night." Biko made them feel small. He was also angry and it was time they got out. He moved towards them, cigarette in one hand and put out the butt in the palm of his other hand. The police got a tremendous fright. He had, in fact, moved to flick it out of the window but they had thought he was going to attack them. He was big and physically strong. They were really thrown. They found it extremely difficult to handle his style, his intelligence, his statements; a man of that calibre. I think that set quite a tone of style for the grouping there' (DR to LW, 1990).

Biko challenged what was ultimately human in others. If those terms were not forthcoming he could be tough, as tough as anybody. Donald Woods reports one occasion when he was in an interrogation room, in detention, with 'seven security policemen standing along the walls all around him. [Warrant-Officer] Hattingh entered the room, walked straight up to where Steve was sitting, and slapped him hard across the face.

"What happened then?" I asked.

"I hit him right against the wall," Steve replied. "Bust his false teeth."

"Then what?"

"He went straight out of the room. I had the feeling he didn't know what to do, or how to react, so he just went out – presumably for further instructions from his superiors."' (Woods, 1987:89)

This unhesitant response to insult, to what was inappropriate in his definition of human behaviour, was a direct display of how Biko exhibited fearlessness of other men and practised Black Consciousness as a way of life. As far as he was concerned he was innocent, should not have been banned or detained, and was certainly not going to be bullied.

Banning was considered as just one more of the innumerable restrictions that apartheid legislation placed on black lives. Biko refused to change his lifestyle in spite of the attempts by the state to watch him night and day. He assessed the conditions of living under the banning order in a very intelligent manner, leaving the state to its own devices without any co-operation whatsoever from him. It was their problem. Although he seldom showed the strain, it may well have been the reason for his occasional, sudden and violent outbursts of anger at something of no great significance, when he would even hit out physically and it became very difficult to calm him.

Biko, like all of the others, consistently broke every single banning condition. In spite of being prohibited from preparing material for publication, he had completed the editing of *Black Review* and, later, was part of a team which prepared material for a regular newspaper column the Black Consciousness point of view secured in the local East London paper, the *Daily Dispatch*. Biko often met more than one person at a time but was careful not to be seen to be doing so. He found a quiet place, within his magisterial district, near a dam, where he would drive with friends or visitors who came to consult him, to avoid the offices, which were bugged. If it was necessary he went out of his magisterial district. On many occasions he drove to see his wife, Ntsiki, when she worked in Keiskammahoek during the week; in 1974 he and Mpumlwana went to Durban after the arrest of most of the SASO–BPC leadership in 1974 to sort out problems there.

Banning failed to destroy the spirit and development of Black Consciousness. The next four years saw the flowering of some of the most imaginative and practical projects it was to produce. Very shortly King William's Town became an important place where many people touched base. The arteries of contact persisted more fiercely. Many of the banned did, in fact, also visit it and, on one occasion at least, at a late-night gumba, Biko was seen to put his hand over his lips each time he opened the door to admit one person after another who, according to the law, should not have been there. Since the gumba was both a forum and an essential palliative for the increased tensions that existed, they, too, persisted and were memorable to anyone who attended them in those besieged days.

Growth of a Community

Biko asked Mpumlwana, who was then 22, to help him settle down and find people with whom to work, and the office in King William's Town was set up. Mpumlwana had already been alongside Biko in Durban. Late at night, after completing an issue or a SASO pamphlet, they would end the long hours of work and politicking with wrestling: 'It was our game. I enjoyed felling him. I'd played rugby. I'd go for his legs, lift him off and throw him down.' This was no mean feat as Mpumlwana was no match for

Biko physically. He is small and slightly built. With his wide-set, dark eyes he is alert to suffering and humour alike. Like Biko his laugh, loud and infectious, cuts through tension. Unafraid of confrontation, he persists in challenging values and pursuing uncomfortable truths and has often mediated in crises involving warring political factions. Mpumlwana came willingly, thinking he could spare a couple of weeks. The weeks turned into months and years; in fact he never left.

A new group quickly formed. Their potential grew and was realised in the tough climate of the Eastern Cape. They became some of Biko's most trusted comrades involved in innovating new ideas. When one person was restricted in one way or another the joint effort protected that person, and he or she went on working. Initially Biko was regional director of BCP; Mapetla Mohapi came in to work for SASO, and Nohle Haya, who married Mohapi, was Steve's administrative assistant. Thoko Mbanjwa worked with Malusi (they later married). She, Biko and others did the research for the *Black Review* and Thoko edited the 1974–75 edition. Mxolisi Mvovo, married to Biko's sister Nobandile, worked as marketing officer for the home industries that the BCP was running. Nobandile worked with Thenjiwe Mtintso for the Border Council of Churches. Her work was closely connected to the BCP work, running self-help projects, bursary schemes and support programmes while Mtintso was field-worker for the Dependants' Conference, funding and working with ex-political prisoners in Dimbaza and elsewhere. Nomsa Williams did research for *Black Review*, and, later on, Peter Jones did the BCP books.

The fact was that designation was irrelevant. Mtintso, for example, though she had had little writing experience was assigned as journalist when Donald Woods gave Black Consciousness an opening on the newspaper he edited, the *Daily Dispatch*.[13] Later, a regular column in the newspaper became Mapetla Mohapi's responsibility. In it the BC viewpoint was expressed. The decision of the content was a group assignment, discussed and debated and even jointly written. Mohapi later became administrator of the Zimele Trust Fund to aid ex-political prisoners, a totally different assignment. King William's Town soon had a research and publishing department running and a showroom to display clothes and leather-work made locally in home industry centres. Several projects got under way throughout the country. A glance at the issues of *Black Review* of 1973–6 indicates the extent of what began to be researched and discussed, and underlines just how much there was to report. It attempted to be faithful to a wide range of aspects, thus making it today an invaluable source of information for those times: youth, workers, education, theatre, writing, political organisations, political trials and so forth. *Black Review* had, as its companions, *Black Viewpoint* and *Black Perspectives*. The creation of cottage industries producing leather goods and cloth garments existed in villages near King William's Town, such as Zinyoka, Njwaxa and Norwood, and,

13 Mtintso later became an active member of the Union of Black Journalists.

later, in Cape Town. The Zimele Trust Fund was set up to aid ex-political prisoners, mainly ANC and PAC people, who were being released into the resettlement areas where there was no employment; bursaries were also raised for their children. The Zanempilo Community Health Centre was officially opened in April 1975; Mamphela Ramphele was its first medical officer and came to live at the clinic. Training courses in leadership, which also conscientised blacks to their reality, continued throughout the country, particularly among the youth. Hierarchy was automatically discouraged. It was literally pointless and diminished what was possible. Apart from aiding the system, dominance by individuals would prevent the evolution of ideas. 'We must not create a leadership cult. We must centralize the people's attention onto the real message,' Biko said (Woods, 1987:190). Curiously the word 'democracy' was not part of the language; rather the word used was 'communal'. More and more people, who were themselves active elsewhere, dropped into 15a Leopold Street from all over the country.

Black Consciousness took root and grew in spite of the awesome restrictions of the 1970s, when each year claimed more banned, and more detentions were made, often under the ferocious Section 6 of the Terrorism Act. With no access to lawyers, no certainty of being charged, detainees were often kept for months in solitary confinement, taken away from their work for long periods of time. Almost everyone whose name is mentioned above suffered detention of one sort or another. Many left the country: Mafuna and Serote went to Botswana in 1974, around the time that the current SASO–BPC leadership was arrested for holding an illegal rally to celebrate the FRELIMO victory in Mozambique. Others left later, many in the aftermath of the 1976 student uprising, some only to return from exile in 1990, after the De Klerk declaration of 2 February.

In a book entitled *Black Theology: The South African Voice* (Moore, 1973; see Biko, 1988:108), Biko defines Black Consciousness as 'an attitude of mind and a way of life'. Its philosophy was to express 'group pride and the determination of the black to rise and attain the envisaged self'; its realisation was to recognise that 'the most potent weapon in the hands of the oppressor is the *mind* of the oppressed'; its methodology was to enable the evolution of ideas to flourish and thereby give a wider range of people the chance to voice opinions, even if some were inarticulate and hesitant at first. Those who lived and learnt through this method and understood it, became a community and took that rootedness with them into whatever area of the struggle they later found themselves. The influence of this BC experience changed the nature of the liberation movements and is an integral part of that history, recognised and acknowledged.

It is essential to place Biko in the context of that community which he helped to create. Within it he was seen as one of the most selfless in character, consistently available to others in ways outlined earlier – his room at medical residence was everybody's room, his house in Natal was everybody's house, his mother's home in Ginsberg became the focal point until the Zanempilo Centre was created – a crucial asset in that time of banning and dislocation. Within this kind of context, because of this type of accepted availability, people were prevented from being isolated and enabled to function. Biko, too, could not have survived without the many others. His personality, however, broke the taboos and had a freeing influence (MM to LW, 1991). So, instead of needing to consult him every day, people found it exhilarating to be independent, seeing him from time to time for sheer pleasure and for rejuvenation in defiance of the authoritarian state. Mpumlwana describes him as the visionary and the adventurer; as being 'like the plough with virgin soil to till; but the field would not bear any fruit without all the other implements, including the seed and the rain' (MM to LW, 1991). Biko knew this. It would be an insult to separate him from the wholeness of the process. He also needed to be cared for, needed love. He sought it in other people as much as they sought it in him, and doubtless Biko spent too much time surrounded by people in excess of this desire. He also needed to be loved and cherished by women, and in spite of the harsh realities he faced and dealt with, had a softness and a gentle sensibility.

There were costs. Enormous dedication and extremely hard work was required. Ramphele remembers: 'I was on duty 24 hours a day, 7 days a week, 52 weeks of the year' at the clinic. This necessitated a submersion of individuality and sometimes the suppression of aspects of individual talent and growth. It became a duty to be tolerant and to listen; it was necessary to be able to accept criticism and act on it (MR to LW, 1989). One of the drawbacks was that having experienced the support of the group and the circle some found it difficult to adapt to other circumstances, especially when they went into exile.

For most, however, it was a nurturing ground for the potential within them that otherwise might not have been realised. Developing trust took its time but was rewarding and cost-effective in the end. Those who built it then have never lost touch, in spite of taking different political roads. Remembrance of Biko symbolised, for those who knew him, the essence of this growth. On 19 October 1977, a month after he died, all the Black Consciousness organisations were banned and people further scattered through banishment and imprisonment. Out of anger over his death and in dedication to what he stood for, many of those who had worked with him refused to let things die. Ramphele, virtually single-handed, built a new clinic at Ithuseng, near Tzaneen, in the district to which she was banished; Mpumlwana continued his mediation work through the churches, preventing many a death in later years; Pityana went into exile and became a priest, later working to combat racism in the international arena at the World Council of Churches; Thoko Mpumlwana stayed in King William's Town and expanded the Ginsberg Educational Trust to include the whole Border region. It became known as the Zingisa Educational Project. Nohle Mohapi joined Thoko and worked for Zingisa until 1990, when she began a new branch in Port Elizabeth, Khanyisa. They all fell under the umbrella of a national Trust, established in the 1970s when the government put pressure on non-governmental organisations through new laws governing fund-raising. This is called the Trust for Christian Outreach and Education, and gives support to a variety of grassroots programmes under the directorship of Nontobeko Moletsane, who had herself been a sister at the Zanempilo Centre. Thenjiwe Mtintso, who suffered shocking treatment and torture in prison, went into exile, joining the armed struggle in Umkhonto we Sizwe (MK) and later became the ANC's ambassador to Uganda. She remembers that 'When we built that community, around Steve, around King William's Town, it really made us. It really made the good parts of me. We were building together, we were fumbling along, starting so many things together, and that made us. And that created the political discipline that we think we have. If you simply look at that lot that came from King William's Town, that went to Lesotho, there were seven of us [who went into exile in January 1979], they were given responsibilities even when we were in Lesotho and we had just joined the ANC. They were young people in their twenties – but quite mature, quite disciplined and very committed and serious. We worked like slaves. Work was not torture, it was part of your whole life' (TM to LW, 1990).

'King was my political home. The group began to be my political school. And Steve began to be my political mentor as a person. But [he] went further than that. He was my counsellor in my own private life. He was a friend, he was a brother, he could actually be all these things, put together. I don't want to put him beyond being a human being. He had his faults, many of them, but one thing I liked about him was the care. Steve could even read your mood, could even take time to talk about your own life; like I was earning this little money and he would sit down and find out: How are you managing? How are you sending money home? He had this attraction for all of us , I think. He was not an enigma – he was, I can't explain it, but I can only say that it was that attraction and that attachment and wanting to spend as much time as possible with Steve, whether in a political or social or informal context. I used to have this craving – if I had not had time [during the day] to be around the group, I'd missed out; or to find he wasn't there, the group [was] not as lively, not as exciting' (TM to LW, 1990).

Political Strategy

The Black People's Convention (BPC) had been established in June 1972 to expand the work of Black Consciousness beyond the student and youth groups of SASO. At its first conference in December it debated two points of view: whether it was to be an umbrella, culturally orientated organisation acting as a parent body to all African organisations, or a direct political body through which blacks would realise their aspirations (*Black Review*, 1972:8-11). Over the next two years it sought to find its feet despite continual harassment of its leadership. In September 1974, in conjunction with

SASO, rallies were planned in solidarity with the victory of the Front for the Liberation of Mozambique (FRELIMO) to mark the installation of Mozambique's new transitional government. The rallies were banned the night before. It was decided, however, that the rally due to take place at Curries Fountain in Durban would go ahead. According to the *Black Review*, about five thousand people had gathered there. The police arrived, broke up the rally and arrested people on the spot. They then rounded up many others from the numerous offices of SASO, BPC and TECON (Theatre Council of Natal), the Black Allied Workers' Union, and so on – all the Black Consciousness groupings, in fact. Those arrested were held under Section 6 (1) of the Terrorism Act, 'which allows for indefinite detention, incommunicado' (*Black Review, 1974–75*:80-1). Seven months after the rally thirteen people were charged in April 1975 under the Terrorism Act, and most of the others were released. Those charged were Sathasivan 'Saths' Cooper (24), Justice Edmund Lindane Muntu Myeza (24), Mosiuoa Gerald Patrick 'Terror' Lekota (28), Maitshwe Nchaupe Aubrey Mokoape (30), Nkwenkwe Vincent Nkomo (24), Pandelani Jeremiah Nefolovhodwe (25), Gilbert Kaborane 'Kaunda' Sedibe (24), Rubin Hare (20), Strinivasa Rajoo Moodley (28), Sadecque Variava (25), Absolom Zithulele Cindi (25), Sulayman Ahmed 'Solly' Ismael (20), and Sivalingham Moodley. *Black Review* carries details of the process which took place before people were finally brought to court. Charges against Ismael and Sivalingham Moodley were withdrawn on 23 June and they were released (*Black Review, 1974–75*:77-90). By the time Biko gave evidence in May 1976, a further two people had been released and there were nine accused.

As Mpumlwana drove the newly released Mohapi from Pretoria to Natal in early 1975, they debated the role that BPC might now play. An idea grew that it should explore its potential as a catalyst for uniting the liberation movements. This idea emerged for several different reasons: the logic that BC's evolving ideology should develop from psychological unity to political unity; the fact that, in spite of the bannings, SASO and BPC still had mobility and continued to operate nationally on the ground; the recognition that the ANC and the PAC were the established political movements and that BPC would not act as a third force but would endeavour to create a national consciousness involving all the existing historical political movements against the common enemy. It was a delicate matter and BPC was a fledgling organisation. The proposal would need to get a mandate. Nevertheless they were convinced, as Pityana asserts, 'that Black Consciousness provided a common programme, one with which the entire liberation could identify', that they had to assert that the stature and leadership of the ANC and PAC were unassailable. 'So, again and again, we acknowledged both the authority of the liberation organisations and the authentic leadership in prison or in exile' (Biko, 1988:11). Pityana explains that 'it was really the only basis on which the ANC or PAC militants could associate with Black Consciousness'.

The idea was discussed with Biko and others from different parts of the country – Thami Zani, Tom Manthata, Kenny Rachidi and others. Influenced by developments in Zimbabwe of unity between ZANU and ZAPU, BPC set out to test their bona fides with the banned PAC and ANC and also with other, smaller political groupings like the Unity Movement. Contact was made with known ANC and PAC supporters, notably the lawyer G. M. Mxenge and Robert Sobukwe respectively. The two were sympathetic to the idea. They in turn agreed to contact their organisations both internally with the underground movements and externally. Confidence grew and BC people travelled extensively. Biko also travelled when necessary.

SASO and BPC had good standing with other political groupings still functioning in South Africa. A joint project was being planned to protest against the impending 'independence' of the Transkei in October 1976. This involved the Unity Movement and other groupings in the Western Cape, where some community programmes were also founded in common, and good personal links were formed. If practical united action was possible along these lines it would later help to build trust for the idea of political unity, they felt.

The next BPC Congress was held in King William's Town in December 1975, the same month in which Biko's new restriction orders prevented him from working for the Black Community Programmes. At the Congress policy documents were proposed and debated. The idea was that these were to be used as working documents in the negotiations with the ANC and the PAC. However, most people at the Congress knew nothing about these planned talks. In the political climate of the time the security risk was too great for the normal open discussion on such matters. The undemocratic approach involved in this must be acknowledged, but there did not seem to be any alternative. It had taken nearly a year of 'delicate shuttle diplomacy to persuade both the ANC and the PAC representatives to agree in principle to a joint meeting to explore the question of mutual co-operation' (MM to LW, 1991). The meeting, due to take place immediately after Christmas, involved not only banned *people* but also the banned organisations.

The economic policy document was written to avoid possible withdrawal of either PAC or ANC, and took its starting-point as 'Black communalism', described in *Black Review* as 'a modified version of the traditional African economic lifestyle which is geared to meet the demands of a highly industrialised and modern economy'. It gave considerable power to the state and local communities but avoided defining itself in Marxist terms or employing the classical class analysis (for details see *Black Review, 1975–76*:123-125). This document, as well as one on the vision of a future state, met with considerable criticism. Mafika Pascal Gwala (editor of the earlier *Black Review* of 1973) saw it as a 'reversal of development and history' (MPC to LW, 1989) and remembers how he really quarrelled with Biko about it. At a further workshop in Mafeking in May 1976, he and others like Diliza Mji, Faith Matlaopane, Norman Dubazana and Nkosazana Dlamini felt that proposing far-reaching policy documents was no business of the BPC but the prerogative of the ANC and involved the 'fleshing-out' of the Freedom Charter (MM to LW, 1991). Such policies could smack of the beginnings of a third force rather than an attempt to find common ground.

This was happening at just about the very moment when Biko was subpoenaed to give evidence in Pretoria in the SASO–BPC trial of the thirteen charged after the FRELIMO support rally. In the confined space of the court, feeling his way through the minefield of cross-examination, Biko chose his words carefully to explain that 'we are advocating black communalism which is, in many ways, similar to African socialism. We are expropriating an essentially tribal background to accommodate what is an expounded economic concept now. We have got to accommodate industry. We have got to accommodate the whole relationship between industry and politics. But there is a certain plasticity in this interpretation precisely because no one has yet made an ultimate definition of it' (Woods, 1987:183–4). He proceeded to talk of bargaining and the importance of dialogue between themselves, who held this African socialist view, and those 'who hold dear a free enterprise system, and out of these two clearly the synthesis will come' (Woods, 1987:184). Although Biko was speaking in the alien environment of the courts, and this can hardly be defined as a clear economic policy, Biko was also speaking to a broader audience. Biko also determined that two things were critical to his agenda: to better understand the nature of economic forces and to further pursue the growing debate about the validity of the class analysis (SB to FW, 1977).

Within a month of Biko's giving evidence in Pretoria, a key political event occurred: the pupils of Soweto protested against the imposition of Afrikaans as a medium of instruction for three of the six subjects required to obtain a matriculation. Dissatisfaction and restlessness had been brewing for some time against many aspects of Bantu Education but this regulation was the last straw. It mobilised into action the enormous peaceful protest which became known as the Soweto uprising. Police bullets claimed the lives of hundreds of young people throughout the country. Reminiscent of Sharpeville, it hardened attitudes. Thousands of students crossed the border to take up arms and join the ANC's Umkhonto we Sizwe or the military wing of the PAC. Their full stories are yet to be told but the Soweto uprising and its aftermath changed the face of South African politics, including Black Consciousness. Biko was insistent that no specific organisation could claim the uprising: 'It took us all by surprise,' he said (SB to FW, 1976). How much of it was psychologically spurred by eight years of Black Consciousness and its contact with youth organisations is yet to be assessed. In the SASO–BPC trial, when cross-examined by the state prosecutor on what image the BPC was giving out about the ANC and the PAC, Biko had stated that 'The struggle is what we attach ourselves to. At different times it is picked up by different people in different methods' (Woods, 1987:195). Black Consciousness organisations were automatically drawn into helping young people to cross the borders.

The SASO–BPC Trial

Professor C. R. D. Halisi, in a paper discussing intellectuals and black political thought in South Africa, states that much of the analysis of Biko's thought has been based upon the testimony he gave at the SASO–BPC trial. It was the only time Biko's voice was heard directly after his banning in early 1973. Halisi acknowledges this as 'at best, a tricky source' (Halisi, 1990:30). This is true, yet, at the same time, re-reading the evidence also gives an indication of the uncompromising manner and confidence of purpose with which Biko handled the case.

Biko was subpoenaed to appear before the court and those charged were mostly people he knew, some close friends. His task was to define Black Consciousness so that they might not be given severe sentences – the mandatory sentence for anyone charged under the Terrorism Act was a minimum of five years.[14] The case tested all of Biko's skills and was an example of his obvious eligibility for becoming a lawyer. He displayed the capacity to walk through a minefield of cross-examination without compromising himself or incriminating the accused. In the dock Biko often appeared to control the argument, either as the astute politician or the story-teller, the humourist or the teacher. In the expression of his answers lies the compassion for his country and its people.

His first test was to assess the situation, having accepted the conditions of participating in the due process of the law of the land. The evidence led by David Soggot, assistant counsel for the defence, gave him the chance to state clearly what Black Consciousness was as well as inspire people once again with dignity and pride, defining SASO and BPC to be concerned with 'the whole development of the human being, in other words the black man [*sic*] discarding his own psychological oppression'. Under cross-examination by both the defence and the state, he emphasised why its historical logic was blatantly obvious and reasonable. His assessment of Judge Boshoff was to draw him into dialogue. He answered his questions as if in a genuine debate, often defining things in the judge's own terms of reference, exhibiting how well aware he was of the judge's own history. He thereby evoked a genuine interest from Boshoff, Biko's manner indicating that they might solve things together. In this style and manner Biko drew the judge into some insights that he had not been aware of before, and there are moments, in the reading of the evidence, where the judge indicates interest beyond what seems to be the scope of the case. After a dialogue about one man one vote, one-party states in Africa, and the meaning of democracy, the judge, in questioning who should have the vote, asked:

'Well, take the gold standard. If we have to debate whether this government should go on the gold standard or off the gold standard, would you

14 It is interesting to note that he had not been in favour of defying the Curries Fountain ban but, once it had taken place, had immediately supported everyone arrested, broken his own banning order by going to Durban to iron out problems affecting lawyers and other matters (MM to LW, 1991).

feel that you know enough about it to be able to cast an intelligent vote about that?'

Biko: 'Me, personally?'

Judge: 'Yes.'

Biko: 'I think probably better than the average Afrikaner in the street, my Lord.'

Judge: 'Yes, well, that may be so. Now do you think you know enough about it to be able to cast such an intelligent vote that the government should be based on that vote?'

Biko: 'Yes, I think I have the right to be consulted by my government on any issue. If I don't understand it I may give it over to someone else that I have faith in to explain it to me... I mean, the average man in Britain does not understand spontaneously the advantages and disadvantages of Britain becoming involved in the European Economic Community, but when it becomes an issue for public decision, political organizers go out and explain and canvass their points of view, and the man in the street listens to several people and decides to use what he has, the vote.'

Judge: 'But isn't that one of the reasons why Britain is probably one of the most bankrupt countries in the world?'

Biko: 'I think I prefer to look at it more positively and say it is one of the most democratic countries in the world.'

Judge: 'Yes, but now it is bankrupt?'

Biko: 'I think it is a phase, my Lord. Britain has been rich before. It may still get up the ladder again. I think it is a phase in history' (Woods 1987:181–182).

Biko displays a certain patience. Throughout the testimony he seems to hold the reins, seldom faltering or appearing to be caught out in any way; he uses statistics well and accurately, and turns what could be dangerous leads into something very reasonable:

Attwell [state prosecutor]: 'In your own view at the moment, do you consider that the blacks are in a position to overthrow the State by violence?'

Biko: 'I do not think so?'

Attwell: 'The military expert also suggested that the most productive sphere in which the blacks in this country could work toward change was the black worker sphere, do you agree with that statement?'

Biko: 'If you are talking about fundamental change perhaps it is a possibility, but I think there are other spheres which lend themselves to easier use. Take the field of sport for instance, which I think is in the vital interests of society also, in that it foreshadows attitudes in other areas. I think the country is now at a stage where considerable pressure can be applied fruitfully in the sphere of sport.'

Attwell: 'But in what sphere in your opinion can the blacks exert the most pressure and be most effective?'

Biko: 'I am telling you now, sport' (Woods, 1987:187–188).

Biko does not treat the prosecutor in the same manner as he does the judge. It is more the cat and mouse game he had practised for so long with the security police. Almost immediately he makes it clear that shoddy definitions and bullying tactics hold no sway with him. He displays his ease of intellect by redefining questions or words, using the very techniques he would expect a good lawyer to use, with skill and apparent confidence. He uses humour and ironic references to whites to express the ironic nature of the society. There is a discussion on the meaning of the system. The definition flows from 'the police' into 'institutionalised racism', with a graphic example of Biko having to use the 'white' toilet in the very building they are in and the marked display of racism he encountered as he did so, even though there was no 'black' one.[15] And when asked whether he describes himself as a freedom fighter he immediately knows where that comes from and challenges:

Biko: 'I did use the expression once to Security Police who wanted to know what my profession was, and I said I was a freedom fighter.'

Attwell: 'I think that was with tongue in cheek, not so?'

Biko: 'Well, it was making conversation, and if you have got to live with the Security Police on your neck all the time you have got to devise a way of talking to them, you know, and this is one of the ways. Generally, they understand only one language' (Woods, 1987:190).

Those four days must have helped to restore any morale that might have been low amongst those who were charged; it would have revitalised the fearlessness and the solidarity, and assured them that they were amongst those pushing forward the struggle. Reading the evidence today[16] makes us forget the tense and dangerous circumstances under which it was given, makes it tempting to assume that this *was* Biko's own true testament and the 1976 expression of Black Consciousness. Partly it is, but there were terrible pitfalls that were set up, which Biko avoided in a remarkable way. The atmosphere was one of deliberate intimidation. The prosecutor constantly led arguments in which he attempted to connect BC, and those charged, with the politics of the banned movements and their leaders. Biko was called at the very time that the BPC was embarking on its unifying role aimed at making contact with those banned organisations, and his genius lay in the way in which he kept many balls in the air at once, not compromising, not intimidating and yet maintaining the attention of the judge. Not everything he said was exactly the way it was. In the film *Cry Freedom*, the director read and used the court record to elicit evidence that Black Consciousness was non-violent. This was not entirely so. The policy of BPC was to explore the non-violent route (SB to The American Committee on Africa, 1977) but many BC people were disillusioned with that and left the

15 Mandla Langa, also called as a potential witness, had the same experience. He used the same 'white' toilet – 'there are no toilets in Pretoria for blacks' – and the police came to throw him out and chased him as he ran up the stairs back to the trial. In the court-room he sought refuge with David Soggot, who, as they went out, gave him his bag to carry, preventing the police from what Langa describes would have been a 'thorough hiding'!

16 It is quoted at length in Woods, 1987:149-205 and Biko, 1988:115-156.

country to follow the political logic of the armed struggle.

The atmosphere of the court was highly charged. Mandla Langa, another witness, feared for Biko's openness and obvious display of a superior intellect, feared his manner would do him harm: 'It was like war, really; you could feel the enmity' (ML to LW, 1989).

Members of the international world began to recognise Black Consciousness, as articulated by Biko, as a key political voice in the country, whereas for most white South Africans, Biko's reply to Attwell's question probably sums it up:

Attwell: 'So you agree with me that the whites basically are afraid of Black Consciousness?'

Biko: 'I would say that the majority of whites are not even aware of Black Consciousness' (Woods, 1987:204).[17]

The Man Within

In spite of not having been in agreement with the decision to defy the ban on the Curries Fountain meeting, it must have been a relief to have performed his task well. When those in the trial and many others had begun to be arrested in 1974 Biko expressed in a letter to Father Stubbs that he felt 'a strange kind of guilt'; he felt a responsibility that 'so many friends of mine have been arrested for activities in something I was most instrumental in starting', a lot of them 'blokes I spoke into the movement'. He comforts himself somewhat by saying that nobody knows why some of them were included and also that no trend in the movement warrants the 'terror act' being invoked. He then reminds himself that 'one does not think this way in political life, of course. Casualties are expected and should be bargained for. An oppressive system often is illogical in the application of suppression' (SB, unpublished letter to AS, October 1974).[18]

In the same letter Biko admitted that for himself the going had been 'tough under the present restrictions'. Again he qualified this with his usual optimism and confidence: 'I am nowhere near despair and frustration but can understand only too well why some of our guys are.' He saw the positives in his life: 'a supportive and defensive township', 'reasonably fulfilling work' and 'I live with a very supportive family, one which is fully committed to my commitment if not to the cause itself'.

Biko seldom revealed his fears openly. Both his sister Nobandile and his colleague Thenjiwe Mtintso say that if banning did get him down, it never showed. Emotionally he took on the mantle of the father to the extended

---

17 The accused were found guilty and convicted to the minimum five years' imprisonment on Robben Island, and as Woods puts it, 'the verbal expression of black anger against white rule had now earned the judicial definition of terrorism' (Woods, 1987:205).

18 His words were carefully chosen. Any letter could be, and usually was, read by the security police. The 'terror act' *was* in fact invoked.

family. Once he had a job he became joint supporter with his elder sister Bukelwa in looking after his mother, insisting that she stop working. After the sudden and tragic death of Bukelwa of a heart attack, in his mother's house in September 1975, he and Ntsiki carried the responsibility. He also displayed a responsibility to everyone he worked with, including those he *had* worked with, now banned or banished.

It was only to the very few that he revealed doubts and his own fears. Father Aelred Stubbs was one of these people, and the evenings he had spent with Russell 'were very good palliatives to the mental decay that so easily sets in' (SB, letter to AS, October 1974). To Ntsiki he expressed the expectation that she would be widowed before he was 30. When his frustration occasionally burst into uncontrolled rage, to the shock of those around him, because it was rare and so uncharacteristic, Ramphele was one of the few people who could calm him and get him to go away to some quiet place. He shared many of his innermost thoughts with her as well.

He talks of his supportive family being committed 'to *my* commitment if not to the cause itself'. Biko was surrounded by women who loved and nurtured him, and Mamcete, Ntsiki and Nobandile, his younger sister, complemented his life with their dedicated womanly care. Certainly they understood and supported his commitment and were drawn in. Men offer women the idiom of including them in the 'just cause' to which they themselves are dedicated although often a woman's functional task under these circumstances is to prepare food and drink, and provide a home, release and comfort. With it goes the assumed superiority of the man's intellect and choice of work, which is given time and space to be expressed. This can be exploitative, and Mtintso remembers, in the mundane way in which it is so often expressed, that 'there was no way you could think of Steve making a cup of tea or whatever for himself!' She herself once refused to do so for him and met the consequences!

Biko expected that traditional support from women, but within the working group around him, he and the others also assumed equality of purpose and capability from women. 'We would have our revolts,' Mtintso remembers. 'They do want women to be political, to be active, to be everything, but they still need a complement of women who are subservient', and this was why outside women ('*khukhuchis*')[19] were always brought into the gumbas 'to add glamour to the party' (TM to LW, 1990). Ramphele also did her fair share of this kind of nurturing support, providing a welcome to all the visitors who came to see Biko at the clinic. He sometimes ate two meals, one there and one at his mother's home, and he put on weight!

But another kind of authority was emerging amongst the women. After Mtintso had withstood, with considerable courage, very rough treatment and torture in prison, Biko was filled with admiration. Ramphele, too, was more and more an example that defied the traditional definition. Had cir-

19 The word 'khukhuchi' was derived from Letta Mbulu's popular song of the time, 'Khukhuchi-khukhuchi wee'.

cumstances not turned the way they did, it was surely only a matter of time
before Biko would also have had to consider the existence of sexism as a
destructive 'ism'. In relation to Biko, not only had Ramphele become the
professional doctor with a secure income, but he had long sounded out his
ideas with her, and expressed his excitement while she helped him to
remain consistent in the application of his ideas. She had been a constant
sounding-board in his political thinking and this made a huge difference in
the restricted environment of King William's Town. He could also unbur-
den himself to her when necessary. Ramphele took little notice of his flirta-
tion with other women, being confident in herself and of the depth of their
own recognition of each other. After 101 days in prison – much of it in solitary confinement – at the end of 1976 , with considerable time to think
about his life, he came clean with some of these flirtations; she couldn't
believe it and laughed and laughed. He admitted that the two of them
seemed bound into a common destiny and that it was partly *that* that he
had been trying to escape. She remembers him saying something like: 'I
know we are two strong personalities and there is no way you are going to
submit to me nor am I going to submit to you, so we have to negotiate our
relationship!' (MR to LW, 1989)

Ntsiki of course understood his nature well, too, and accepted it in a different way: 'It needed somebody with strong convictions, or strong – I
don't know whether to call it love for somebody – to stay with him. I doubt
very much, even if I had left him, I am sure he would have married several
times. I know he wouldn't have lasted in marriage. And I know he was
very fond of his kids' (NtB to LW, 1990). However, by early 1977, Ntsiki
took her own independent stance. She had handled more than she was
willing to take. She had constantly raised issues with Biko, which he understood, but he did not long comply with her wishes. She began to look for
another post, and when a job came up in June–July at All Saints Hospital in
Engcobo in the Transkei, she told Biko she intended to move away and set
about filing a divorce. No matter how much she had challenged Biko, he
did not change. His approach to her as his wife remained what is perhaps
best described as traditional, with that expectancy of a role-model wife
who was supposed to understand and accept whatever her husband chose
to do. Ntsiki loved Steve but circumstances went beyond her endurance.
Particularly as his wife and, maybe one should add, as the daughter-in-law
of Mamcete, for whom Ntsiki had deep respect, there was the added difficulty of making personal demands against the powerful circumstances
which she had fallen into: her husband was banned and deeply committed
politically; people came to consult with him night and day; there was the
necessity for her to have a job to survive, not only financially but also personally; the job was outside her husband's magisterial district; there was
the knowledge that Steve was bound in with Mamphela, politically deeply
committed to the work she was doing and all that surrounded her, including the powerful status which being a doctor carried in the community,
especially as a woman; the fact that the clinic had become his logical politi-

cal base. Ntsiki was not aggressive, did not expect to perform the undignified task of fighting for her committed rights as a wife, her inalienable rights as a married woman. They had talked through the things that upset her, constantly, and she had conceded a great deal regarding his work 'but the relationship part was becoming too much,' she said. 'It was beyond my acceptance' (NtB to LW, 1990). Ntsiki never stopped loving Steve.

The Power of the State

King William's Town was changing. On 15 July 1976 Mohapi was arrested and detained at Kei Road police station under the Terrorism Act and died in detention three weeks later on 5 August. This was a tremendous shock. It was alleged that he hanged himself with a pair of jeans (*Black Review, 1975–76*:95). It was clear that he hadn't. The post-mortem was conducted by Dr R. B. R. Hawke, a pathologist, in the presence of Ramphele and Dr Msawuli, who were themselves then detained on 13 and 29 August respectively under the Internal Security Act. Biko was detained on 27 August, and Mvovo, Mpumlwana, Mbanjwa and Mtintso in the same month. Mohapi's widow, Nohle, ran the office for four months until they were all released in December, when Mtintso was banned to Johannesburg and Mvovo to Dimbaza. In March 1977 Mpumlwana, now married to Thoko Mbanjwa, was held under Section 6 of the Terrorism Act for another four months. At the beginning of April, Father Stubbs was stopped by police on his way from Port Elizabeth airport to a local church where he was to preach on Good Friday; he was body-searched and ordered to strip, an indignity Biko thoroughly disapproved of. In the same month, Ramphele was banished to the northern Transvaal. She was removed, suddenly and swiftly, from the BCP offices in Leopold Street by the police – only having time to grab her handbag – and driven hundreds of miles. Within days of her arrival, having been told where she was to work in a particular hospital, she realised that the number on the warrant for her arrest and banishment did not coincide with her Reference Book.[20] Even her name was spelt wrongly. She rang her lawyer, Raymond Tucker, who agreed this made her banning order null and void. Her young brother, Thomas, had just arrived to see her at Trichardtsdal. 'All she said was, "Good! I'm glad you've come. Now we're off!", bundled him into the car and drove the 200 miles odd to Johannesburg' (Biko, 1988:225–226). At 4 a.m. Ramphele and Father Stubbs left St Peter's Priory in Johannesburg and drove to the Zanempilo Centre, arriving twelve hours later. Great reunions, but only for ten days, before the system, slightly embarrassed, got its act together and banished her again for seven years. In those defiant days Hlumelo Biko was conceived, to be born after his father's death, miles away in Lenyenye, where Ramphele, having refused to work in the place assigned to her by

20 The hated pass book all blacks had to carry in South Africa, which controlled their every movement.

the system, began to establish the remarkable clinic of Ithuseng. After the long detentions of 1976 the state continued to break up and destroy continuity all over the country by consistently removing people. Staff in the office and the clinic went down to the minimum, the column in the *Dispatch* ceased, the signs were ominous and the state was menacing, but there was nothing to do except carry on.

Peter Jones, who was an activist in the Western Cape region of BPC in 1975–76, was asked by Biko to come and help manage the office in King William's Town. He had been part of a team, including Mpumlwana, Mvovo and Thandisiwe Mazibuko, who travelled widely to enlist support for the campaign to protest against the 'independence' of the Transkei. By now it was conceded that the Black Consciousness Movement had become 'the least contentious' of the political organisations in terms of forging some kind of unity of focus for all the liberation movements in spite of the fact that the planned meeting between the banned organisations had had to be postponed in December 1975. Events, including the arrest of the PAC leadership, had subsequently prevented its taking place internally. This idea had to be abandoned in favour of engaging the liberation organisations outside the country (MM to LW, 1991). 'The relationship with anyone outside was based on the nature of the relationship we had with people inside the country,' says Jones. By 1977 'people were very close to us. There was no credibility problem. And because of Steve's quiet position he [was] the best placed to personally promote it.' In January 1977 Biko was appointed honorary president of BPC in order to provide him with the leadership identity necessary. He was 'more visible than a lot of other leadership within our organisation, not media visibility but a crucial kind of visibility' (PJ to LW, 1990). Unity talks needed to take place outside the country as well. It was decided that Biko should secure an invitation from abroad. In April, when Father Stubbs had delivered Ramphele back to the clinic, Biko asked him to procure some such invitation in the UK or Europe, which he did.[21] Biko made the same request of Lein van den Bergh, a Dutch lawyer who, representing a Dutch funding agency, visited King William's Town around that time.

International Perspective

Representatives and diplomats of foreign countries, constantly on the look-out for personalities representing opinion, began to consult Biko as someone who held the key to what was going on in the black world (MM to LW, 1990). This was partly the result of his performance in the SASO–BPC trial but also because of the arrest of virtually all the leadership of the Black Consciousness Movement after the Soweto uprising, including himself.

In December 1976, Senator Dick Clark, who was attending a conference

21 Stubbs never returned to South Africa. His visa exemption was withdrawn on 16 July 1977.

of the African–American Institute in Lesotho, applied to the government to see Biko while he was still in detention. Biko was released just before they were due to meet. Mpumlwana reports that immediately Biko knew this, he 'sent word to us in prison that he was out, was seeing Dick Clark[22] and asked, "What should I say to him?" That evening we battered our way at a statement, which we smuggled out early to influence his presentation.' Even under these circumstances there was consultation. Biko presented Clark with a memorandum entitled 'American Policy Towards Azania' (MM to LW, 1990).

After a polite preamble the memorandum pointed out that although words had been abundant by US politicians in condemning apartheid, 'very little by way of constructive action has been taken to apply concerted pressure on [the] minority white South African regime'. It then outlined 'a few minimum requirements' (nine in all), including a reversal of the policy whereby the US looked 'to the South African government as a partner in diplomatic initiatives in Africa'; a more severe economic policy on trade and arms embargoes; the withdrawal of investments and the introduction of living wages and proper employment practices by US firms in South Africa; no tolerance towards Bantustan leaders but US officials should insist on seeing 'authentic black leadership' in the country and that Carter (then president) should move fast on Namibia, noting that SWAPO was 'recognised by us black people as indispensable in the formulation of any independence plans'. Another 'requirement' was the legitimation of 'non-government initiated platforms' like the BPC and the banned organisations; also the release of political leaders (Memo to Dick Clark, 1 December 1976).

Clark made a press statement after meeting Biko that 'I talk to Vorster [the prime minister] when I want to find out what the Government are thinking. I have talked to Mr. Biko to find out what blacks are thinking' (Haigh, January 1977).

Soon after this Biko was invited to the US, under the auspices of the USA–SA Leadership Exchange Programme, but he refused, explaining that he would only accept such an invitation when 'America had given proof of a radically changed policy towards South Africa' (Stubbs, 1988:229). In most of the liberation movements, the US was considered 'imperialist', a country whose foreign policy towards other countries preferred 'economic stability' under an oppressive regime, rather than supporting a people's struggle for democratic human rights which invoked radical political views in order to attain that. Biko expressed to Donald Woods how Western countries merely 'slapped the wrist' of the South African government but 'maintained their diplomatic and economic links that helped to bolster the regime' (Woods, 1987:139). Moreover, 'The Andy Youngs are nice enough guys, but their approach is doing us no damn good. If we are to have a peaceful solution here the Andy Youngs must stop talking and start really getting tough with Vorster – sanctions, blockades if necessary, the lot. We

22 Chairman at the time of the Senate Sub-Committee for Africa.

blacks reject the theory that sanctions will harm us more' (Woods, 1987:140).

As repression closed in on the Black Consciousness Movement, contact with the outside world became more and more important. It was the only 'court of appeal' in the increasingly dangerous atmosphere in South Africa, where the judiciary was virtually castrated by the legislature. Biko immediately recognised the usefulness of diplomacy amidst the growing danger that surrounded him and his colleagues. More and more people were dying in detention. The strategy was to inform the outside world as precisely as possible about the nature of that detention and the necessity to act against the South African government.

In a recorded interview with an American businessman, probably made around January 1977, Biko speaks about what detainees were up against. It was after Mtintso had been beaten up and tortured, and Biko was very angry about that: 'When I went into jail, my friend [Mohapi] had just died. He was the 24th person to die in jail since 1973. When I came out, they were talking about number 27. And this is happening increasingly now, because of the frustration the police are having. They want quick information. Now, there's an extent to which a person can absorb beating without revealing information. But sometimes it so happens that, in fact, the person being assaulted doesn't [have the information]. And they simply go on and on with a towel around your neck saying "Speak" – and you say nothing – "Speak" – you say nothing – and the bloody brutes are not trained well enough to realise when enough is enough. So by the time they release the towel you have been dead for a couple of minutes' (*The New Republic*, 7 January 1978).

In January 1977 he met with Bruce Haigh, second secretary in the Australian Embassy. As they drove out to a quiet and secluded place of Biko's choice (to avoid the bugged BCP office), Biko expressed interest in the current political and economic situation in Australia, stating that he looked to that country and others, like Scandinavia, Britain and the US, for some answer as to how the process of democracy would deal with the demands of an evolving technocratic society.

Biko led the discussion throughout, covering a wide range of topics, giving Haigh important information – for example, what he felt were the reasons for his own detention. Haigh reports: 'they [the police] were trying to find out how many students had fled to Botswana and Swaziland and what they were doing there. They knew very little and he had been unable to help them.' Biko then gave Haigh the real information: that several thousand students *had* fled (since the Soweto and country-wide uprising), that 'lines of communication had been established between them and the students still in South Africa', and that Biko believed demonstrations would now be smaller in order to avoid loss of life; his expectation was 'that in future small groups of two or three people would probably start using explosive devices against selected buildings and government installations'.

Further, it was his opinion that 'the students felt that as activists they had a legitimate claim to lead the protest movement', that 'the ANC and PAC were building up their organisations within South Africa once again, but this was only after the students had created the pre-conditions for their return and re-organisation'. The youth who went into exile helped inject new energy and life into the liberation movements, informing and influencing them directly in assessing the thrust of the current political climate. They also went to take up arms.

Biko treated Haigh as an intelligent ally, giving him careful political information throughout the visit. Haigh himself was strongly aware of the danger surrounding Biko. In his very last entry in his report he wrote an appeal to his government: 'Please protect Biko' (Haigh, 13 January 1977).

In these last recorded interviews with Biko – notably by foreigners – the strategy was to get information out fast. It was important to understand each interviewer and assess what would be the best information for each one of them so that it could be carried as far as possible to the right quarters. In reading these interviews, even superficially, we again witness Biko's astute understanding of the people he is meeting and of the situation at hand. In August 1977, speaking to the American Committee on Africa he explained that BPC's 'line' was to explore the non-violent road within the country, but that there was also the view 'that the present Nationalist government can only be unseated by people operating a military wing'. His own opinion was that 'in the end there is going to be a totality of effect of a number of change agencies operating in South Africa'. He would also like to see fewer groups. 'I would like to see groups like ANC, PAC and the Black Consciousness Movement deciding to form one liberation group and it is only, I think, when black people are so dedicated and so united in their cause that we can effect the greatest result.'

Arrest

When he spoke those words, Biko had long since set out on that course. Only a few days later, he left for Cape Town on 17 August, once again breaking his banning order. Through Peter Jones he had a long-standing plan to meet with various people there. There was also a need to settle some possible dissension within the BC ranks and to consolidate discussion around the possibility of their formally adopting the class analysis (A. W. Marx, forthcoming book). Another reason was to deal with some criticism of his having met with Clark (NA to LW, 1991). Biko also hoped to see Neville Alexander, who, having once been a member of the Unity Movement in the 1960s, now represented an important political grouping in the Western Cape. Alexander had served ten years in prison on Robben Island with the major ANC and PAC leadership and had been banned and house-arrested on his release in 1975. He was an articulate exponent of the class analysis and had considerable influence in this regard. Although Biko wished to see Alexander for other reasons, he had expressed interest in his political views (SB to FW, 1977) and might have hoped for a stimulating debate as well. But the times were very risky, and before he left King William's Town, Alexander had said he would not be able to see him. This message was not communicated to Biko, who only discovered it on arrival.

It was getting in and out of a magisterial area that was the greatest risk for those banned. Once out it was less likely that a person would be recognised. Perhaps it was a bad omen that Pityana was detained, once more, two days before Biko left. Ramphele was banished, Ntsiki had gone, Mpumlwana was only recently out of jail. Nobody thought the trip was more risky than usual. However, when they arrived in Cape Town things did not go as expected. Because of the controversy within the BC ranks, the policy decision made by those around Alexander was not to discuss things directly with Biko until the local BC position had been ironed out. 'We asked Biko not to come down but he came, both to see us and to settle the BPC rift in the Western Cape' (NA to Marx, in the latter's forthcoming book). There must have been some expectancy that, once Biko was there, Alexander would feel obliged to see him. This was not the case. Alexander was, politically, strictly disciplined. 'I had not been mandated to see him and could not get such a mandate in time,' he said (NA to LW, 1991).

This attitude was difficult for Biko to accept, and he waited for three hours outside Alexander's house while an old Robben Island friend of Alexander's, Fikile Bam, who also happened to be in Cape Town, was brought in to discuss whether he might change his mind. This was a high-risk operation for all three of them: Alexander was banned and house-arrested and under constant surveillance; Bam was virtually banished to the Transkei homeland and had to get special permission to be in South Africa; and Biko could have been recognised at any moment.

Jones intimates the growing unease they felt: 'A few other things happened in the course of that night. We just felt that we were not in control of the situation. There were too many shadows around us. By the morning – it was very dark still – we decided [to] get into the car, say to people we were going to have a party – because they expected us to have a party – and disappear' (PJ to LW, 1990).

Driving back to the Eastern Cape, Biko obviously had things on his mind: 'For the first time we were actually talking personal things. We were going through his life, his marriage and stuff, and I was going through my girl-friend at the time – I wasn't married – and my aspirations, and so on. What hit me was I couldn't recall any other time when we spoke with so much clarity,' recalls Jones (PJ to LW, 1990).

Nearing the end of the long journey, round about 10.20 p.m., Jones was driving into Grahamstown. Biko had a tape-recorder on his lap and they were listening to a tape. Both were lighthearted and relaxed. As they came round the bend they ran into a roadblock of uniformed policemen and 'a number of plainclothes men I realised were Security Police' (Woods, 1987:377).

When requested to open the boot, Jones had difficulties because it was not a car he knew. While waiting for this to be executed, one of the plainclothes officers asked Jones where he was going. 'East London,' he had replied. Then the man looked at Jones and said: *'Jy gaan seker vir ou Biko sien'* ('You're no doubt going to visit that chap Biko'). Peter showed no reaction and said: 'Who's Biko?'

Impatient with the intransigent boot, the same plainclothes officer, Lt. Oosthuizen, 'suggested I should follow them to the charge office where the car could be searched,' Peter remembers. 'He [Oosthuizen] started to walk to his car, then as an afterthought he said: *"Daai groot man kan met my ry, en julle kan saam met hom ry"* ("That big chap [Biko] can ride with me and you [the police] ride together with him [Jones]".)'

At the charge office, having identified Peter Jones by his wallet, the police then asked Biko what his name was. '"I am Bantu Stephen Biko," he replied. For several moments there was absolute silence with police just looking at both of us. "Biko?" Oosthuizen asked. "No, Bantu Stephen Biko," said Steve, giving the correct Xhosa pronunciation to the *b*'s'[23] (Woods, 1987:377-378).

Next morning they were 'viciously handcuffed' and removed to Port Elizabeth to the sixth floor of the police headquarters at the Sanlam Building, handcuffed by one hand to the bars, then photographed, taken back outside, 'separated by two squads of police who surrounded each of us... I was in front and Steve a few paces behind me.

'My entourage stopped at a Kombi [van] and I was told to enter and lie face down on the floor between the seats. I turned to look at Steve who just passed and called his name out loud. He stopped to look at me and called my name and we stared, smiling a greeting, which was interrupted when I was slapped violently into the Kombi. That was the last time I was to see my close comrade ever – alive or dead' (Woods, 1987:381).

Peter Jones was held for 533 days without trial. He was finally released in February 1979. On his release he immediately wrote down all he could remember. During those first twenty-five days during which time Biko was also held, he tells us what happened to him in the hands of the Port Elizabeth police.

After his last glimpse of Biko, the Kombi took off on 'a very fast journey with many turns... I couldn't fit into the floor space comfortably and had to lie on my side. We stopped outside a police station [Algoa Park] ... and I was taken into the charge office ... [where] I was subjected to another search by Nieuwoudt, who then slapped me around. Later, I was taken handcuffed to the cells. The Security Police, six of them, threw the blankets and mats outside, except for one blanket and one mat. I was unhandcuffed and stripped naked. Immediately the six policemen began shouting abuse and hitting me, before forcing me into a shower where the cold water had been turned on full force.

'As I stumbled into the shower [still being beaten] I turned and grabbed

23 'The events of this night and subsequent events convinced me the Security Police had absolutely no knowledge of our movements during the 17th and 18th of August 1977,' reflects Peter Jones.

the hand of Nieuwoudt and pulled him with me into the shower. This led to more severe beatings. I stood in that cold shower capable of nothing but hating them as I looked at them laughing at me... This became routine for the next five days...

'That first week of detention I spent mostly trying to get warm. It was very cold in Port Elizabeth ... I would wrap myself completely in my blanket and try to sleep, which I did most of the time as the cold showers and beatings used to thoroughly exhaust me. I was never questioned really during this time of "softening up" except for the Security Police constantly accusing me and Steve of having been in Port Elizabeth...

'Meals consisted of dry bread three times a day. Sometimes there was coffee in the morning and less frequently at lunch a mug of some brew referred to by prisoners as "Kupugani" which I never ate. It took weeks for me to settle down to being able to eat any sizeable amount of this dry bread... I ate very small portions when I experienced real hunger pains. My normal bodily functions became alienated from my normal mental processes to the extent that I had to consciously decide that I should try to make use of the toilet... I had no exercise, could not wash... I had to drink water from the toilet bowl, as well as try to wash some of the worst accumulated dirt from my body.'

Six days after his arrest formal interrogation began: 'The first session lasted for more than twenty hours. I left my cell at about 2200 hours [on 24 August] and was brought back at about 1800 hours the following night... We drove at high speed to Sanlam Building ... immediately I entered the room I was held by several police while one of my hands were freed and my clothes taken off. I was made to sit naked on a chair with my left hand chained with the handcuff to the chair. Snyman and Siebert occupied chairs at desks respectively to the left and right of me.

'On the desk in front of Siebert was a length of green hosepipe. I was able to look right into the hole of the pipe and noticed that the hole was filled – with what, I cannot say, but it was something metallic.' General questions followed. 'Then suddenly they focused on the trip Biko and I had been on... I repeated my original story that I had gone down to Cape Town to attend to a newly established project there (a clothing factory) and that Steve's presence was incidental and unplanned with no other intention than giving him an "outing"... Siebert suddenly jumped up and hit me with the hosepipe across my face and chest and arms, and then returned to his seat... Siebert told me they knew we had been in Port Elizabeth, that we had dropped pamphlets and that we had seen or met some people with whom we distributed these pamphlets.[24] After some time of following this trend I told the police that in fact we had been in Cape Town to have discussions with our BPC men there.' Jones was given pen and paper to write two statements: his political history and the story of the trip. This did not satisfy Siebert who ordered two policemen to put him *op die stene* (on the bricks).

24 As it happened, 20 August was the anniversary of the student uprising in Port Elizabeth.

'Soon after this Siebert re-entered, accompanied now by Snyman, Nieuwoudt, Marx and Beneke.'

After some resistance Jones was forced onto two small pieces of brick. 'Two chairs (heavy steel ones) were placed one on top of the other (the one upside down), and both Beneke and Nieuwoudt had to lift these until I could hold them high above my head. Siebert told me that should the chairs lower or fall I would "get it". I told him it was impossible to hold. I was already experiencing cramps in my legs.' Questions followed on Jones's involvement in BPC and BCP. Jones lowered the chairs to his shoulders. They were taken away and he was again chained to the chair and, again, the subject of the pamphlets and Port Elizabeth came up. When he repeatedly said he knew nothing, he was again placed on the bricks. 'Snyman started calling me names and calling me a liar. He got up from his chair and kicked me on the left leg. I stumbled and the chairs came tumbling down, one hitting him on the head and the other landing on Siebert's desk... I was taken from the bricks, on which I had by now spent several hours, and both hands were handcuffed. Siebert got up and asked me when I was going to stop lying, and started to deliver heavy blows with both hands (open) to my face. I grabbed both his hands and pulled him down towards me. I told him that the treatment was unnecessary as I was answering their questions. Siebert, who is smaller than me, told me to let go of him, and did I want to fight? Two fist blows followed delivered by Nieuwoudt and Beneke ... these two grabbed my arms and held them firmly.

'Siebert removed his watch and rolled up his sleeves. For a very long time he slapped my face with both hands (open) continuously and without pause. I remained silent, felt my senses dimming gradually to the stage where I could with a detachedness just feel the blows going through my head while I looked straight into Siebert's eyes.

'Just behind Siebert was a mirror hanging on the wall and I could see my face in it. As the blows continued I would from time to time look into the mirror, amazed that my face could assume such dimensions. Another "lip" was forming, blood from my mouth and nose, mixed with spittle, dribbled down my face onto my chest... Marx and Snyman now stood to the left and right of Siebert, facing me, and Nieuwoudt started delivering fast and heavy blows to my head with the hosepipe, which was excruciating in the kind of shocks it sent through my body.

'Then Beneke started hitting me with his fist in my stomach and I started to stumble. Marx got a boot to my right leg as a warning to stand still. Beneke left and from a drawer of a filing cabinet took another hosepipe, black this time. Marx shouted: "Give him both – black power and green power!" Beneke took up his position again, on my left, and from then on he and Nieuwoudt hit me mainly on the head with hosepipes while Siebert carried on smacking my face. Snyman and Marx delivered kicks to my shins whenever I moved out of the way.

'Every time I tried to defend my head with my hands the pipes would move to the back, the kidney area, or attack the hands. I found it impossible to cope with all the immense pain and I turned and faced the wall and, closing my eyes, hoping for oblivion, which never came, as blows rained down on my head and back.

'After some time this assault stopped, with everybody panting for breath. I was just able to swallow the groans wanting to escape my mouth. When spoken to I couldn't reply. My mouth was very cut and swollen and I would just nod a reply' (Woods, 1987:381-389).

This interrogation of Jones took place on 24–25 August. Biko's interrogation began on 6 September, according to the evidence at the inquest. He was interrogated by precisely the same team: Warrant-Officer Ruben Marx, Detective Sergeant Nieuwoudt, Captain Siebert and Warrant-Officer Beneke, under the leadership of Major Snyman.

Peter Jones lived to tell his story. Bantu Stephen Biko did not.

At the inquest into Biko's death – Jones was still in prison – Lt.-Col. P. Goosen, head of the Eastern Cape Security Branch, said: 'Major Snyman reported to me that Mr. Biko had become very aggressive and had thrown a chair at him and had attacked Warrant-Officer Beneke with his fists. A measure of force had to be used to subdue him so that he could be hand-cuffed again. I immediately visited Mr. Biko. He was sitting on the sleeping mat with his hands handcuffed and the leg-irons fixed to an iron grille. I noticed a swelling on his upper lip. There was a wild expression in his eyes. I talked to him but he ignored me' (Woods, 1987:257).

We do not yet know the whole truth of what happened to cause the fatal injury in Biko's case. It is still a secret.[25] At the inquest into his death in detention Advocate Sydney Kentridge put the security police 'on trial' in so far as was humanly possible in a state that ensured police protection. Callousness and brutality were in evidence day after day. The doctors who supposedly examined Biko displayed a pathetic weakness in the face of the security police – or fear, or simple lack of care or compassion – and dis-graced their profession. At a point when Biko's brain was damaged, when he was deranged to the extent of no longer being in control of his bodily functions, the head of the Eastern Cape Security Branch, Lt.-Col. Goosen, cynically described his condition as that of 'shamming' – 'Neither I nor any of my colleagues, nor the doctors saw any external injuries' – and he put in the order for Biko to be transported, naked, in the back of a Landrover for the distance of hundreds of miles from Port Elizabeth to Pretoria.

In the judgment, Magistrate Marthinus Prins pronounced that 'on the available evidence the death cannot be attributed to any act or omission amounting to a criminal offence on the part of any person' (Woods, 1987:354).

Whether or not Biko threw a chair at Snyman or whether what happened to Jones happened in more or less the same way in his case is not of major significance now. South Africa's security laws enabled policemen to be unaccountable. Protection of the most irresponsible policemen ensured that

25 There has been a recent (June 1991) report that the case may be re-opened.

no court could condemn them. Beatings and other torture resulting in deaths were safely, symbiotically, locked into a protective conspiracy between police witnesses and the state. What happened in police room 619 happened countless times. The security laws allowed detainees to be held in terror without any protection. Doctors, magistrates and others were willing to compromise the integrity of their professions in the presence of these laws, thus making the law a mockery but ensuring that it was played out as if it was not.

Through the exposure of this particular death (and subsequent inquest), white South Africans would surely have understood what had happened to justice in their land. However, the supreme arrogance persisted into and throughout the 1980s. At the time of Biko's death, the Minister of Police, Mr Jimmy Kruger, was at a National Party congress in the Transvaal. In his first announcement reporting it, he said that Biko had died 'following a hunger strike', adding that 'Biko's death leaves me cold'. Surrounded by fellow travellers and spurred on by his leader, a party delegate from Springs, a certain Christoffel Venter, stood up among the sniggers of appreciation to commend Minister Kruger's 'democratic principles'. Venter added that Mr Kruger was so democratic that 'he allowed detainees "the democratic right to starve themselves to death"' (Woods, 1987:214).

Twelve years later Father Aelred Stubbs – now a contemplative member of the Community of the Resurrection – cast his mind back on Biko and the preservation of the innermost person in that extreme situation: 'I am trying to work from my knowledge of Steve and my knowledge of his deepest values and instincts,' he said. 'I am sure that there was a kind of inner fortress of integrity that he would not suffer to be violated.' He knew that Biko was prudent with a sense of self-preservation and, although only a stupid person would have no fear, Biko had conquered fear in an intelligent way: 'He had a much greater fear of betraying himself than a fear of physical violence even to the point of death. He had conquered fear by his inner conviction of his outer undefeatability if he was prepared to give everything. That kind of quality grows with exercise. A deep instinct. Very very deep, absolutely rooted in the roots of his culture. Steve grasped the essential goodness of what was there and worked from that, allowed that to work within him, always broadening it as his own horizons did' (AS to LW, 1989).

A Man for All Seasons

Pityana was still in prison on 12 September, the day Biko died, and was not told of his death. That night he had a dream. He dreamt that he had 'this enormous discussion with Steve where he was saying, more or less, "I am leaving. You must look after my children", and I saying, "You know it's not *my* business to look after your children – you must do something responsible."' Biko had insisted in a friendly sort of way until Pityana had reluctantly agreed that, all right, if he *had* to go somewhere, he, Barney, would look after his children. The next day Pityana was allowed to have a shower, something not allowed before, and 'this white boy was reading the paper and I managed to see in his paper a statement by Kruger. I would otherwise never have known and then suddenly this sort of funny discussion I was having in the middle of the night came back. I was in a very very lonely state in that cell. I was absolutely distraught, angry – much more [I was] almost suicidal' (BP to LW, 1989).

'Steve?' Strini Moodley puzzled, 'Which Steve? I couldn't connect death with him. It was something I, you know, I just couldn't – I just couldn't believe it for a long time' (Strini Moodley in the film *Biko: The Spirit Lives*).

'It was the fire – the fire went out,' Ramphele looked out of the window. 'When Thenjiwe phoned me on the thirteenth of September I was in hospital. When I heard, everything went dead. I literally wondered if I could walk across that room, if I could survive physically. Everything was dead.' Mamphela Ramphele was banished, isolated in the northern Transvaal, in hospital, trying to save the life of her unborn child – Biko's child (MR to LW, 1990).

Biko's funeral took place at the King William's Town stadium. Oxen drew the coffin until it was lifted and held shoulder-high, an impulsive gesture which was to become the hallmark of funerals of comrades to come. The only visible presence of the state was one lone soldier seen on a tower high above the crowd. Otherwise the police were not present. But, as Mafika Gwala explains, not everyone made it:

'I missed Steve's funeral. Most Natalians missed it too. The result of police action in turning the cars and buses carrying mourners back on the Transkeian borders. Although I missed the funeral for yet another reason, I did not miss the symbolism that such burial carried...

'Those who have attended the funerals of all those who have died in detention must have gone to these funerals with an inner understanding that a scratch on a black man is a scratch on every black man. And that death in detention at one centre is death in detention all over the country...

'When we heard that Steve was dead many of us must have said, deep down in our minds, if the time must come let it begin now' (Mutloatse, 1981:229-231).

As Biko explained, it had already begun. The youth of Soweto, of Natal, of the Eastern Cape, of Langa and Guguletu, and therefore of the whole country, had understood, and as Biko explained further, 'The dramatic thing about the bravery of these youths is that they have now discovered, or accepted, what everybody knows: that the bond between life and death is absolute. You are either alive and proud or you are dead, and when you're dead you can't care anyway. And your method of death can itself be a politicising thing; so you die in the riots. For a hell of a lot of them, in fact, there's really nothing to lose – almost literally, given the kind of situations that they come from. So if you can overcome personal fear for death, which is a highly irrational thing, you know, then you're on your way' (*The New Republic*, 7 January 1978:12).

Biko's mother understood this too. 'In truth he was not my child. He was the son of the people. I have come to understand that I must comfort myself and accept that truth: that this child was not my child. Moreover, there are many children of other people who have gone before Steve. When a battle is fought not all the soldiers come back home. It is God's will in which this whole thing happened. After such a long time *ube ubomi bom bakhe busombiwa* [his life is still dug out]. Accepting that, I have a humble view of myself as a person from whom he comes' (MB to LW, 1989).

Biko foresaw his death in the nature of what he was doing, and was prepared to die. Thus, along with many others, he became a martyr in the struggle for freedom in South Africa. He fulfilled his own concept of obedience to God, which was, as he explained, 'at the heart of the conviction of most selfless revolutionaries, a call to men of conscience to offer themselves and sometimes their lives for the eradication of evil' (SB in a document to DR, 1973).

To kill has always been the basic instinct of frightened men, of men who refuse to accept change or, in particular, those who stop neither at corruption nor torture nor murder to entrench power and control: Christ, King, Cabral, Allende, Malcolm X, Gandhi ... and in South Africa, where the list is very long: Tiro, Mohapi, Turner, Goniwe, the Mxenges...

Biko was only 30 when he died. Dying so young leaves a life of such promise in the air, so to speak. What would its future have been, we wonder. A useless question, but one which all Biko's friends raise and to which they give disconcertingly different answers. Lein van den Bergh, a Dutch lawyer, who was a member of the Resistance in World War Two and experienced imprisonment at Dachau, met him only once and saw in him the qualities of a man whom he would expect to become 'the leader of the government' (LVDB to LW, 1989). Woods, in his exuberant style, said that he was simply 'the greatest man I ever met'. And for those who worked with him and were daily touched by his life he was irreplaceable: 'we all each individually experienced it. You can't replace the catalyst that he was. None of the other people we related to were *that* to you – and yet he didn't get to you. He was best at not making you grovel with gratitude. We couldn't have another Steve' (MM to LW, 1990). Some of his political critics were less impressed. In the *African Communist*, for example, Biko was accused of 'being a "liberal", an idealist, insufficiently anti-capitalist, a pacifist, and lacking any understanding of the mass struggle' (Halisi, 1990:29).

What cannot be denied is that Biko's contribution was to have had insight into the psychological nature of his time, which had resulted in momentary political impotence. It was to recognise the necessity and, above all, the political potential for the growth of an identity for the oppressed, which was called Black Consciousness. It was to work with consensus decision-making as an essential part of making that consciousness grow, if it was to result in independent thinkers and actors for the future of the country. With this understanding and by living this to the full, Biko and his contemporaries broke the stunned silence of the mid-sixties. This was what he saw as the first task.

As the political situation changed with the implementation of the homeland policy and its newly emerging 'elite' – with the added logic of separate parliaments on the drawing-board for the 'Coloured' and 'Indian' communities, with the worker strikes of 1973 and the subsequent strengthening of the working class through the emerging trade unions, with the uprising against Bantu Education of 1976 and the exodus of thousands of young people to join the armed struggle outside the country, Biko and others saw the potential for 'black' unity becoming the wider political unity which he had expected to emerge. In pursuing this he had become aware that the political analysis was moving strongly in the direction of defining the South African situation in terms of class oppression alongside the steadfastness of racial discrimination.

Biko must be respected as a man, not a myth. He was so essentially *living*. He was a life-force, an antidote to pessimism with his huge smile and raucous laughter and the 'no bullshit thing'. He used every opportunity available, weighing up a situation precisely and swiftly, seeing its limit as much as its potential, seeing how to make it work for the common purpose, knowing nothing was perfect and that you had to work very very hard to transform anything. He also saw the essential potential of individuals, and that without the recognition and subsequent growth of that potential they could not function fully. He worked with whomever came his way. He was not elitist in spite of having commenced initially from a university. There was no time to waste and he knew he had to sacrifice his formal education. The strength of his particular style of leadership stemmed from his capacity for astute political insight coupled with his faith and recognition that anyone could grow, learn and participate once challenged with meaningful ideas, which led to a meaningful life.

Five weeks after his death, on 19 October, all the Black Consciousness organisations were banned, the Zanempilo Centre was handed over to the Cape Provincial Health Department, the police removed the machinery from the Njwaxa leather-working cottage industry and smashed the recently built workshop. Many new people and organisations were banned and many of those not yet detained were detained. These included Mtintso, Mpumlwana, Mvovo and Dimza Pityana. Two nights before this, Francis Wilson, a friend of Biko's, had a dream. He was in an old European city with his wife. There was a coffin lying on the ground. On top of it was a Christmas tree, and Wilson knew he had to pick up this coffin and that Biko's body was inside it. As he leant down to pick it up he felt the Christmas tree prick his cheek and wondered how on earth he would manage because Biko was so big and had a very heavy body. 'Suddenly I heard an unmistakable, deep chuckle and Steve stepped out from under the tree wearing an old, comfortable sports jacket, very relaxed and very alive and his chuckle was more or less saying: "How the hell do you think you're going to pick me up?!" and I was very relieved I didn't have to! He was very concerned about Mamphela. He wanted to know how she was. Did we know where she was? And I said, Yes, we did. So we three walked down the street in this city to a building where I knew Mamphela was. (During my dream I didn't recognise the building, and when I wrote the dream down shortly afterwards I still didn't know but I now know it was a hospital.) We went through the door of this building, up some stairs, turned left down a passage, but Steve didn't want to be seen by anybody so one of us stayed with him at the entrance while the other went to find out where Mamphela was. She was no longer there but we were told she was OK. As we clattered down the stairs and out of the building I thought to myself, "Oh, well, this is only a dream", and then I thought to myself, "This is much too vivid so it can't be a dream", and the next step in this thinking was, "If this isn't a dream, Steve is alive; he's OK", and I woke up laughing, feeling a sense of indestructibility about things and felt exhilarated the whole of the next day; and then, on the following day, when we ourselves were raided [by the security police] early on the morning of the nineteenth, a big raid – the day I thought I would be banned and a lot of my friends *were* banned – I had this sense: "Well, it's OK. The forces of evil cannot overcome the forces of good", and that "Steve is still alive." Ten years later, in December, I was with Mamphela at a research conference, organised indirectly by the ANC, in Amsterdam and I recognised the city' (FW to LW, 1991).

The refusal of blacks to be subservient or humiliated, even in the face of death, changed the nature of the struggle and ensured Biko's legacy in perpetuity, in a form which he would have most desired. The Biko generation inspired the culture of fearlessness. It was carried by the youth, a decade younger, in the 1976 uprising, when the government inadvertently strengthened that resolve by killing hundreds of young people. This fearlessness was sustained throughout the 1980s, in the face of a country on the verge of declared civil war, with troops in the townships and the growing infiltration of guerillas. Black South Africans never felt inferior again. This was given expression all over the country, even in the smallest towns. After Biko's death and the bannings of the Black Consciousness organisations, those who had been involved found themselves in all kinds of roles and places. Through a defiance and a refusal to be subservient, many young people faced the same fate as Biko, yet the oppressed were spurred on, wherever they were, in claiming their rights, disrupting apartheid and demanding their own true identity, which had nothing to do with the fenced-in 'green pastures' of the whites. It has, indeed, seemed like an 'awakening of the people,' people who finally made politicians move. It was in the ghettos, where so many lives were lost, that the seeds of democracy began to germinate. It has been in the ghettos that the rebirth has taken place for South Africans. And, while the jumble unravels itself and the bid for power begins, Biko would surely never have lost sight of that.

Biko's perception and energy freed people psychologically to take their destiny into their own hands. How they will now pursue this is, as yet, uncertain but his memory would be served best by the growth of a broader consciousness that remains wary of mindless authority, that recognises that ideas are strengthened through consensus decision-making, which has the capacity to be persuaded by a majority vote, even if it seems inappropriate, and, simultaneously, has the ability to then work with that decision, ensuring its soundness.

3

Medical Ethics and South Africa's Security Laws: A Sequel to the Death of Steve Biko

N. BARNEY PITYANA

'The prison doctor was the interrogator's and executioner's right-hand man...' (Solzhenitsyn, *The Gulag Archipelago*).

André Brink, in his novel *A Dry White Season*, records in an agonisingly real manner the puzzlement and wounded sense of justice of one man, an Afrikaner, who learns of the death in custody of his black servant who had become his friend. Until then he had accepted the social and political situation, feared God and paid due reverence to the teachings of his church, the Dutch Reformed Church. But more than that, Ben du Toit was a remarkably compassionate man. It was his sense of the justice of Afrikaner institutions that led him to launch a private investigation into the mysterious circumstances surrounding the death in police custody of his friend. He discovered that at every turn he was met with intrigue and hostility, and as layer after layer of the onion unfolded a cover-up in high places was exposed. The judicial system was implicated; the politicians were not to be trusted; the Church was cynically in theological collusion with the system. His personal life changed, he lost his job, his wife left him, but he was drawn closer to the victims of the system that had become so much a part of his own life. What began, in his view, as a simple unfortunate error, ended with him suffering persecution, threats, intimidation and a criminal death in a road accident.

André Brink, an extraordinarily liberated Afrikaner writer, is making a perceptive comment on the ethical state of South Africa. His vehicle, in this instance, is the death in detention of a black detainee which exposed an intricate web of involvement of the police and medical practitioners employed by the state. What draws the attention of a writer like Brink is a matter to which mortal humanity must pay attention.

This chapter takes its cue from Brink and examines the dilemma of medical practitioners who attend to prisoners detained under South Africa's security laws. It examines whether clinical independence is possible and the extent to which doctors tend to subordinate their clinical judgment to that of the security police. How does a doctor uphold the interests of the patient even while his own political commitment is contrary to that of the patient and, as a government employee, he has to carry out his duties? The question of human rights is suggested by my brief, particularly the rights of prisoners. How can international codes of medical ethics like the Geneva and the Tokyo Declarations co-exist with security laws that seek to deny the prisoner those very rights? We have then the proverbial ethical dilemma for the doctor. I hope to attempt to outline how these competing forces can be dealt with.

Case History

The death in detention on 12 September 1977 of Black Consciousness leader Bantu Stephen Biko raised to prominence some of these dilemmas for the South African medical establishment. Up to this point the profession had no adequate means of ensuring that doctors abided by their professional oath in their dealing with political prisoners. In the prevailing culture of repression, political prisoners were regarded as non-persons towards whom there was no moral duty.

Steve Biko was arrested by the South African security police on 18 August 1977 and detained under Section 6 of the Terrorism Act. He was held in solitary confinement, kept naked and manacled for 20 days at Walmer Police Station in Port Elizabeth. On 6 September he was taken to the Sanlam Building in Port Elizabeth, the headquarters of the security police. There he was interrogated under torture and in the early hours of 7 September he received physical injury to his head. That same morning he was examined by Dr Ivor Lang, a Port Elizabeth district surgeon, who discovered Biko's lip lacerated, bruising near his second rib, his hands and feet swollen and his gait ataxic (staggering). Lang made out a certificate that he had 'found no evidence of any abnormality or pathology on detainee'. The next day he was seen again by Lang and by Dr Benjamin Tucker, Port Elizabeth's chief district surgeon. According to Tucker, Biko was incontinent and had a 'possible extensor plantar reflex' (both may indicate brain damage). He was transferred to the prison hospital and examined by Lang and Dr Colin Hersch, a specialist physician. Biko was again found to have an extensor plantar reflex, and Lang recorded in Biko's bedletter that no pathology had been found.

On 9 September a lumbar puncture was performed on Biko and found to be blood-stained. Lang recorded this, too, as normal. On 10 September, Hersch recommended that Lang consult a neurosurgeon because of the presence of blood in the cerebro-spinal fluid and that if necessary skull X-rays be done. Lang claims to have discussed these findings with a neurosurgeon who thought they were not indicative of cerebral haemorrhage or any other brain damage. The two of them agreed that Biko should be transferred back into the custody of the security police, 'provided he was examined daily by a doctor'.

On 11 September, Tucker examined Biko. He found him apathetic, frothing at the mouth, hyperventilating and weak in the left arm. He recommended that Biko be taken to a hospital with trained staff. The security police objected, and instead they confined him to a prison hospital. At this point during the inquest into Biko's death, Mr Sydney Kentridge SC, counsel for the Biko family, asked Dr Tucker:

'In terms of the Hippocratic Oath, to which I take it you subscribe, are not the interests of your patient paramount?'

Dr Tucker: 'Yes.'

Kentridge: 'But in this instance they were subordinated to the interests of security. Is that a fair statement?'

Dr Tucker: 'Yes, I didn't know that in this particular situation one could override the decisions made by a responsible police officer.'

On the afternoon of 11 September, Tucker phoned Lang, who recommended that Biko be taken to the hospital at Pretoria Central Prison, where he could be under the observation of trained staff. It is fair to assume that this decision was prompted by the security police. Lang was also aware of the deterioration in Biko's condition but nevertheless recommended that he be taken to Pretoria, over 700 miles away. At this point in the inquest Lang admitted that had his patient been a child with the same signs and symptoms Biko showed, he would have insisted that the child go into hospital immediately.

Kentridge: 'Why didn't you stand up for the interests of your patient?'

Dr Lang: 'I didn't know that in this particular situation one could override the decisions made by a responsible police officer.'

Kentridge: 'In terms of the Hippocratic Oath are not the interests of your patients paramount?'

Dr Lang: 'Yes.'

On the night of 11 September Biko, evidently a seriously ill patient, was driven to Pretoria, naked and manacled to the floor of a Landrover. Eleven hours later he was carried into the hospital at Pretoria Central Prison and left on the floor of a cell. Several hours later he was given an intravenous drip by a newly qualified doctor who had no information about him other than that he was refusing to eat. Sometime during the night of 12 September Steve Biko died, unattended.

Medical Practitioners and the Statutory Bodies

Biko's death aroused controversy world-wide. The inquest magistrate returned an open verdict and gave no reasons for his decision. He did, however, in terms of Section 45 of the Medical, Dental and Supplementary Health Services Act of 1974, refer the record of the proceedings to the South African Medical and Dental Council. The said Act makes provision for referral to the Council of the proceedings of any court of law 'if it appears that there is a *prima facie* proof of improper or disgraceful conduct on the part of a registered person or of conduct which, when regard is had to such person's profession, is improper or disgraceful'. The court left open the possibility that one or more or all of the medical practitioners were *prima facie* guilty of professional misconduct.

The South African Medical and Dental Council is a statutory body established to 'control the training, practice and standards of conduct of medical practitioners, dentists and practitioners in supplementary health service professions'. It consists of representatives appointed by the Minister of Health, university faculties of medicine and dentistry, the nursing and pharmacy professions, and a few individuals directly elected by doctors and dentists. The Council sees itself as 'an instrument to protect the interests of the public and that it should remain imbued with the spirit of responsibility in its service to the public' (*SAMJ*, 27 March 1965:259-261).

However, when the matter of the professional conduct of the medical practitioners was referred to the Council for investigation, a preliminary committee decided in April 1980, thirty months after the death of Biko, that 'there was no *prima facie* evidence of improper or disgraceful conduct on the part of the practitioners. The Committee resolved that no further action be taken on the matter' (MASA, n.d.).

The decision of the preliminary committee was ratified by the full Council, meeting *in camera*. No evidence was made public, neither were the reasons for this extraordinary decision given, even though the Council had overruled the opinion of the inquest court. The conclusion is inescapable that the Council was motivated by political considerations rather than the upholding of professional standards.

A feature of the conduct of both Drs Lang and Tucker was the ease with which they told half-truths or lied. Their medical records were unreliable. Dr Lang, who was called to examine the prisoner, signed a certificate that declared: 'I have found no evidence of any abnormality or pathology on the detainee.' Yet, in a later report, he stated that on this first examination he found 'a cut lip, a bruise on the stomach, an inability to move the limbs, swollen hands and feet and slurred speech.' During the inquest, he admitted that his certificate was inaccurate. He had been warned by the police that Biko was 'shamming'. He assumed that Biko's uncoordinated walk was the result of his refusal to cooperate. He left no instructions for the patient's observation and gave no treatment (*SAMJ*, 22 August 1981).

Dr Tucker, the district surgeon, together with Dr Lang, had examined Biko and found him to be incontinent. Biko complained of pain in the head and back. Dr Tucker found a possible extensor plantar reflex, which is indicative of brain damage. He did not, however, ask the patient about the cut on his lip, neither did he in his report mention the abrasions on his ankle and wrists that he had observed. The doctors were not keen to find out how these injuries had been sustained. Cross-examined about his lack of curiosity, Dr Tucker testified: 'If I am called to see a patient and he has a cut on his head, then I am interested in treating him and not how he got his cut.'

The fact of the matter, however, is that Dr Tucker did not treat his patient on this occasion. Counsel's summary of the evidence points to the irresponsibility of these actions: 'The doctors, for whatever precise reason, felt themselves beholden to the security police. They did not query the origin of Biko's injuries and symptoms, either from Biko or the security police. This studied lack of curiosity can only be explained either by their collective collaboration with the police or a deliberate election not to embarrass the police, nor indeed themselves, by asking questions to which the answers were obvious.'

Commenting on the brevity of Dr Lang's certificate, a Committee of Enquiry set up by the Medical Association of South Africa in the wake of the aborted proceedings of the SAMDC, observed that 'it [the certificate] can only be described as being inaccurate or even highly inaccurate ... it was incomplete and could mislead a third party' (*SAMJ*, 22 November 1980, 7 March 1981). The Committee drew attention to Rule 17 of the Rules of the SAMDC which were promulgated in 1976, specifying the omissions in respect of which the Council may take disciplinary action. One of these stipulated that 'Granting a certificate in his professional capacity, unless he is satisfied from personal observation that the facts are as correctly stated therein' constituted a disciplinary offence.

Dr Hersch, the specialist physician, was equally guilty of a gross act of omission because, although he suspected brain damage, he did not specifically declare as much in his report. He also failed to record his observation that the patient had a scar over the left eye. That should have led him to investigate the possibility of a brain lesion.

The Relationship of Doctors to the Security Police

It seems clear that what influenced the unprofessional conduct of the doctors was the fact that they constantly felt beholden to the security police in the way in which they carried out their duties. Clinical independence was therefore sacrificed and subordinated to the wishes of the security police.

The police apparently believed that Biko was feigning an illness. They had no medical evidence for this, save their knowledge that the prisoner had once been a medical student. At the inquest the doctors alleged that Lt.-Col. P. J. Goosen, the head of the Eastern Cape Security Branch, had expressed concern about the condition of the detainee, but Goosen's own testimony betrayed no such concern. He expected the doctors to give their stamp of approval to the conclusion he had arrived at on non-medical grounds. This police opinion was in turn communicated to Drs Tucker and Hersch and seems to have formed the basis of their professional conduct.

Colonel Goosen seemingly believed that he was solely responsible for the detainee. In his understanding his duty to investigate an alleged threat to the security of the state gave him power to override any laws which he felt would undermine his execution of this duty. Therefore, whatever medical advice might have been given, he believed that the final and sole decision as to whether that advice should be followed rested with the security police

– despite the explicit wording of the Police Standing Orders by which he was bound.

These Orders do not have the force of law. They do, however, constitute a code of conduct, the breach of which is not visited with criminal sanctions but may be the subject of an internal, departmental disciplinary inquiry. Standing Order 319 stipulates that 'there is a duty upon the police to call in the district surgeon or another medical practitioner ... whenever a person is seriously injured or shows signs of illness ... he should be called in by the speediest means available [and] any instructions given by the district surgeon ... are to be carried out without delay. If removal to hospital other than a jail hospital is ordered, precautions have to be taken to guard the prisoner.' The Order appears to give the police power to judge the seriousness or otherwise of a complaint, but it is clear that once called, a doctor takes charge of the management of the patient and has the power 'to give instructions'. What it does not state or suggest, however, is that, as far as political detainees or prisoners are concerned, a different set of considerations applies or that these regulations can be vitiated by Section 6 of the Terrorism Act, in terms of which most political detainees have been held.

Nonetheless, it is apparent that the doctors felt that they had no clinical independence in the treatment of their patient. Biko was kept in a prison cell in unclinical conditions. There were no nursing facilities and no trained staff who could be relied upon to maintain regular observations. When the Committee of Enquiry of the Medical Association of South Africa requested to see the cell in the police station where Biko was held during the time of his treatment, permission was refused. After Biko was transferred to the Sydenham Prison Hospital for examination by Dr Hersch, instructions were left by Drs Hersch and Keely, the neurosurgeon, that the patient be kept under observation. Dr Keely made clear that by this he meant that the patient must be kept under 24-hour observation by trained nursing personnel. Such facilities were not available. Despite Biko's condition, a decision was made, which Dr Lang authorised, to transfer him by road to a prison 700 miles away. The Committee of Enquiry noted: 'Dr Tucker wanted the patient to be admitted to a provincial hospital in Port Elizabeth where there was trained staff. Colonel Goosen flatly refused this request for security reasons. Dr Tucker apparently felt himself unable to insist but agreed that he be transferred to Pretoria by motor vehicle ... unaccompanied by any medical personnel on this journey which was taken at night' (SAMJ, 7 March 1981).

No medical records accompanied the patient, and Dr Lang's predilection for inaccurate reports found expression in this final entry: 'Dr Hersch and myself can find no pathology.' Dr Lang insisted during the inquest that the statement was not 'false' but 'incorrect'. What he meant, he said, was that there was no 'gross' pathology. For him, nervous and brain damage diagnosed by his colleagues Tucker and Hersch did not constitute 'gross pathology'. Semantics, however, could not come to his rescue regarding the indubitable fact that no medical or nursing care was provided for the patient: no temperature was recorded, no urine examined, no blood tests were performed. The medical practitioners felt that they had to yield to the security police, and that 'their actions were subject to the control at that stage of the police and of prison authorities'. It is clear that the doctors accepted beyond question what Colonel Goosen told them. They both testified that they had subordinated their clinical judgment and independence to the police in the interests of state security. They never asked Biko for his own account of how he sustained the injuries. Questioned why Biko was not taken to a proper hospital, Dr Hersch confessed: 'Unfortunately this was not in our hands.'

In the light of the evidence, it can confidently be asserted that the decision of the SAMDC was a cover-up, unfortunate because it further undermined confidence in the body and the profession it represents. It confirmed the popularly held view that the Council was a tool of the state and could not act independently when it came to a matter of public interest. An editorial in the Johannesburg *Rand Daily Mail* made this point in a pithy manner: 'It leaves ... the inescapable conclusion that because Mr Biko was black, a political activist and a Security Police detainee, his life as a medical patient somehow mattered less. It makes mumbo-jumbo of fine phrases of the Hippocratic Oath, phrases which apparently do not preclude doctors in such cases from filling in false medical certificates or ignoring serious signs or from leaving a patient naked, urine-soaked, manacled ... or from being driven 1 100 km through the night in the back of a Landrover' (19 June 1980).

Ethical Provisions in the Professional Code of Doctors

The Medical Association of South Africa (MASA) is a voluntary organisation whose aims and objectives are to promote the medical and allied sciences and to maintain the honour and interests of the medical profession. It has no statutory power. MASA is, however, strongly represented in SAMDC and its president at the time of the Biko inquest was then chairman of SAMDC. The public reaction to the verdict of SAMDC stung the organised medical profession. Their public image as a caring profession had been damaged and their reputation in international medical circles dented as it became clear that doctors had subordinated professional interests to the expediency of a repressive political system. The profession could no longer project itself as independent of the apartheid state. MASA felt that the strong public reaction placed them undeservedly in a position where their standards, as well as their bona fides, were being queried.

Thus grieved, MASA swung into action. On 13 October 1980 it issued a statement expressing concern about the medical services available to detainees. Representations were to be made to the responsible Minister. Recommendations were to be made for changes in the rules governing the medical treatment of, and facilities for, detainees which would allow the best possible medical service to be rendered to them at all times. As a result, new rules were promulgated. These were to ensure the clinical independence of doctors and unfettered access to their patients under optimal clinical and security conditions. The Federal Council of MASA then resolved that 'the primary responsibility of a doctor attending a prisoner is towards that individual as a patient. Laws and regulations curtailing the principles of clinical independence and autonomy were unacceptable,' it declared.

It also set up a Committee of Enquiry to:

(a) give consideration to and make recommendations regarding the ethical issues which were raised as a result of the medical care received by Mr. S. B. Biko;

(b) make recommendations regarding the procedure to be followed where, in terms of existing legislation, there is apparent conflict or clash of interests between the medical profession and MASA on one hand and the state or persons or bodies under the control of other statutory bodies;

(c) make recommendations regarding the maintenance of clinical independence despite the provisions of the relevant Acts, for example the Act on Terrorism and others.

The organisation also adopted a Code of Conduct to regulate the behaviour of medical practitioners responsible for the care of prisoners. It comprised five points:

1. The health of his patient must be a doctor's first consideration (Declaration of Geneva), and he owes his patient complete loyalty and all the resources of his science: whenever an examination or treatment is beyond his capacity he should summon another doctor who has the necessary ability (International Code of Medical Ethics).

2. A doctor must have complete clinical independence, and laws and regulations curtailing the principles of clinical independence and autonomy are unacceptable (International Code of Medical Ethics).

3. Under no circumstances is a doctor permitted to do anything that could weaken the physical or mental resistance of a human being except from strictly therapeutic or prophylactic indications imposed in the interest of the patient (International Code of Medical Ethics).

4. A doctor may not permit considerations of religion, nationality, race, party politics or social standing to intervene between his duty and his patient; he shall in all instances be bound to relieve the distress of his fellow-men, and no motive shall prevail against this higher purpose (Declaration of Tokyo).

5. A medical certificate should always be correct in point of fact and must be acknowledged even by the highest authority and accordingly the facts stated must be beyond doubt (Principles of Medical Certificates, World Medical Association).

It needs to be recalled, however, that, as a voluntary association, MASA can only *influence* its members. By contrast, any code adopted by SAMDC would have the force of law with the power to ensure compliance by all medical practitioners in the country. Further, MASA's own federal structure has meant that matters can only be dealt with in the first instance in the regional bodies, and only when referred from there can the national machinery come into action. In the case of three doctors attending Biko, only one was a member of MASA and subject therefore to the disciplinary procedures of MASA. Even in this case, once the regional body had thrown out the complaint, there was no further course of action.[1]

Security Provisions

The point has already been made that the Police Standing Orders do not necessarily apply to prisoners detained in terms of security legislation. Detention for political reasons at the time of the Biko case was covered, in the main, by three pieces of legislation: the Terrorism Act of 1967, Section 6 in particular, the General Law Amendment Act and the Internal Security Act of 1976. None of these made any provision for dealing with the medical treatment of detainees. In the Terrorism Act 'terrorism' is broadly defined to include 'any act whatsoever committed with the intention to endanger the maintenance of law and order'. If the facts are proved in evidence to have been committed, then there is a presumption that the offence was committed with the necessary criminal intention for a conviction in law, unless the accused can discharge the onus beyond all reasonable doubt. In other words, the burden of proof is placed upon the accused to prove his or her innocence.

Theoretically Section 6(6) of the Terrorism Act (under which Biko was held) should enable medical practitioners who are state employees access to the detainee, but the practitioner depends on the police for a call and not on the detainee–patient. If the doctor has not been called by the police, then he or she is not on duty and the prohibition applies.

Over the years the South African courts have pronounced on the scope and interpretation of Section 6 of the Terrorism Act. In *S.* v. *Moumbaris* 1973(3) SA 109(T) the court held that Section 6(6) means no more and no less than that only the Minister or an officer in the service of the state shall have access to a detainee or shall have a claim or a right to (that is, shall be able to demand as of right) any information relating to or obtained from a detainee. This judgment goes on to state that 'whilst the detainee is in detention, he is under the control of the police and any information so obtained can be used in court'. This ruling clearly shows that the Police Standing Orders which make provision for the prisoner to call a medical practitioner of his own choice, provided that he can meet his own medical expenses, cannot apply in respect of persons detained in terms of Section 6 of the Terrorism Act. The

1 MASA has since amended its Constitution (May 1981) so as to empower the Federal Council to hold an investigation into alleged misconduct of a full member, and to expel or reprimand or admonish those found guilty of misconduct.

clear statement that the police have complete control of the detainee does not seem to allow for the exercise of clinical independence.

The Act also states that any information obtained by an officer of the state in the performance of his duties may not be disclosed even to a court of law (*Cooper and Others* v. *Minister of Police* 1977(2) SA 209(T)). This implies that not even a statutory body like the SAMDC can obtain information from a medical practitioner about his dealings with a person detained under the Act. The district surgeon can be shielded by the Act and avoid censure by SAMDC or MASA. For that reason codes of conduct can be rendered ineffective when enforcement is sought in cases under the Terrorism Act. According to the judgment in *S.* v. *Mothopeng and Others* 1979(2) SA 183(T), since this provision is intended to benefit the interests of the police, it is only they who can relax it.

This interpretation was necessary, the judge felt, because not to allow it would result in an absurdity: 'doctors who visit detainees and must be able to visit them would ... be unable to do so because the doctor is not necessarily a person who is a Minister or officer in the service of the state, and if a doctor did visit a detainee he would be unable to testify for the detainee in any civil action.' This is a classic case of bending the rules not in order to ensure justice or the clear intention of the legislation, but to guarantee the protection of the interests of the state. An opposing view, a more liberal interpretation, was taken by Mr Justice Didcott in *Nxasana* v. *Minister of Justice and Another* 1976 (3) 745 (D). He held that evidence gained from a detainee about his health, notwithstanding its conveyance to the court by a magistrate who visited him, 'could not be said to be official information or state secret'. Accordingly the judge argued that the court had a right to authorise that information be obtained from a detainee which can be disclosed to the court. It can only be regretted that this view has not proved popular with the South African judiciary. If this position had applied, then Peter C. Jones, detained at the same time as Steve Biko and at the time of Biko's inquest held under Section 6 of the Terrorism Act, could have been called to testify about his own treatment and torture in the hands of the same team of security police who handled Steve Biko. Such powerful circumstantial evidence could have thrown more light on the events surrounding Biko's death.

Conditions for the detention of prisoners in South Africa are regulated by the Prisons Act of 1959. In terms of this Act a prison means 'any place for the reception, detention, confinement, training or treatment of persons liable to detention in custody'. Therefore, a police station cell or even the back of a Landrover or a hospital becomes a prison for the purpose of this Act. A prisoner means 'any person, whether convicted or not, who is detained in custody in any prison or is being transferred in custody'. The Act also provides that for every prison there shall be a medical officer who shall perform such duties as are assigned to him by and under the Act, and if there is no full-time medical officer his duties shall be performed by a district surgeon.

The only medical officers a detained person is likely to come across are those employed by the state. Proceedings in the Biko case showed very clearly that such medical practitioners are wont to subordinate their professional autonomy to the interests of the state. The role of the district surgeon and the nature of the cooperation expected of him are underlined in the following extract from *A Guide to the Health Act*, which was published by the Department of Health in July 1978, soon after the Biko debacle: 'the services which district surgeons render to prisoners and persons detained by South African Police [also] fall within the definition of personal health services. These services, however, can have far-reaching legal implications and for this reason they can also be described as medico-legal services. In view of this and for security reasons it would be advisable that specially selected medical practitioners be allocated by the Department to undertake these services.'

The Guide does not spell out the criteria for this careful selection process but the juxtaposition of 'security reasons' and 'specially selected' leaves one with the chilling thought that medical practitioners might be selected not on the basis of their professional competence, but on their reliability in matters relating to the security of the state.

Another result of the Biko controversy was that a new Police Standing Order, specifically applicable to detainees in terms of Section 6 of the Terrorism Act, together with a new Warrant of Arrest, was issued by the Department of Justice. The reference in paragraph 8 of the Police Standing Order to the Prisons Act effectively limits the right of detainees to a medical practitioner of their own choice, as Police Standing Order 319 clearly allowed. The new Order stipulated that in the case of complaints by and symptoms of illness of a detainee:

> (i) The services of a competent medical practitioner must be obtained forthwith.
>
> (ii) Effect must be given to the instructions of the medical practitioner, but should it be necessary for the detainee to be removed for treatment in a hospital other than a prison hospital and such a removal is regarded as involving a security risk, Head Office must first be consulted.
>
> (iii) The fact of any illness must without delay be reported to Head Office by telex, so that the Minister can be informed if necessary.
>
> (iv) No sick detainee must, without Head Office's approval, be removed from one city or town to another city or town.
>
> (v) Sick detainees must in regard to sleeping and eating facilities enjoy special attention and must be visited more often than in normal circumstances.
>
> (vi) Save in exceptional cases, for instance where disclosure of the fact of detention of a terrorist will harm the investigation, the nearest blood relation or relation by marriage must be notified of such a condition of illness which in any way may be regarded as serious. Visits

to the sick detainee must, however, not be permitted without permission having been granted by Head Office.

This Standing Order brought a measure of clarity to a very confused area, in particular the demarcation of authority between the police and the medical officer, and might have saved Steve Biko's life had it been in operation at the time of his detention. What limited its effectiveness was the fact that Standing Orders have no force of law. They are obligatory on the police as professional conduct. No comparable regulations are available, to our knowledge, for medical practitioners selected to provide medical services to the detainees. The Committee of Enquiry of the Medical Association also pointed out that two paragraphs (8 and 9) of the new Warrant for Detention posed difficulties of interpretation. Paragraph 8 apparently related only to the provision of prescriptions and did not solve the problem of who had the authority for the removal or otherwise of a patient–detainee. The Committee also correctly noted that the insistence on permission having to be obtained from Head Office was undesirable and incompatible with a doctor's duty to maintain clinical independence. Its report noted that 'it is undesirable that some unknown person sitting in authority in Pretoria should have, as it were, the final say as to the proper treatment to be given to a person whom a medical practitioner has instructed should be removed to a hospital other than a prison hospital'. (MASA, n.d.:7)

In the light of this, the Committee of Enquiry held that Regulation 17 of the SAMDC Rules on Medical Certificates did not go far enough inasmuch as it seemed to enable a blatant *suppressio veri* by Dr Lang in particular and, to a lesser extent, Drs Tucker and Hersch as well. The Committee underlined strongly the need for 'full and complete certificates in addition to their being correct'. It also recommended that 'unless there are compelling reasons to the contrary, the medical examination of the detainee should not be carried out in the presence of a police officer and, in all cases where this is possible, the medical practitioner should obtain from the detainee himself (in addition to any information that he might have obtained from the police officer in whose custody he is) what complaints the detainee has'.

On the question of the desirability of the reserve powers of Head Office, the Committee advised that in the event of the views of the medical practitioner not being accepted by Head Office, the medical officer should be able to seek the opinion of another independent medical practitioner. Where medical opinion determines, Head Office should be bound by that advice. If the directions of the medical officer are still ignored or overruled, continues the report, 'we believe that it is ethically the duty of the medical practitioner to report directly to the Minister'. Such conduct, it was felt, would be consistent with the clinical independence of the medical practitioner.

If one can point to an inadequacy in the ethics of the Committee's report, it is that the Committee does not seem to have considered how long it would take for all these various levels of appeal to happen. No consideration is given to the condition meanwhile of the patient–detainee. It seems to be envisaged that while the appeals are in progress the legal authority of the security police would operate unchallenged. In its anxiety to protect the medical practitioner, the report dabbles in legalism. It fails to encourage doctors to act according to their conscience. After all, moral responsibility is an individual matter. In response to the report of the Committee of Enquiry, the Medical Association resolved to seek an interview with the responsible Minister to discuss the possibility and advisability of introducing legislation dealing specifically with the medical treatment of prisoners detained under the Terrorism Act of 1967, and other related laws.

A Commission of Enquiry into the security laws was set up under the chairmanship of Mr Justice P. J. Rabie by the government in 1980. The Commission saw it as its task to remove vagueness and confusion in current legislation. In a report released in February 1982, the Commission found that there was 'no doubt that security laws were necessary and that, generally speaking, existing legislation was adequate, but additional measures were needed'. So the Commission limited itself to justifying the retention of existing security provisions and merely streamlined and consolidated them. It rejected pleas for the abolition of Section 6 of the Terrorism Act, but recommended:

> 1. A detainee must be visited at least once a fortnight by a magistrate or a district surgeon. An inspector should visit detainees and report his findings to the Minister of Law and Order.
> 2. The Commissioner of Police should be given the discretion to decide if a detainee may be visited by relatives or lawyers.
> 3. The police must provide reasons for continued detention to a review board if a detainee is not released after six months. The board may hear evidence from and consider written representations made by the detainee (*Rand Daily Mail*, 4 February 1982).

It is clear that the Rabie Commission had no intention of limiting the powers of the security police. Even visits by a magistrate and district surgeon were left to the discretion of the police. No consideration was given to the fact that what encourages the personal abuse of detainees is both the enormous power and unaccountability of the police and the absence of any 'watchdog' body supervising their conduct. Doctors and magistrates need to be given authority to take corrective action to protect the detainee and, if necessary, institute legal proceedings. Visits by magistrates had proved ineffective. But the *status quo* was left intact; no judge was given the right to visit any detainee, and detainees were denied a right of hearing in a court of law while in detention. Police always held the right to call the district surgeon, but the individual requiring a doctor or magistrate most was the detainee, who still had no right to call them. Though both the magistrate and the district surgeon are commonly seen as part of the system against which most detainees bear anger and resentment, yet in the context of prolonged spells of solitary confinement, these officers can provide a listening ear and access to the outside world.

Thus, in my view, we are back to square one. The ethical problem has not been solved. What is the ethical basis for any action that the medical practitioner might take? This problem raises questions both about medical ethics and about the human rights of prisoners and the Christian approach to moral judgment. The next section addresses these questions.

Ethical Principles

In the detention camps of Stalinist Russia, it was the doctor who would determine whether interrogation or torture could continue; it was the doctor who, because he signed the death certificate, could always be trusted to provide 'sound' medical reasons for death and conceal the truth. Moreover, any doctor who behaved differently was not kept on the prison staff. That cannot be surprising where the police have such complete authority, as in South Africa.

André Brink in *A Dry White Season* testifies in similarly horrid terms about the complicity of the district surgeon in the death of a prisoner. A cold and uncaring attitude comes across when the district surgeon, challenged at the inquest hearing by defence counsel as to why he had not made a thorough examination of the deceased, brushed this aside: 'Why should I? He only complained about his teeth.'

Perhaps because doctors have so much power and their undoubted skills may well be open to abuse, the provision of a code of medical ethics helps to ensure the optimum conditions for the doctor to perform his duties whilst having regard to and respect for the patient–detainee as a human being. Problems of moral judgment, right and wrong, do arise in the course of medical practice. Although, in the final analysis, doctors must act according to conscience, nonetheless an ethical code can guide them in reaching a clinical judgment that will, by and large, be seen to be ethically correct. The issues of clinical independence and the rights and duties of doctors and patients–prisoners need to be discussed in the light of the code of medical ethics enshrined in the Declaration of Geneva (1948) and the Declaration of Tokyo (1975).

The concept of clinical independence or autonomy is intended to safeguard not only a doctor's professional freedom but also the patient's interests. Ultimately the doctor is responsible for making clinical decisions affecting the management of a patient, and no outside force or interest must be allowed to interfere with this autonomy. It is quite clear that where the doctor abdicates this autonomy, responsibility for the well-being of the patient is forfeited. This may be tempered by the doctor's consulting with the patient and seeking advice from other professional colleagues, but the doctor must take ultimate responsibility for any clinical decisions.

The critical element in any clinical practice is trust: trust among the medical team, and trust between patient and doctor. Society must also be able to put its trust in the medical profession. It is an important element of this trust that the doctor's integrity must not be impugned or subjected to suspicion. To some extent this can be ensured if the doctor takes patients into his or her confidence, treating them seriously and with respect as human beings. Patients may be vulnerable, particularly if they are also detainees, but that they retain their own rights as individuals should be indisputable. Even detainees retain their human rights except those which, according to Mr Justice M. Corbett, are taken away by law expressly or by implication, and those necessarily inconsistent with the circumstances in which the detained is placed (in a dissenting judgment in *Goldberg* v. *Minister of Prisons* 1979 (1) SA 14 (A)).

It is an essential part of medical ethics that patients retain the right to information about their health: 'Failure on the part of doctors to talk intelligently and sensibly to patients is an ethical as well as practical failure.' The *Dictionary of Medical Ethics* rightly concludes that 'clinical success is less probable in an atmosphere of mutual suspicion. If doctors wish to retain the respect of their patients, they must in turn treat their patients with respect and recognise not only their needs but also their sensitivities and their rights' (1977:233). In the Biko case, none of the doctors ever bothered to communicate with their patient. The clinical management was conducted not just in primitive and unconducive conditions, but also in an atmosphere of fear and suspicion. The point of reference of the doctors was the security police rather than the patient.

I have suggested that a detainee–patient may well feel vulnerable and degraded, and hostile to anyone in authority. As a political activist he or she may be resentful and angry. The doctor needs to hear fully the patient's story and win the patient's confidence if there is to be cooperation. In an environment of hostility and suspicion, the possibilities of the proper performance of medical care and clinical management are reduced. It seems quite obvious that doctors must be able to deal confidentially with their patients for, to a doctor, there is no detainee but a patient. As MASA's Committee of Enquiry noted, the doctor should be allowed to treat the patient in private. That would show respect for the patient's privacy and would enable conditions of confidentiality to prevail. In the event that the doctor is called upon to disclose confidential matters, the British Medical Association believes that it must be the overriding consideration of a doctor to uphold the benefit of the patient and the protection of his interests. There may be occasions, especially in prison situations, when the prisoner wishes to share confidences with a doctor. It is incumbent upon doctors to declare the parameters of their participation, determined either by their status in the prison or the conflicting expectations to which they may find themselves subjected. Only in cases where the clinical relationship is not prejudiced should they make a full disclosure to the patient, offering the patient the opportunity to reach a free decision about what should or should not be disclosed.   .

What then is the role of a doctor in prison, especially in instances where interrogation is taking place? In *Medicine, Science and Law* (vol. 17, no. 14,

1977) D. O. Jopp argues that the intention of Howard (the pioneer penal reformer) was that doctors as professional people of integrity, primarily motivated by an ethic to care for people and especially the sick, the poor and the socially handicapped, would bring into the penal situation a permanent critical and progressive influence for good. The introduction of doctors into prisons was seen as a way of ensuring that a humanising element would be ever present. But there was more to it than that. If prisons were to discharge the healing task entrusted to them by society, emphasis should not just be on penalty and revenge, but on restoring wholeness in the human being.

Jopp, however, is not oblivious to the dilemma this involvement poses for doctors. Their professional integrity, impartiality and independence may easily be compromised. There will be a clash of interests and loyalties. It is expected of a doctor as a law-abiding citizen and as a state employee that the integrity of the judicial system be upheld and nothing be done that will undermine the need to protect the public from anti-social elements. Jopp echoes the *Dictionary of Medical Ethics* in recommending that 'when doctors interview or examine individuals in custody they must of necessity proclaim in what capacity they intend to deal with the inmate and in what way information obtained will be treated' (1977:263).

In South Africa, however, detainees are kept in custody without recourse to the judicial process even though, in principle, they may be innocent of any crime. However, in the matter of *Goldberg v. Minister of Prisons* the highest court in South Africa came to its decision on the basis of the professional or expert evidence of a prison doctor who regularly visited the prison. He testified that despite the withdrawal of reading material and listening to the radio, 'from his observations applicants were not suffering from any psychological deviations'. It is worth noting that no other medical opinion was open to the prisoners. The court held that 'it was questionable whether prison regulations confer legal rights on prisoners' and that 'a distinction had to be drawn between the furnishing of necessities, on the one hand, and comforts, on the other'. Basic rights or necessities had to be confined to items such as food, clothing, accommodation and medical services, and only those things that are basic to the maintenance of a reasonably civilised manner of living. If it is accepted that medical services are basic to the needs of the prisoner, how should, and in what conditions can, that right be exercised? The learned judges remain silent.

In its new Code of Conduct, MASA has incorporated the Geneva and Tokyo Declarations and the International Code of Medical Ethics. In the wake of the widespread use of torture of Jewish prisoners during the Nazi regime and particularly the involvement of medical personnel in those episodes, the international community sought to limit the recurrence of similar affairs. According to the Tokyo Declaration, the presence or otherwise of a doctor during interrogation is meaningless if the doctor acts as an accomplice after the fact by providing false information or by maintaining a studied indifference to the cause of the ailment the doctor has been called to attend to. Yet it may be important for a prisoner to be examined before and after detention, preferably by a doctor of his or her own choice (United Nations Recommendation 20 read with the Standard Minimum Rule for the Treatment of Prisoners Rules 32 and 33). The MASA Code also affirms the right of medical practitioners to clinical independence, and the fundamental principle that 'the health of my patient will be my first consideration', and that considerations of race, class or religion will not be allowed 'to intervene between my duty and my patient'.

What is significantly absent from the MASA Code is what the Geneva and the Tokyo Declarations refer to as the 'utmost respect for human life'. This does not mean that a doctor has a duty to preserve life at all costs. But it does mean that a doctor has a moral obligation to employ the skills of his profession to help heal a patient, that is, to bring a patient into well-being and wholeness. MASA itself seems to have come to the conclusion that 'if the required medical and nursing care [conforming to the guidelines determined by the World Medical Association] ... had been made available to Mr Biko, the subsequent unfortunate events would [not] have occurred'.

The attitude of the doctors in the Biko case seems to have fallen far short of the Kantian maxim 'to treat men as men and not as means'. In the clinical management of Steve Biko it can be said that the doctors withheld from him his human dignity and respect as a person. They abdicated their moral duty. Such a duty, to be ethically appropriate, must be unconditional and universal. Moral guidance must be applicable in all comparable situations. In this case, other considerations tempered the clinical judgment of the doctors. The fact that the patient was a detainee held under security laws and a black person seems to have affected their attitudes. In the circumstances, the duty of care which the doctors owed to the patient as an unfettered *prima facie* duty, or Kant's categorical imperative, which overrides all other considerations, was abandoned.

In the *Dictionary of Christian Ethics*, McEwing defines a *prima facie* duty as a 'possible action for which there would be a compelling moral reason in the absence of any moral reason against it, so that it is always obligatory to fulfil a *prima facie* duty if it does not conflict with another which states that a moral principle can only be overruled by another moral principle' (1967:98). He constructs a sort of table of priorities which gives precedence to those rules which prohibit the taking of life. I would question that there was a conflict of duty of this proportion in the Biko case. At the Nuremberg trials, the defence of 'following orders' could not be sustained. In the face of an obvious wrong, it is hard to justify moral failure to perform a professional duty. At any rate, the doctors in the Biko case did not put this as a defence save to say that they did not feel able to question the integrity of a responsible police officer. The effect of such a defence was to use the police as scapegoats. There is no suggestion that they were prepared to examine their own conduct against professional norms.

Clearly the norm of reverence for human life is one which, in normal circumstances, the medical profession in South Africa and everywhere would support. Finnis (1980:86) refers to the right to life as a basic value 'corresponding to the drive for self-preservation'. Life is that which gives vitality, personalised wholeness, 'which puts a human being in good shape for self-determination'. Life, accordingly, includes bodily health, freedom from pain and the right to pursue well-being and happiness. It is a cliché to say that without life there can be no being. Therefore, to allow physical and mental suffering by torture or other acts of omission is to invade this basic right. Life must be lived in its fullness and certainly not in misery because of the acts of commission or omission of another human being. Finnis again points out that a principle forbidding torture in all cases is a principle of justice. The right to life, therefore, as a basic human right imposes obligations on all to respect life. That is a sense of justice. Human rights, therefore, limit somehow our expression of our selfish desires and instincts and temper them with an obligation towards the humanity of others.

The problem with many notions of human rights is that they do not have the force of law, but rely on the morality and reasonableness of the individual. In a world of the good or virtuous, human rights are preserved. Moral judgments are arrived at, according to Finnis, 'by a steady determination to respect human good in one's own existence and the equivalent humanity or human rights of others, when that human good and those human rights fall directly into one's case and disposal'. Sadly, the doctors in the Biko case fell short of these principles. The principle of the right to life imposes a duty on a medical practitioner to minister to the best of one's ability, as one's conscience would allow and according to one's professional integrity and moral judgment, to any whose needs as mere human beings constitute a claim for the doctor's services.

Increasingly, though, in a morally unjust world, the determination of international principles of human rights, such as first enshrined in the Universal Declaration of Human Rights (1948), has meant that universal and objective standards are being established. International law has advanced to the stage where action can be taken against a state and its officers, overriding concerns about interfering in the internal affairs of states, where there is evidence of gross violations of human rights. That is so even if that state has not ratified the Universal Declaration, as is the case with South Africa. Other states have gone so far as to make human rights' concerns justiciable in law. Instruments like bills of rights protect the basic rights of individuals against arbitrary state power. European governments can be taken to the European Court of Human Rights at the instance of an aggrieved citizen. The need to give teeth to human rights legislation is imperative in a country like South Africa.

It could be supposed that the principles of Christian ethics would find ready acceptance among officials of the South African government. After all, the Preamble to the Republic's Constitution claims to be conscious of 'our responsibility towards God and Man' and 'to further the contentment and spiritual and material welfare in our midst'. Christianity believes in the sanctity of human life; that all are made in the image of God with power to reason and the capacity to choose. Human life, to a Christian, is a matter of deep reverence. Implicit in this is a proper regard for the human body and a refusal to inflict, willingly, any mutilation of it. Humanity therefore has a right to life. This implies the duty of cherishing and preserving human life and taking all moral means for the relief of suffering and the eradication of disease.

Human rights, therefore, are self-evident truths. They are based on humanity's concept of justice and of 'the good'. They regulate humanity's competing claims to happiness and self-fulfilment and, as such, they ensure the optimum conditions for the fulfilment of human worth: 'What a man may morally expect of his fellows, what he can demand from them morally' (Ward, 1976:64). Therefore, anything that subtracts from or frustrates this achievement will be resisted by society because it is society that extends these rights and recognises them from natural rights. All moral persons will incline to uphold these rights rather than deny them.

Conclusion

The problem, as I see it, for the medical profession in South Africa is that in a country that affirms the sovereignty of parliament, the only way in which medical codes of conduct can be enforceable is when they are enshrined in the law of the land. Despite its allegedly Christian foundation, the South African state has never seen it as its task to uphold human rights. Quite clearly, a culture of universal morality is not a major concern of the South African regime.

In the strange South African circumstances, society is judged from the perspectives of the white electorate. 'The law cannot remain and does not remain wholly neutral as to what are the basic ideals of society' (Mitchell, 1970:60). Whatever the difficulties inherent in Lord Devlin's concept of the law's concern for morality, in South Africa this will always be difficult to judge. In such circumstances, there can be no shared morality, no universal principle. The ultimate judgment on the South African legal system is its capacity to defy universal norms and principles and to hold in contempt natural law. There is no way of determining whether laws passed under these conditions command the respect of most reasonable people who are subject to them. Basil Mitchell makes the point that 'The mark of a just society is not that it abstains from making [such] judgments, but that it enables them to be made freely and responsibly after the fullest possible discussion'. Inherent within the South African system is the incongruence between moral ideals and the security interests enshrined in the law.

Moral responsibility is not compatible with a Pilate-like ritualistic washing of hands. Moral agents cannot 'pass the buck'. They take responsibility for their actions which they make as free agents. Therefore, for the medical profession to be content to say that it has done all that it could according to the law, is not sufficient. One notes in the attitude of the South African medical profession in this case, an anxiety to be seen to take full consideration of the security aspects and to emphasise cooperation with the government.

Professor J. N. de Klerk, then chair of the Federal Council of MASA, argued: 'When the medical profession is called upon to provide services to the community within a particular political milieu whether it be in South Africa, Russia, USA or Britain, it must, while not for a moment deviating from its ethical and moral standards and its obligations to the community to provide services to the best of its ability within the political climate that prevails in the country, reflect the ordering of that society and its ideals at that time' (*SAMJ*, 30 November 1981). What if conditions are such that doctors cannot carry out their grandiose ethical codes in practice? All that was called for, by those opposed to the decision of the SAMDC, was for the profession to dissociate itself explicitly from the evil inherent within the system and not to seek to maintain a dubious neutrality. The profession was challenged to uphold the ethical standards enshrined in its own codes and to act decisively against those who breached them, as well as to distance itself from the security machinery of the state. That is what De Klerk and his colleagues were not ready to do in 1980. For that we return to Alexander Solzhenitsyn, who states:

> Evidently evil-doing ... has a threshold of magnitude. Yes, a human
> being hesitates and bobs back and forth between good and evil all his
> life. He slips, falls back, clambers up, repents, things begin to darken
> again. But just so long as the threshold of evil-doing is not crossed,
> the possibility of returning remains, and he himself is still within
> reach of hope. But when, through the density of evil actions, the result
> either of their own extreme degree or of the absoluteness of his
> power, he suddenly crosses the threshold, he has left humanity
> behind, and without, perhaps, the possibility of return (1974:175).

The Biko affair marked a moral threshold in public life in South Africa. The reputation of the medical professional had never sunk as low. Confidence had evaporated. It was no longer just a matter of moral wrongdoing by a few medical practitioners. Through the actions of MASA and the SAMDC, the whole organised medical profession became implicated in that wrongdoing. It seemed that Biko uncovered a veneer which exposed the roots of evil in South African society. The medical doctor deals with people at their most vulnerable. The doctor is taken into the confidence of the suffering. Without that relationship of trust, healing cannot take place. This distrust and suspicion became the characteristic of the whole South African society: a divided society. This was not, however, just the separation caused by apartheid, but it reflected a moral breakdown of society.

The Biko affair also marked the lowest ebb in South Africa's international relations. South Africa lost friends and supporters who had been arguing that South Africa must be given a chance. The matter went beyond the declaration that apartheid was a crime against humanity; it now seemed that there was no possibility for the reversal of the downward spiral short of a

bloody revolution. Campaigns for the isolation of the apartheid regime
were stepped up. Actions to expel South Africa's medical profession from
international forums in medicine, psychiatry and nursing were intensified.
Their once-high reputation had now been impugned by the Biko affair.

Inside South Africa, however, the case sparked a revolt among many
doctors who sought to distance themselves from the actions of their association. For the first time there was what one might call an ethical dimension to the voluntary choices doctors make about belonging to an association. The National Medical and Dental Association was born, a group
devoted to a quality of medical care abdicated by MASA. It sought to
examine the social context of medical practice imposed by apartheid and to
resist it. So NAMDA set itself apart and campaigned against apartheid, and
sought the expulsion of official South African medical bodies from international organisations. In addition, NAMDA made such ideological choices
as to struggle for a democratic future. Thus professional practice and the
aspiration to a just society were considered interlinked. Through NAMDA
a new climate emerged in the medical profession. There was now vigorous
debate and confrontation. It is in such a climate that one must understand
the case of Dr Wendy Orr, a Port Elizabeth district surgeon who lost her job
because she testified about the condition of detainees. Significantly, she did
so against the instructions of her unrepentant senior, Dr Ivor Lang.

What of the future? South Africa is now changing and the struggles of
the democratic movement are being vindicated. Though the security police
has been disbanded and their duties transferred to the Detective Branch,
most repressive security legislation remains in place. The medical profession has paid dearly for its past actions. Minds now need to be concentrated on the challenges of the future. In a democratic South Africa, there
should never be another Biko affair.

PART TWO

4

Biko and Black Consciousness Philosophy:
An Interpretation
C. R. D. HALISI

Black Consciousness philosophy began as the theoretical expression of a younger generation of black South Africans compelled by circumstances to rethink the very meaning of politics in the South African struggle. As a student-led movement rather than the youth wing of an adult political organisation, the South African Students' Organisation (SASO), harbinger of the Black Consciousness Movement (BCM), emerged as an independent political and intellectual force. The temporary lull in internal political opposition existing at the time of the BCM's formation partially accounts for the innovative character of Black Consciousness philosophy.

Given the repressive political mood of the period, the initial critical impulse behind Black Consciousness philosophy revolved around the basic question of continuing black submission to apartheid. Steve Biko believed that Black Consciousness philosophy, by providing an alternative to psychological complicity with racial oppression, could expedite the subjective prerequisites needed for black liberation.

Simply stated, the central contention of Black Consciousness philosophy was that resignation to racial domination was rooted in self-hatred and this had major political implications: the black person's low sense of self-esteem fostered political disunity, allowed ethnic leaders and other moderates to usurp the role of spokespersons for the black masses, and encouraged a dependence on white leadership. Conversely, a heightened sense of racial awareness would encourage greater solidarity and mobilise mass commitment to the process of liberation.

However, an understanding of the 'liberation process' had to be reappropriated by the BCM generation. Biko's examination of the social psychology of racial repression intuitively led him to deconstruct the black nationalist tradition from a new generational vantage-point. Biko, who possessed a natural inclination for social theory, understood that 'political traditions' were social and intellectual constructions. He respected the wisdom of his predecessors but did not reify past perspectives. For Biko, political traditions were raw material to be reworked into new forms of awareness. Thus, at one level, Black Consciousness philosophy was a synthesis of the fundamental political principles of the three most prominent black liberation organisations, the African National Congress (ANC), the Pan-Africanist Congress (PAC) and the Non-European Unity Movement (NEUM).

This chapter will argue that Black Consciousness philosophy reconstructs both African and black nationalism from a different generational and theoretical perspective. Theoretical reconstruction 'signifies taking a theory apart and putting it back together again in a new form in order to attain more fully the goal it has set itself' (Giddens, 1982:100). Furthermore, the chapter contends that Black Consciousness philosophy incorporates three distinct traditions of political thought, two of which are international in scope: the complex tradition of black South African political thought, theories of anti-colonialism and racial liberation developed in Africa and in the African diaspora, and New Left student radicalism with its straightforward recognition of the legitimacy of black power politics.

At the core, Black Consciousness philosophy embraced the existentialist view that individuals and communities choose freedom or enslavement. In order to overcome fear, it was essential for the oppressed to confront their oppressors. For the BCM, political action had to approximate 'a way of life' or a 'gut reaction'. By striving to be indistinguishable from everyday life, Black Consciousness philosophy sought, at once, to articulate mass sentiments and fuse intellectuals and masses.

The political flexibility of BCM activists was deliberate – a practical outgrowth of their theoretical inclinations. BCM activists gravitated in many political directions; they joined the ANC or PAC, organised trade unions and civic associations, formed new black consciousness-oriented organisations or were forced into prison or exile. In all these venues, BCM members discoursed with cadres of previous generations. Indeed, many, if not most, of the harshest critics of the BCM were members of an older generation who considered its basic political premises naive.

Ironically, radical black students hoped to revitalise a demoralised and divided older generation. Student idealism and commitment to confrontation politics renewed the search for a strategy of internal politics. In generational terms, Black Consciousness philosophy was an agenda for ideological realignment and political revitalisation. Needless to say, the BCM's views on realignment were rarely appreciated by members of older generations whose politics had been coloured by the factional divisions of the past.

As a concept, 'generation' implies a specific historical circumstance in which intellectuals form a concrete bond of cooperation and solidarity as a result of their exposure to the social and intellectual processes of change. Intellectuals usually form more concrete bonds within generational cadres where together they interpret the material of their common experience usually in ways distinct from other cadres (Mannheim, 1974).

Black Consciousness philosophy was informed by a distinct generational perspective. Seen as a generational cadre, former BCM members may, over time, have found themselves in many different places but continued to share an intense understanding of what politics meant. Biko was extremely sensitive to the fact that his generation – the SASO generation – was politically pivotal. Thus his observation that if his generation failed to confront government repression, the younger generation of students, represented at that time by the South African Students' Movement (SASM), would consider them 'sell-outs'.

Irrespective of their organisational affiliation, leadership cadres of the established liberation movements initially regarded the BCM with scepticism and suspicion. Perhaps there is no better indication of the theoretical significance of Black Consciousness philosophy than the reaction it elicited from intellectuals of older generations. In June 1972, Oliver Tambo, president of the African National Congress, did not consider the BCM an organisational challenge but candidly remarked that 'Black Consciousness posed a tremendous threat at the theoretical level only' (Turok, 1974:369). Tambo's observations of the BCM can be set in a larger context.

Internationally, intellectuals of older generations were threatened by the New Left's dismissal of established ideologies, on the grounds that they were either irrelevant or reactionary. New Left social theory

> rejects capitalist reform, socialist and communist social systems as well as the social theories that justify them. Social inequality, elitist authoritarian hierarchy and repressive manipulation are seen as the common coordinates of bureaucratic domination which lie behind ideological mystifications buttressing each of these systems. In place of such structures, New Left social theory posits the possibility of an egalitarian society free of the alienation characteristic of contemporary society (Hirsh, 1981:6).

Consistent with New Left thought, the Black Consciousness Movement offered a critique of capitalism that was radical without being explicitly Marxist, and democratic while offering a critique of the limits of South African liberalism.[1] Older-generation socialists criticised Black Consciousness philosophy on the grounds that it did not adequately address working-class interests and was the ideological expression of the black petty-bourgeoisie. Liberal critics tended to take exception to the strident race-conscious pronouncements of the BCM and its absolute refusal to endorse multi-racial cooperation.

Black Consciousness philosophy openly confronted the pathology of racism in South African society and its impact on both black and white South Africans. Today, even in an atmosphere of political reform, the race-conscious political assumptions of Black Consciousness philosophy remain controversial among intellectuals. The key question remains whether the legacy of racial domination created a 'black consciousness' manifested in some form among all classes of black South Africans. If so, political parties,

---

1 The importance of this double-edged critique became clear to me after several days of conversation with Biko in May of 1977.

despite their formal platforms, cannot totally suppress the race relations dynamics addressed by Biko and his generation. The distorted political economy of apartheid has had to operate in conjunction with a racist social psychology. Racism is a personal imperative of white rule: the internalisation of racial norms is a requirement for white mobilisation on behalf of racial privilege. In a racist political culture, the erosion of a black person's sense of self is unavoidable. Consequently, both non-racialism and black nationalism will endure as legitimate, if competing, responses to the legacy of racial domination.

Black Consciousness philosophy did more than explore racism and psychological obstacles to black solidarity. By contesting specific racist policies, the BCM forced open new arenas of struggle at a crucial period. Biko's own analytical animus, like that of the BCM, was aimed at the government's Bantustan programme – the central policy framework of apartheid. He and his colleagues were directly affected by attempts to transform the black intelligentsia into a part of the 'Bantustan bourgeoisie'.

In many respects, the BCM evolved as a counter-ethnicity movement; its young members were the victims of government experimentation with retribalisation policies. They were compelled to speak their ethnic languages in elementary school while having their academic futures determined by proficiency in the two official European languages. Biko recognised that the policy of Bantu education amounted to a state-engineered process of class formation. By linking education to the homeland policy, the white government sought to 'tribalise' the black intelligentsia's racial consciousness and to divert its energy into ethnic-based development.

After Biko's tragic death in detention, his writings rapidly gained international renown. In addition to his collected essays, Biko's published testimony at the trial of the South African Students' Organisation and Black People's Convention leaders exposed the world public to the thoughts of this important black intellectual (Biko, 1978; Arnold, 1978). In his speeches and writings, it is apparent that Biko assiduously avoided the temptation of trying to convert Black Consciousness into a form of racial fundamentalism. In other words, without compromising racial liberation as a core political value, he did not reduce all political conflict to racial factors. For this reason, most commentators rightly assert that there is no evidence of reverse racism in Biko's thought.

To give his message greater universal appeal, Biko adroitly situated his version of Black Consciousness philosophy within a humanist framework; he knew that racism was the aberration. From its inception, Black Consciousness philosophy had a humanist bent which allowed the development of a theological counterpart. The black caucus of the University Christian Movement gave birth to Black Theology, the religious complement of Black Consciousness philosophy. Black Theology encouraged black South Africans to reinterpret the Christian faith in the light of the specific realities of their situation.

As a social theorist, Biko was sensitive to the philosophical tension between freedom as a universal aspiration and racial oppression as a particular form of enslavement. Thus, Biko's best-known essay, aptly entitled 'Black Consciousness in Quest of a True Humanity', considered the particularities of the 'black experience' without dismissing its place within universal processes of change, those which have shaped the political development of the modern world. As an activist, Biko's immediate concern was with the brute reality which racial oppression imposes upon its victims. As a thinker, he understood, better than most, that situations characterised by long periods of resistance to racial domination encourage a distinct tradition of political theorising – a black political tradition.

With this in mind, Biko was confident of his ability to interpret the relevance of other intellectual traditions, and in particular the recurring themes, questions, and debates unique to struggles for racial liberation. This led some of his critics to charge him with being contaminated with foreign ideas and to dismiss the BCM as a parody of America's Black Power Movement. Political discourse was not new to Biko. Before attending university, he had already become a student of black South African politics.

Black South African Nationalism: Biko's Synthesis

Exactly how the nationalist tradition was to be defined was, for Biko, a crucial question; he was one of those entrusted to formulate the BCM's position on black nationalism. In South Africa, the appropriation of African land by white settlers has made race a consideration in the competing definitions of territorial nationalism held by rival African nationalist groups. As a central issue in African nationalist thought, differing views on the so-called 'land question' do not neatly coincide with organisational membership. In contrast to one another, Africanist and multi-racialist interpretations have galvanised around a basic question: should the land belong to all, including descendants of European settlers, or be returned to the dispossessed African majority? Biko's synthesis, his reconstruction of black nationalism, can be seen as a theoretical compromise between contrasting political positions.

Biko upheld the principle of racial nationalism, confirming the view associated with the PAC that the land belonged to the African people. However, he departed from African exclusivism by including Africans, Coloureds and Indians in the designation 'black'. Although the BCM objected to separate ethnic-based organisations, it was influenced by the idea of a multi-racial confederation of organisations, or Charterism, associated with the ANC. At least in theory, Biko resolved the PAC's objection that ANC Charterism amounted to minority control of the black movement. The BCM made *black* nationalism superior to ethnic – African, Indian or Coloured – nationalisms. By placing stress on black nationalism, the BCM strengthened the call for non-European unity that had long been championed by the NEUM. Coloured and Indian communities were not only invited to unite with the African majority but to regard their own oppression as similar to that of those they had been encouraged by apartheid to abhor. In this way, the BCM usurped the power to decide who counted as one of their political group, rather than leaving the right to define 'the people' in the hands of the minority government. The central policy of apartheid had been to allow smaller 'non-white' population groups greater privileges than those enjoyed by the African majority.

Just as Biko modified the Africanist definition of 'black people' to incorporate all 'non-Europeans', he altered the notion of multi-racialism to exclude formal alliances with whites. The decision to avoid alliances with whites was based on the assumption that their participation would undermine the prospects for black unity. Formally, the ANC endorsed alliances with progressive whites over PAC objections, but in reality the issue remained difficult to resolve in both camps. In time, the PAC came to define 'African' in non-racial terms and progressive whites were given a role. The BCM contended that white South Africans who opposed apartheid should educate their racist brethren, should not attempt to control black organisations, and should learn to accept terms of interaction established by the black majority. This amounted to a call for a white consciousness movement that ran parallel to the activities of the BCM.

In actuality, Biko did not see 'race' purely as a biological category; it too was a social construction. He, like the BCM, realised that black people, despite class and ethnic divisions, shared a common oppression. Biko concluded that class and race dynamics operate in tandem as a system of power relations. The BCM's reconstruction of intra-black relations was, at once, its most radical and its most utopian vision. It was radical in its desire to abolish ethnic divisions among the victims of white racism, and utopian in its assessment of the tenacity of ethnicity and what was required to refashion social relations.

As a utopia, Biko's synthesis redefines civil society on terms unfavourable to the state; in practice, it revives the NEUM's principle of non-collaboration with government-sponsored institutions as a new theory of community-based protest. Biko realised that black South Africans could choose *not* to participate in 'the system'. Non-collaboration, as a positive act of refusal to participate, constitutes a negative theory of political participation. Put another way, the refusal to participate in racist institutions empowered majority communities, required a reformulation of legitimate standards of civic participation and, in turn, necessitated a re-evaluation of the prospects for internal politics. Biko put it this way:

> I completely discourage the movement of people from the left to join the institutions of apartheid. In laying out a strategy we often have to take cognizance of the enemy's strength and as far as I can assess all of us who want to fight within the system are completely underestimating the influence the system has on us. What seems to me to be logical at this stage is for the left to continually pressurise the

various apartheid institutions to move in the direction of testing the limits of possibility within the system to prove the whole game a sham and to break off from the system (Biko, 1978:143-151).

In summary, while Biko had a strong temptation to relate Black Consciousness philosophy to past traditions of African resistance, he also realised that the ideology and tactics of the BCM had to be extricated from them. On the other hand, he recognised that ideological and political developments are part of an ongoing social dialogue. Consequently, for Biko, ideology, along with other resources necessary for social revolution, had to be mobilised, and could never be completely original. That is, even a revolutionary ideology always consists of elements drawn from previous radical interpretations (Bouchier, 1977:26-29). A revolutionary movement can use ideology in an innovative or non-innovative manner. Thus, the major question posed for analysts of BCM is whether or not Black Consciousness philosophy constituted an innovation, an advance?

Black Consciousness Philosophy and Black Political Thought

The very phrase 'Black Consciousness philosophy' suggests a discourse unique to the victims of white racism; it posits the existence of a transnational tradition of black political thought. By contrast, African nationalism is far more parochial and, unlike Black Consciousness philosophy, often rejects the idea of 'black power'. Black power politics does not limit itself to identification with a particular nation-state or even to Africa as a continent; people of African descent are called upon to seek empowerment wherever they find themselves and to fight racial oppression wherever it exists. Black power represents the internationalisation of black nationalism, and this has important theoretical implications.

Just as with the dialectic of racism and humanism, Biko grasped the primary antinomy in black political thought – non-racialism and racial nationalism. The theoretical permutations that result from the interaction of these two poles of possibility are rarely appreciated in interpretations of black politics. Given the situation of racial domination, these two approaches reflect an unavoidable dimension of black political life that usually confounds conventional ideological distinctions. In the United States, the debate over 'separation' or 'integration' as viable policies surfaces in black political discourse as another manifestation of these two polar distinctions in racial liberation ideology (Cruse, 1962:16). Reflecting the experience of racial domination, non-racialism and black nationalism are analytical categories unique to black politics.

Theoretically, both non-racialism and racial nationalism offer alternative prescriptions for political action although practically they entail similar social outcomes. Within the framework of black political discourse, cooperation with non-blacks can be read alternatively as 'negotiation' or 'co-optation', and black leaders seeking to transform the racist character of the dominant institutions from within the system can be subjected to the charge that they perpetuate those very institutions simply by cooperating with them. On the other hand, black leaders who claim to operate independently of dominant institutions rarely ignore *legitimate* opportunities to work with non-blacks to transform the system.

Thus, within the South African context, distinctions between the racial ideologies of ANC Charterists and PAC Africanists can never prove clearcut since both groups claim to desire a society in which racial distinctions would be irrelevant. As Leo Kuper perceptively remarks, 'the fact of the matter is that both groups shade off into each other' (1965:379).

The BCM was one of the few African organisations to identify unashamedly with blacks in the diaspora by assimilating the international resistance against racial domination in its political outlook. Biko and other members of the BCM encouraged a dialogue between intellectuals in Africa and in the African diaspora. It was almost inevitable that the two most historically significant struggles for racial liberation would draw sustenance from one another. More specifically, the comparisons between SASO and the Student Non-Violent Co-ordinating Committee (SNCC) were striking. SASO shared characteristics and identified with all radical student movements; however, its strongest identification and most pronounced characteristics were shared with the black student movements, primarily SNCC, which were active in the United States. Each in its own way, these two student organisations were largely responsible for internationalising the concept of black power.

Initially, SASO and SNCC were closely allied with white student groups; ultimately, however, they came to articulate 'go-it-alone' positions. Both groups drew their following from segregated campuses but several of the early leaders had been active in multi-racial politics. Both in South Africa and the southern United States, students came to stress the unique aspect of the black struggle in their respective countries, on the African continent, in the black diaspora and the 'Third World'. The focus on racial domination formed an ideological bond between the two black student struggles. So it was that these two movements, with very few formal links, drew upon one another for inspiration and as evidence of the international significance of their domestic struggles (see Carson, 1981). The identification of the Black American students with African liberation was in part revitalised by Malcolm X's fervent belief in 'linking the national struggle to the international one' (Wolfenstein, 1982:23).

Black Consciousness Philosophy and the New Left

Often termed the decade of protest, the 1960s rocked the universities of many industrial as well as industrialising nations. Whether in Berkeley or Beijing, Paris or Johannesburg, students organised themselves into formidable campus-based movements; they formulated radical ideologies coloured by their own youthful experiences and developed strategies and tactics designed to confront the inequalities in their respective societies. So pervasive and prominent were radical student politics that Edward Shils compared these worldwide student solidarity movements to the Communist International (1969:1).

As a social myth, student and left-wing internationalism envisioned a world without class, racial or gender oppression – one that had triumphed over all forms of psychological alienation. Speaking of the New Left, Martin J. Sklar and James Weinstein observe that 'their radicalism is not created by a consciousness of material poverty, however; they are more concerned about the poverty of human relations and values' (1966:64). Barney Pityana, Biko's closest collaborator, confirmed the identification of the BCM with the New Left: 'there was a serious examination of the norms of society and an attempt at evolving societal values, meaningful examination of the self and a redirection of the collective perspectives of the oppressed people' (1979:3).

In South Africa, racial privilege undermined student solidarity and obscured many of the obvious generational commonalities that black and white university students shared. For, although it was true that the government routinely intimidated white liberal students willing to pursue non-racial politics, black students faced raw repression of a harsher sort. They were denied the most fundamental of rights, ones taken for granted by their white counterparts.

Nevertheless, the National Union of South African Students (NUSAS) and SASO members shared important political assumptions, which were ultimately rooted in New Left thought. It is clear from NUSAS reports, records, and minutes that the organisation took progressive stands on a wide range of national and international political issues. Domestically, NUSAS also made an effort to monitor developments on black campuses. After black students proclaimed their autonomy by forming SASO, Biko's first political task was to expose the inadequacies of NUSAS. However, when placed in relationship to New Left thought, the theoretical interaction between NUSAS and SASO proves more complicated than most accounts of the BCM tend to reveal. In retrospect, while there were differences in theory and approach, there were also significant political assumptions held in common.

Although primarily concerned with black liberation in South Africa, Biko was aware that a significant political discourse was emerging worldwide. During this same period, many white radicals were engaged in a similar process of rethinking the definition of class, the relationship of class struggle to politics, and the meaning of 'revolutionary subject' in contemporary capitalism. New Left experimentation with revolutionary thought transcended ideological boundaries and revived concern with the issue of human emancipation as a trans-ideological and trans-national project.

As an historical occurrence, Black Consciousness philosophy coincided with the world-wide development of New Left critical theory. In the South

African case, Biko saw that aspects of liberalism, Marxism, and even African nationalism could uncritically function to defend the *status quo* or to define liberation in a way that obscured the political and psychological dynamics of racial oppression. Although psychological liberation is common to both Africanist and Black Consciousness thought, the intellectual influences that shaped the New Left stress both psychological and cultural liberation. Frantz Fanon, Aimé Césaire, Malcolm X, Mao Zedong, Antonio Gramsci and Amilcar Cabral can all be read as 'cultural nationalists'. Each of these radical thinkers was specifically concerned to relate psychological liberation to culture.

Although Biko did not denigrate the Old Left, there was a critical juncture in his thought regarding Old and New Left perspectives. Black Consciousness philosophy departed from both conventional African nationalism and Marxist socialism. As with African nationalism, black power thought has often resulted in a peculiar ideological legacy – a melding of anti-colonial, anti-capitalist, and anti-racist ideology. Frantz Fanon, the most important theoretical influence on the black New Left, was not far from the truth when he observed that in order to accommodate such a diverse array of struggles, 'Marxist analysis should always be slightly stretched' (1968:32).

A student of Fanon, Biko stressed the role and the responsibility of intellectuals in political and social movements. Like Fanon, many black populists consider coalitions between intellectuals and masses a catalyst for social revolution. Both Biko and Fanon saw Western education as a process of socialisation which often undermines the black intellectuals' commitment to their people and their respective cultural values (Biko, 1978:69-70).

In the light of the times, Biko and the BCM adapted a new theory of political consciousness to the black South African experience. Biko considered the transformation of consciousness to be a catalyst for mass action. Common to most of the student ideologies of the decade was a concern with consciousness, culture, alienation, community and the dimension of everyday life as the most important reference for political activity. In addition, the mass upheavals which characterised the decade of the 1960s led to a belief on the part of many student radicals that a mass movement was the most genuine organisational expression of mass consciousness.

Assessments of the success or failure of the BCM, in large measure, depend on whether the movement is viewed as a student vanguard organisation or a more diffuse intellectual and cultural movement. The New Left detached the notion of an advanced political consciousness from that of the vanguard party. For most Old Leftists, education of the masses can only be brought about by the activities of a vanguard party. Biko concluded that mass education could be accomplished by committed intellectuals armed with a knowledge of popular culture. Popular culture could be harnessed to help 'breathe life back into the oppressed' (Howard & Klare, 1972). Biko strongly believed in the unique capacity of humankind to make and remake its own conscious life:

This is the first truth, bitter as it may seem, that we have to acknowledge before we can start on any programme designed to change the
status quo. It becomes more necessary to see the truth as it is if you
realise that the only vehicle for change are these people who have lost
their personality. The first step therefore is to make the black man
come to himself; to pump back life into his empty shell; to infuse him
with pride and dignity, to remind him of his complicity in the crime
of allowing himself to be misused and therefore letting evil reign
supreme in the country of his birth. This is what we mean by an
inward-looking process (1978:29).

Through Black Consciousness philosophy, the BCM evolved what can be
referred to as a prefigurative approach to politics. In other words, the BCM
concluded that in order for emancipatory politics to achieve a social transformation, new values and practices would have to be *prefigured* in the
opposition movement. This prefigurative view of politics is consistent with
Biko's contention that politics has an undeniable psychological dimension.
Even now, it can be argued that the 'conscientisation' of the masses remains integral to the process of liberation.

Biko and many other black intellectuals have played a vital role in
reshaping society, have initiated interim strategies of struggle built on the
existing culture of resistance and have opposed the indoctrination of the
masses with ideas antithetical to genuine liberation. Biko identified the psychological foundations of apartheid as a terrain of struggle. In the final
analysis, he understood Black Consciousness philosophy in terms consistent with his own personal sense of mission – a combination of theoretical
honesty and devotion to the cause of liberation.

5

The Emergence of Black Consciousness: An Historical Appraisal

SIPHO BUTHELEZI

The purpose of this chapter is to analyse critically the emergence of the Black Consciousness Movement in South Africa from the late 1960s. Most of the literature on this question is devoid of structural and scientific analysis and is characterised by stereotypes, distortions and omissions of important political events and their interconnection, sequence and periodisation. In this literature, political developments are not regarded as a process but as an illogical stream of events without structure or laws.

The basic proposition advanced here is that in order to understand the historical development of Black Consciousness as an ideology of struggle, one must understand its historical roots during its formative years, as well as its form and content as determined by the concrete historical and objective conditions of the South African social formation.

A second key element in our theorisation of Black Consciousness will be the central concepts and ideas that influenced and shaped the ideology of the movement. Those ideas were of two types: the core notions that expressed the historic goals and methods of the movement, and the tactical and strategic ideas that expressed the conjunctural struggles and immediate needs of strategy and organisation.

Simultaneously, we will attempt to identify the social forces represented by the Black Consciousness Movement, and in what ways they determined its ideological orientation. Three social forces have played an important role in South African social movements – intellectuals, rural labour and the urban working class. The social characteristics propelling these forces into an active and specific role in the mass democratic movement have rarely been identified adequately. The task here is to redress the situation.

Historical Background

The South African Students' Organisation (SASO) came into being as a response to the relative political vacuum that existed after the banning of the African National Congress (ANC) and the Pan-Africanist Congress (PAC) in 1960. By the late 1960s, black youth could no longer accept white leadership and political representation in matters that affected them and the rest of their community. Biko himself put it this way: 'So what happened was that in 1960, effectively all black resistance was killed, and the stage was left open to whites of liberal opinion to make representations for blacks, in a way that had not happened before in the past, unaccompanied by black opinion.'

The immediate concern of SASO, therefore, was to build an organisation that would represent black student opinion and generate a sense of solidarity between black campuses. The existence of such an organisation, it was hoped, would break the isolation of these centres and bring them closer together. The SASO communiqué issued at the July 1969 conference at Turfloop (the University of the North) stated:

> That there is a need for more effective contact is unquestionable, especially in view of the ever-increasing enrolment at the non-white institutions of higher learning, particularly the university colleges. For all intent and purpose, these students have remained isolated, not only physically but also intellectually. There we find institutions which seek to breed pseudo-intellectuals with an absolute bogey for anything which associates them with the society in which they live, particularly if this is related to some kind of disagreement with any particular aspect of the general policy of the powers-that-be. There is no way of stopping this except by interfering with the programme of indoctrination and intimidation so effectively applied at all South African universities.

The acute feelings of isolation, frustration and alienation repeatedly referred to in SASO's literature reflected the general mood of this generation of students and was experienced individually and collectively in various ways. On the campuses themselves, such feelings were deliberately fostered by the authorities at various levels. This inevitably led to divisions which expressed themselves politically. The existence of faculties tended to foster balkanisation and, in some cases, feelings of superiority and inferiority. All too often students studying the natural sciences tended to look down on those in the social sciences. These attitudes were often reinforced by faculty staff. Law and medical students occupied a distinct position in the occupational pyramid, probably because of the lucrative nature of their professions in the outside world. Social work and theology students occupied the lowest position in this pyramid, usually being seen as destined to play a collaborative role in the apartheid state and its Bantustans. These divisions frequently expressed themselves politically during debates at student body meetings, and more especially at Student Representative Council elections. Students tended to elect those from their own faculty, probably because they could identify a common interest. It was not until SASO's emergence that student representatives began to be elected on the basis of their political astuteness, ability and experience. Consequently, and not surprisingly, most of the SASO leadership of this time had ANC, PAC and Natal Indian Congress (NIC) family backgrounds.

Within faculties themselves, students at this time resented the organisation and content of their curricula. In many subjects, especially in the social sciences, students were critical of what was regarded as an overdose of ruling-class ideology. This was particularly the case in regard to anthropology, history, theology, sociology and psychology. This resentment against the curriculum was galvanised by the fact that most reading lists prescribed textbooks, pamphlets and articles written by Afrikaans-speaking academics, and omitted well-known radical texts.

Poor communications and generally hostile relations between the university administration and white members of staff, on the one hand, and black students, on the other, aggravated frustration and tension on campuses. Severe restrictions on students' social and political lives, with frequent expulsions for transgressions, kindled a live volcano that erupted from time to time. Outside the campus, students experienced alienation from their local communities, particularly at Turfloop (University of the North), Ngoye (University of Zululand) and Fort Hare, which were located in rural areas. Likewise, the police, white shopkeepers and railway officials demonstrated their own racial hostility towards university students, whom they regarded as 'cheeky kaffirs-in-the-making'.

During vacations at home, many students experienced difficulties in their attempts to find vacation or temporary jobs. Many prospective white employers viewed educated blacks with grave suspicion and could not countenance the idea of being confronted by politicised and unionised workers. This hostile attitude became more generalised as SASO hit the headlines from 1972 onwards. From this time, black graduates found it difficult, and sometimes impossible, to secure satisfactory employment in the private sector. Most discovered they could only find work as teachers, social workers or government employees.

In their various townships at this time, university students found themselves becoming alienated from their own people, including their childhood friends, who regarded them with awe as educated persons and felt socially inferior. It was partly for this reason that SASO was later to help form a number of youth organisations, composed of both secondary school pupils as well as unemployed youth. One of these was the National Youth Organisation (NAYO) founded in 1972. More significantly, many of this new generation of students, especially those in urban areas, found it relatively difficult to associate with members of their own class – the professionals – who generally despised them as products of the Bantu Education system and the 'tribal' colleges. The SASO militants were later eager to make a distinction between politically committed black intellectuals and the educated 'middle class' whose blackness was only 'skin-deep' (Biko, 1971).

This educated, middle-class professional group had largely been educated at missionary institutions and at Fort Hare, and some had been members of the ANC Youth League. They were drawn from well-to-do families, the sons and daughters of chiefs, rich peasants and relatively wealthy petty traders and professional people. Unlike many of their predecessors who formed the Youth League in the mid-1940s, most of the SASO militants in the late 1960s and early 1970s were products of the locations and townships. Many of them had managed to acquire university entrance largely through the efforts of their own labour during school vacations when they worked in factories and even in the mines.[1]

Thus the black youth of this period knew at first hand the harsh reality and the brutality of the apartheid system and the appalling conditions under which their families lived and worked. This was a generation also keenly aware that their marginal status in South Africa's racially structured social and economic system rendered them incapable of getting past the barriers thrown up by racism. In the context of Portuguese Guinean society, Amilcar Cabral characterised the dilemma of this social stratum in these words: 'It is within the framework of this daily drama, against the backcloth of the usually violent confrontation between the mass of people and the ruling colonial class, that a feeling of bitterness or a frustration complex is bred and develops among the indigenous petty-bourgeoisie. At the same time they are becoming more and more conscious of a compelling need to question their marginal status and to rediscover an identity' (1973:62).

In South Africa, it was within the context of this daily drama that many black students began to question their marginal status and felt the need to seek an identity with the mass of the oppressed; hence the popular slogan among SASO militants: *'We are Black students, and not black Students!'* The urgent need for this process of integration and identity was expressed by SASO president Steve Biko at the First National Formation School at Edendale in December 1969. He enunciated the aims of SASO as, *inter alia*: 'To heighten the degree of contact not only among non-white students but also among these and the rest of the population; to boost the morale of the non-white students, to heighten their own confidence in themselves and to contribute largely to the direction of thought taken by the various institutions on social, political and other current topics' (Biko, 1969).

Before black students could set up a common political agenda and elaborate an ideology of liberation, they first had to overcome the problem of inter-campus communications. Two ways were envisaged by which to attain this objective. The first was to initiate and regularise correspondence and the exchange of information and material about matters of mutual concern in the form of letters and publications. This was to be supplemented by inter-SRC visits.

Prior to the formation of SASO, little contact existed between students of various centres. Only during vacations did students get a glimpse of the

1 Onkgopotse R. Abraham Tiro, who was killed by a bomb whilst living in exile in Botswana in 1974, and Harry Nengwekhulu are typical examples of SASO cadres who had working-class experience. Incidentally, they succeeded each other as SASO national organisers.

social, academic and political life of their colleagues elsewhere. One centre of contact was metropolitan Johannesburg, and it was from this city that many students were scattered among the various colleges. It is hardly surprising, therefore, that students from Johannesburg played a leading role in student politics, especially at Fort Hare. Johannesburg soon became the melting pot of national student politics and the first city outside the Durban SASO headquarters to establish a SASO branch and office, known as REESO (SASO Reef). Many high-school student leaders were active at the REESO office and were to play a leading role in the 16 June uprising in 1976.

These early contacts were facilitated by such prominent SASO leaders as Onkgopotse Tiro, a history teacher at Morris Isaacson High School who taught student leaders like Tsietsi Mashinini, as well as veteran SASO and BPC leaders like Tom Manthata, Aubrey Mokoena, Fanyana Mazibuko and many others. It was at Morris Isaacson where the initial organisation of the 16 June uprising took place.

The second method of communication which, it was felt, could help forge links among the student population was a 'loose structural alliance' provided for by the SASO constitution. When the two tactics were weighed against each other, it was found that the first was inadequate in the absence of a formal mechanism which could ensure its smooth functioning. The other tactic of setting up a formal organisational structure gained more support, although it also had certain shortcomings. There was an overriding fear amongst some students, especially those who had been associated with NUSAS, that any form of division in student ranks along 'racial lines' amounted to tacit conformity to the policy of apartheid. This feeling was particularly strong among former NUSAS members at Fort Hare and University of Natal (Black Section) at Wentworth where the liberal tradition of 'non-racialism' had been a dominant ideological perspective. The debate on the formation of SASO as an independent black organisation, dubbed by some as 'second-class' apartheid, was clearly reflected in the report of the Turfloop conference of July 1969. It was summed up as follows:

> Any move that tends to divide the student population into separate laagers on the basis of colour is in a way a tacit submission to having been defeated and apparently seems in agreement with apartheid. In a racially sensitive country like ours, provisions for racially exclusive bodies tend to build up resentment and to widen the gap that exists between races, and the student community should resist all attempts to fall into this temptation. Any formation of a purely non-white body shall be subject to a lot of scrutiny, and so the chances of the organisation lasting are very little (Biko, 1970).

Throughout this debate, militants associated with Biko at Wentworth and Harry Nengwekhulu at Turfloop argued in favour of organisational independence. The debate on both campuses was, however, complicated by the thorny issue of the role and position of Indians and Coloureds, not only in

SASO but in the liberation movement in general. At Wentworth, this issue was most pointed because of the presence of Indian and Coloured students on the same campus as Africans. The great divide, according to Biko, was between pro-NUSAS (ASA) and the pro-PAC (ASUSA) elements.[2] The Biko group, which was not part of either of these political factions, was viewed with suspicion by the PAC-oriented faction, who regarded them as a 'middle extension' of NUSAS because of their previous associations with this body.

The pro-PAC group argued that minority groups like the Coloureds and Indians could not be included in SASO since they saw their interests in the maintenance of white political and economic power. Biko later complained in an interview with Dr Gerhart in 1972 about the Coloured and Indian students' failure to defend themselves and asserted that this did not help their case for SASO. Nevertheless, the Biko group argued that as far they were concerned, all the oppressed were involved in the struggle for freedom, and each had its own grievances. It was necessary, they argued, that they should work with all who were committed to the removal of the source of those grievances, be they African, Coloured or Indian. They also argued that SASO was not a movement of Africans or any other group, but of the oppressed people, and that those who experienced oppression in South African society and were committed to the struggle against that oppression should be free to join SASO. According to Biko, their argument weighed heavily in the minds of the majority of students. As a result, the Africanists of ASUSA were defeated and Biko's group carried the day.

Their victory was important for two reasons. First, the Wentworth campus was the only one where Africans, Coloureds and Indians studied together, and any demonstration of unity here was bound to have a positive impact on other universities. Second, the University of Natal's authorities had long professed a policy of 'non-racialism' and had thus tolerated the activities of NUSAS on the black medical campus. It was for this reason that other campuses looked to Wentworth not only to give firm support to SASO but also to give 'strength and direction in the long struggle towards the realisation of the aspirations of these students, which in the long run are the aspirations of any "sane" South African' (SASO, 1969).

At the Turfloop conference itself, some students argued for a 'fight within' NUSAS. This view was rejected by an overwhelming majority who pointed out that NUSAS's 'protest-after-the-fact' politics only served to provoke victimisation of black students, and the result was general political apathy among them. When this position was defeated, some students called for an undertaking from the SASO leadership that the new organisation would at least affiliate to NUSAS. Although no such undertaking was given, the idea of affiliation was not rejected out of hand for fear of alienating those who still had some lingering loyalties to NUSAS. For some stu-

2 The African Students' Association (ASA) and the African Students' Union of South Africa (ASUSA) were formed after the bannings of the ANC and PAC in 1960.

dent leaders like Biko and Barney Pityana, the idea of affiliation to NUSAS was untenable, although they could not state as much publicly. The result was a cautiously worded constitution aimed primarily at uniting people of various political outlooks. It was not, however, a reflection of uncertainty about SASO's new role, as some analysts have suggested (see Herbstein, 1978:65).

According to the first SASO constitution adopted at Turfloop, SASO's main objective was to promote contact and practical cooperation among students studying at the affiliated centres. In order to alleviate the fears of those students who had argued for a fight within NUSAS and those who had sought an undertaking for affiliation of SASO to NUSAS, the constitution made room for 'contact among South Africans generally'.

The conference went further to contradict the impression that SASO had been formed in opposition to NUSAS or that it was its black equivalent. The point was made that 'SASO makes no claim of being a "national union" but simply an organisation formed to promote contact' among black students (SASO, 1969).

The issue of affiliation was deliberately avoided by Biko and his colleagues at the conference, and it was decided that it should be shelved for the time being. In order to reach a compromise and to achieve maximum unity, a resolution was passed which maintained recognition of NUSAS as a national union. It read:

> SASO makes no claim of being a 'national union' but is simply an organisation formed under protest and makes no claim of being a pure organisation. The malicious claim [that SASO claimed to be a 'national union'], therefore, cannot be reconciled with the draft Constitution, nor the Preamble thereto. Neither we nor NUSAS or any other body should seek to thwart the attempts of student leaders who wish to try to effect this kind of contact, for it is the lifeline to intellectual salvation of not only the students at the university colleges, but of the non-white population as a whole since they shall draw their future leaders from these students (SASO, 1969).

It should be noted that the issue of affiliation to NUSAS was limited to a few vocal individuals who had actively participated in the organisation. Whilst many students might have been cautious about the emergence of SASO as a blacks-only organisation, it was less because of their faith in NUSAS than the fear that an independent black organisation like SASO might be seen to be in conformity with the Bantustan programme, of which the black universities themselves were a product.

For the new SASO leadership, their most urgent task was to cultivate a broad front of all black students and to identify this with the struggles of the oppressed majority. As the July conference resolutions stressed, identification with the struggle of the oppressed was not in itself enough unless the student played a significant role in that process.

During this crucial formative period of the new student movement, its perception of the role of black students in the liberation process itself eventually crystallised into what came to be known as the ideology of 'Black Consciousness'. This was a conscious attempt at negating the dominant ideologies of 'white liberalism' and 'apartheid', as well as an instrument for unifying all oppressed people, irrespective of their class background. It is this articulation of the ideology of Black Consciousness that I propose to deal with presently.

The Definition of Black Consciousness

The years 1970 and 1971 saw SASO rapidly increasing its membership and gradually extending its influence beyond the university student community. The basic method of affiliation was 'centre affiliation' through Student Representative Councils. Where there was no SRC, as in the case of Fort Hare, a majority decision at a meeting of the student body was accepted as an act of affiliation. Provision was also made for individual affiliation, especially for students studying by correspondence through the University of South Africa (UNISA) and for those who had completed their studies (Biko, 1970).

In order to attain greater unity among the membership and to establish a common political identity among students, the SASO leadership began to address the question of ideology which had been deliberately avoided at the 1969 General Student Council (GSC) meeting at Turfloop, and which since then had been avoided in favour of the urgent task of consolidation and the building of a popular base.

To achieve their political objectives, the SASO leadership felt it was necessary to destroy any political influence that white liberalism might still have at Fort Hare and Wentworth. In this process, a critique of NUSAS as an organisation for white people 'asserting and dialoguing about White causes, and looking at the aspirations of White people' was seen as crucial if any links that might have existed with NUSAS were to be broken off. In order to distinguish themselves effectively from white liberal politics, the SASO leadership decided to set up a common agenda geared towards the process of liberation. Barney Pityana summed this process up retrospectively as follows: 'We realised that the black people in the townships, in the length and breadth of the country, were talking a different language, and we felt that what needed to be on the agenda of black students was the language of liberation, the language of freedom, the language of independence' (Personal communication).

In order to clarify among themselves the kind of language of liberation they sought to popularise, student leaders had to acquaint themselves with the history of the liberation movement in South Africa. This educational process was embarked upon at 'formation schools' as well as leadership-training seminars organised in 1970 and 1971. These sessions normally lasted four days and involved in-depth discussions on many topics. Participation at the seminars and formation schools was limited to the core cadres from centres and branches; these were locally selected in consultation with the SASO national executive.

In an effort to facilitate communication amongst the black student population, and to spread the message of Black Consciousness, a SASO newsletter was published by the headquarters in Durban. Through this medium, students were urged to engage in dialogue amongst themselves and to 're-assess their position, role and responsibility within the South African student movements and society in general' (*SASO Newsletter*, June 1970).

The *SASO Newsletter* of June 1970 pointed out that too often in the past black students had 'thoughtlessly' aligned themselves with white student protests and tended to ape the attempts by white liberals who, 'operating from their comfortable circumstances in Lower Houghton [an affluent white suburb in Johannesburg], have toiled to ameliorate the suffering caused by apartheid'. The newsletter's editorial observed that although white liberals had their own role to play in opposition to apartheid, the role for black students was different: 'We'll have, we believe, to close our ranks before entering the open society, not because we are racialists, as some will charge, but because our sympathetic White countrymen, sincere and well-meaning though they may be, have been rendered by circumstances unable to view the problem from the Black man's viewpoint.'

The significance of the SASO attack on liberalism was that it amounted to a categorical rejection of the Congress Alliance: SASO regarded this as an unholy alliance which had in the past led most black leaders to rely too much on the advice of white liberals. In SASO's view, a priority of the Congress Alliance's leadership had been 'to "calm the masses down" while they engaged in fruitless negotiation with the status quo'. The old ANC methods of struggle were in this context regarded as a 'programmed course in the art of gentle persuasion through protests and limited boycotts' with the hope that the troubled conscience of the 'fair-minded' English folk would exert some pressure towards political change in South Africa (Biko, 1971a).

Many SASO militants were also hostile towards the Freedom Charter of 1955 which, as far as they were concerned, was the product of the influence exerted by white liberals on the ANC. Biko's view (1971) that 'the biggest mistake the Black world has ever made was to assume that whoever opposed apartheid was an ally' summed up the feelings of many leading SASO figures of the time. The scepticism about old methods and perceptions of the political struggle associated with the ANC, which had engaged itself in 'coalitions with organisations other than those run by Blacks', led SASO members to identify with the ANC Youth League, which in their view had precipitated the emergence of Black Consciousness with its 'go-it-alone' stance.

This rejection of old forms of political struggle compelled the SASO leadership to grapple with developing new ideological and political forms of struggle. This need was also underlined by the huge enrolment into SASO of students with no previous connections with, or knowledge of, the old political traditions. Ten years on from 1960, very few students knew at first hand anything about the older nationalist organisations, particularly the PAC, which had existed for only a year before its banning. It was not until the mid-1970s when some key PAC and ANC activists were released from Robben Island, that these organisations became the subject of debate within the Black Consciousness Movement. Even then, for reasons of security, the discussions were largely restricted to a few individuals in leadership positions. What is more, contact with the ANC and the PAC by newly exiled SASO–BPC cadres from 1973 onwards had triggered discussions about relationships and cooperation with these various organisations.

In the meantime, SASO had to evolve new forms of struggle within the horizons of its own historical context and experience. In the view of Steve Biko, probably the most articulate exponent of Black Consciousness, an ideology of liberation should be the product of life experience under the harsh realities of the apartheid system. Born shortly before the election of the National Party in 1948, Biko summed up his own life experience in these words: 'My friendships, my love, my education, my thinking and every other facet of my life have been carved and shaped within the context of separate development. In stages during my life I have managed to outgrow some of the things the system has taught me' (*SASO Newsletter*, September 1970).

According to the Black Consciousness viewpoint, the fact that apartheid was tied up with white supremacy, capitalist exploitation and deliberate oppression made the problem much more complex (Biko, 1977). For the advocates of Black Consciousness, therefore, the struggle meant conscious resistance against the 'dehumanising and demoralising' effects of apartheid ideology and practice. Blacks were defined as those 'who are by law or tradition politically, economically and socially discriminated against as a unit in the struggle towards the realisation of their aspirations' (SB to GG, 1972).

The definition of the term 'black' to include Africans, Indians and Coloureds was crucial in the development of the movement. It is worth noting here that neither the ANC nor the PAC had at this time arrived at such a precise and strategic definition which embraced all the oppressed and sought to unite them within a single ideological discourse. Even in SASO ranks, the debate about the wisdom of including Coloureds and Indians in the organisation was by no means over. As was indicated earlier, at Wentworth this debate had become more ferocious, and in 1970 a special meeting was called to resolve the issue.

To Biko the debate was not new. In his own home in King William's Town, most of his blood relatives, who were members of the PAC, had debated the same issue with him. According to Biko, he was never convinced that it was right to exclude Coloureds and Indians from the liberation movement because, like Africans, they were also victims of the same system of oppression. By the time he became a medical student at Wentworth, the question never arose, because 'I never had to adjust my mind to accept Indians and Coloureds ... because I never rejected them' (SB to GG, 1972).

The crucial importance of Black Consciousness ideology was emphasised by Don Mattera, a leading member of the Coloured Labour Party and its Public Relations Officer who resigned to join the BPC in 1973. He noted that 'never has democracy been suppressed and crushed as in this country... It is when all Black groups – Coloured, African, Indian – can come together in a common brotherhood that there will be hope for us' (*Rand Daily Mail*, 11 July 1972). Similarly, Strini Moodley, an ex-member of the Natal Indian Congress, spelled out the basis and need for black solidarity in an article in the *SASO Newsletter* in May–June 1972: 'We have come together on the basis of our common oppression and do not separate on the basis of superficial cultural differences. I say superficial ... because culture is dependent on behaviour and in the light of the realities of our oppression... We have similar fears, the same desires and the same experiences. We have to use the same trains, the same buses, the same restaurants.'

SASO militants repeatedly emphasised that being black was not a skin pigmentation 'but a reflection of a mental attitude', and that only those who had committed themselves to the liberation process could be described as 'black' in the political sense. Those who did not identify with the process would continue to be referred to as 'non-white'. It is significant to note that the latter reference was specifically meant for the Indian capitalist group (particularly concentrated around Durban), and those individuals who served in such apartheid institutions as the Bantustans, the South African Indian Council, the Coloured Persons Representative Council, and the so-called mayors in Urban Bantu Councils. In this sense, therefore, SASO's definition of 'black' was not all-inclusive: 'The fact that we are not White does not necessarily mean we are all Black. Non-whites do exist and will continue to exist' (Biko, 1977).

In an editorial prior to the issuing of the SASO Policy Manifesto (hereafter referred to as the Black Students' Manifesto), a lengthy explanation of the concept of 'blackness' appeared in the September issue of the *SASO Newsletter*. Here it was argued:

> The term ... must be seen in the right context. No new category is being created but a re-Christening is taking place. We are merely refusing to be regarded as non-persons and claim the right to be called positively... Adopting a collectively positive outlook leads to the creation of a broader base which may be useful in time. It helps us to recognise that we have a common enemy... One should grant that the division of races in this country is too entrenched and that the Blacks will find it difficult to operate as a combined front. The black umbrella we are creating for ourselves at least helps to make sure the various units should be working in the same direction, being complementary to each other.[3]

In order to foster a sense of self-respect among blacks in South Africa, the Black Students' Manifesto declared: 'The basic tenet of Black Consciousness is that the Black man must reject all value systems that seek to make him a foreigner in the country of his birth and reduce his basic dignity. The Black man must build up his value systems, see himself as self-defined and not defined by others.'

As part of this process of self-definition, 'black' was used to refer to Africans, Indians and Coloureds. The definition of Black Consciousness as 'an attitude of mind, a way of life' was interpreted to imply the awareness by blacks of the potential power they could wield as a group politically and economically, and hence group cohesion was regarded as an important facet of Black Consciousness. The mobilising function of the ideology of Black Consciousness was seen as decisive in the advancement of what was called 'the totality of involvement of the oppressed people'.

The implications of SASO's adoption of Black Consciousness as an ideology of liberation were far-reaching in practice. When Barney Pityana succeeded Biko as president in July 1970, he set about rewriting the SASO constitution, and the executive was enlarged to accommodate action-oriented development programmes designed for political mobilisation at grassroots level.

The amended SASO constitution, adopted in July 1971, committed the organisation to the struggle for the emancipation of the black people of South Africa and the 'betterment of their social, political lot'. The new constitution also unconditionally declared SASO's 'lack of faith' in the genuineness and capability of multi-racial organisations and individual whites to effect rapid social change in South Africa. Accordingly, given that black students had 'unique problems pertaining to them', it had become imperative for blacks 'to consolidate themselves and close their ranks' if their aspirations were to be realised.

Although no strategy was mapped out to achieve these objectives, this task was left to the national executive and planning commissions. These bodies set out the primary aims and objectives as follows:

1. To promote contact, practical cooperation, mutual understanding and unity among all black students in South Africa;
2. To represent the interest of students on all issues that affect them in their academic and community situation;
3. To heighten the sense of awareness and encourage them to become involved in political, economic and social development of black people;
4. To project at all times the Black Consciousness image culturally, socially and educationally;
5. To become a platform for expression of black opinion and represent these internationally.[4]

SASO's General Student Council held at Wentworth in July 1971 laid the foundations for the political direction that SASO was to follow throughout

3 This document was tabled by S. Biko (Wentworth) and Alex Mhlongo (Ngoye) at the conference (mimeo). The policy manifesto was later called the Black Students' Manifesto.

its period of legal existence. At this meeting, SASO declared itself to be a black student organisation working for the liberation of blacks in South Africa, firstly from psychological oppression brought about by inferiority complexes and, secondly, from physical oppression 'accruing out of living in a racist society'. According to Pityana, it was necessary to make a distinction between psychological oppression which was self-inflicted in the sense that blacks had internalised feelings of inferiority and 'dared not ·challenge the system', and physical oppression, which is an external and visible condition of existence. Pityana nevertheless acknowledged that there was no real demarcation between psychological and physical oppression because liberation was a unified, single process (Personal communication).

In this context, the central proposition of Black Consciousness was that blacks in South Africa had a certain common historical experience which arose out of colonialism and of which they needed to be collectively aware. They therefore needed to mobilise themselves as a group in order to translate this awareness into political action and then to overcome racist oppression. As a consequence, Black Consciousness placed great emphasis on freedom from the constraints of psychological oppression, which was a 'result of 300 years of deliberate oppression, denigration and derision' (*SASO Newsletter*, August 1970).

The conclusion arrived at from this premise was that in the South African historical setting where both blacks and whites live and 'shall continue to live together', each group was 'either part of the solution or part of the problem'. In view of the historical circumstances that accorded whites a privileged position, and because of their 'maintenance of an oppressive regime', whites had defined themselves as part of the problem. What this meant in essence was that SASO envisaged a common non-racial society in an undivided and unified South Africa. The organisation contended that this could not be achieved through the introduction of selected reformist measures as advocated by white liberals.

SASO also believed that a non-racial society could only come about with the overhaul of the socio-economic system which apartheid had built and sustained over many decades. It was argued, therefore, that the only people who had a genuine interest in and commitment to this objective were the victims of the system. This observation led SASO to declare that 'in all matters relating to the struggle towards realising our aspirations, Whites must be excluded' (Black Students' Manifesto).

The SASO statement had a far-reaching impact on student relationships in South Africa as a whole. The immediate influence was felt directly on

4 The Planning Commission's task was to deal with the administration of the organisation, such as the nomination of a second layer of leadership in case of banning orders, arrest or imprisonment of the current leadership. The Commission also dealt with political and ideological questions in conjunction with the secretary general of SASO. All its deliberations and decisions were secret.

SASO's relationship with NUSAS. Initially, SASO had expressed the need to establish contact with other student and professional organisations, including NUSAS (SASO, 1969). As noted earlier, SASO had originally recognised NUSAS as the 'national union' of South African students and rejected the idea that SASO sought to compete with NUSAS in the recruitment of members. At the 1970 SASO conference, however, this position was reversed, and SASO withdrew its formal recognition of NUSAS as a body purporting to represent all students in South Africa. It declared: 'The emancipation of the Black people depends on the role the Black people themselves are prepared to play ... In the principles and make-up of NUSAS Black students can never find expression for the aspirations foremost in their minds' (SASO, 1970).

The decision not to recognise NUSAS shocked the liberal establishment in South Africa, and the challenge was met with equal vigour, although without any positive success. The liberal response only served to polarise the already existing political cleavages amongst the student population.

Towards a Political Organisation

The withdrawal of recognition from NUSAS became a major issue at the University of Natal (Black Section) and at Fort Hare. At UNB Ben Ngubane, then a senior medical student,[5] was most vociferous in defending the multi-racial tradition of student politics. Donald Woods, the editor of the *Daily Dispatch* of East London and patron of NUSAS, played a central role in discouraging Fort Hare students from affiliating to SASO. He saw SASO as a black capitulation to the separate development ideology of the Nationalist government and NUSAS as upholder of a cherished multi-racial liberal tradition.

Black Consciousness spread in spite of all the criticism it received both on and off university campuses. But its growth amongst predominantly black students posed a dilemma for its proponents. There are few, if any, historical examples of students successfully leading major movements of social change. In the case of the Black Consciousness Movement, SASO found itself as the leading light of a new social movement without an adult base of support. However, critics of BCM are wrong in accusing it of having been completely ahistorical in its analysis and strategies for action. Long and heated debates were conducted amongst BCM adherents about the advisability or otherwise of establishing a political movement to popularise Black Consciousness and to mobilise the oppressed into a united force against racist exploitation.

These debates also involved non-students, whose opinions were sought and valued. There were two positions on the issue. The one side argued for the formation of a political organisation with a strong political programme

---

5. Dr Ben Ngubane is now senior member of Inkatha Freedom Party's executive committee.

which would lead blacks out of the apathy they found themselves in since the banning of the ANC and PAC in 1960. Those supporting this view were impatient with the notion of conscientising people outside of a clear-cut political programme. They referred contemptuously to those who held opposing views, as proposing a gradualist, supra-cultural approach. Those on the other side of the debate maintained that blacks had to learn from their past experience and not just respond in a predictable way which would expose them to a ruthless repressive system. They further argued that the fear which had gripped blacks after the banning of the PAC and ANC would not simply disappear once a new political organisation came into being. Those holding this view felt that it would be better to invest in conscientising blacks through non-threatening vehicles such as existing community, church, youth and cultural organisations. They also contended that it was only when a critical mass of blacks had been psychologically liberated that they would be in a position to challenge those responsible for their physical oppression, socially, economically and politically.

In 1971, SASO leaders started to explore the possibility of bringing together all black organisations to debate this issue openly and launch a major adult thrust of the BCM. An initial meeting of six organisations, including IDAMASA (Inter-Denominational African Ministers' Association), ASSECA (Association for the Educational and Cultural Advancement of the African People), and the Old Boys' Association of St Peter's seminary, was held in Bloemfontein in April 1971. A follow-up conference was later arranged in Pietermaritzburg and was addressed by both Steve Biko and Chief Gatsha Buthelezi.

In December 1971, a third conference was held in Orlando West, Soweto. Tensions ran high between those advocating the formation of an overt political organisation, and those calling for greater caution and the need to strengthen the cohesiveness of the black community.

Nchaupe Aubrey Mokoape and Harry Ranwedzi Nengwekhulu were the most prominent spokespersons of the more militant demand for an overt political organisation. Steve Biko, who had always been of the view that more time was required to develop self-confidence amongst blacks through conscientisation and psychological liberation, found himself, together with Ben Khoapa, in the company of the older generation including M. T. Moerane and Dr William Nkomo. Gail Gehart is thus mistaken in claiming that it was simply a matter of the SASO militants against the older generation (Gerhart, 1979:292). This was a critical and complex debate which cannot simply be reduced to a division between militants and conservatives. It involved strategic choices about how to operate effectively in a tight political space. The choice was thus between accepting one's weaknesses at a particular historical point and devising strategies to address these weaknesses under a broadly based cultural umbrella organisation, on one hand, and assuming that one could mobilise sufficient support amongst oppressed people by appealing to their aspirations for freedom, on the other.

The latter choice was made, and the Black People's Convention (BPC) was launched at the Orlando West meeting in December 1971. Drake Koka, a veteran trade unionist, was elected president, and Mthuli Shezi, Saths Cooper, the Rev. A. Manyathula and five others became members of the first executive. Although Steve Biko had originally been opposed to the formation of an overt political organisation, he gave his full support to BPC once it became a reality.

BPC struggled to gain support on a mass basis, and tended to have the same overall membership as SASO. Various reasons can be advanced for this failure to mobilise more broadly amongst adult black South Africans. Firstly, there was difficulty in attracting funds for a political organisation such as BPC in 1972. Few donors, local, national or international, saw it as a horse they were prepared to back. Secondly, many black people felt uncomfortable about identifying with an overt political organisation, as a result of their experience in the 1960s, thus vindicating the view held by Steve Biko and others that black people had first to be liberated from fear.

Thirdly, police repression was intensified against all those involved in political mobilisation. Mthuli Shezi, then vice-president of BPC, was pushed in front of a moving train at Germiston railway station by a white railway policeman who had taken exception to his protection of a black woman commuter against the policeman's abuse some days before. Shezi died five days later of his injuries, and no one was held responsible for his death. Many other activists at that time were subjected to harassment by the security police.

BPC found it difficult to thrive in such a harsh environment. It continued to operate in the shadow of the more highly organised SASO and relied on SASO for both resources and political direction – an incongruous position indeed. The banning of eight BC leaders in early 1973 further weakened BPC. While SASO was able to mobilise the next layer of leadership to take over from those lost to the organisation, BPC struggled to find able and willing people to take over leadership positions.

Mrs Motlalepula Kgware emerged as president of BPC at its December 1973 conference, thus becoming the first black woman to head a national political organisation. Her age and respectability gave BPC a boost amongst adult blacks, but fear remained an important deterrent to participation by most people.[6]

Mosibudi Mangena served as a national organiser under Mrs Kgware. He became the first BC activist to be charged under the Terrorism Act of 1967 and sent to Robben Island. His detention and trial arose out of a train trip to the Eastern Cape; a police plant who travelled with him claimed that Mangena had been trying to recruit people in the train compartment for

6 Biko believed firmly that fear was an important determinant of South African politics. Out of fear of repression blacks acquiesced in oppression, whilst whites, from fear of black domination and loss of privilege, gave support for racist policies to keep blacks down (Biko, 1978:87).

military training. How anyone would have dared to recruit strangers in public in the harsh political climate of 1973 is beyond comprehension. But it was Mangena's word against that of the police, and in terms of the Terrorism Act, one was presumed to be guilty until proven otherwise – a complete travesty of justice.

The victory of FRELIMO in Mozambique in 1974 created euphoria amongst blacks in South Africa. It aroused hope that even an entrenched repressive regime could be toppled through the sheer determination of the oppressed. BPC and SASO leadership, particularly those based in Durban at the time, wanted to celebrate the event and use it as a mobilising occasion. The Durban-based BC leadership decided to defy the ban and go ahead with the rally in spite of the advice of Mr Justice Poswa, then SASO's legal adviser, and Steve Biko's appeal for caution in the face of the costs of defiance.

Ironically Steve Biko and those BC activists based in the Eastern Cape were left to pick up the pieces and keep both BPC and SASO afloat during the long detention and trial of the BC leaders arrested after the rally. Mapetla Mohapi and Malusi Mpumlwana were sent to run the SASO office in Durban and to repair the damage done to relations with those offended by the BC leadership's handling of the pro-FRELIMO rally.

It was thus logical that in December 1975 the BPC conference would be held in King William's Town. At this conference BPC policy was clarified on a number of issues: the difference between Black Consciousness as a way of life, and black solidarity as a political strategy; and the BPC's stand on socio-economic issues. Black communalism was adopted as a framework for future socio-economic policy formulation.

The BPC resolution on socio-economic issues was referred to a working group, which later reported to a workshop held in Mafeking in May 1976. At this workshop a document, sometimes referred to as the Mafeking Declaration, was adopted. It sparked off a controversy within BC ranks between those who saw BPC as a holding operation for banned organisations, and those who believed the BPC had to take a position on socio-economic issues if it was to function as an effective broker of unity between liberation organisations. The former regarded the document as a challenge to the ANC's Freedom Charter and resented it.

At the King William's Town conference, Hlaku Kenneth Rachidi was elected president of BPC and Steve Biko honorary president. The honorary presidency was created as a strategic move to enable Biko to occupy an official position within the BCM, without falling foul of the conditions of his banning order, which prohibited him from membership of and participation in BPC, SASO and BCP. He was thus able to pursue clandestinely the unity talks he was involved in at the time with other liberation organisations.

Although BPC failed to grow into a mass political organisation, its strategic use of the media, notably the regular weekly column in the *Daily Dispatch* which appeared under Mapetla Mohapi's name, and the release of

well-positioned press statements, established BPC as an important voice in
South Africa. When the Soweto schoolchildren rose up in June 1976 the
political temperature was raised considerably. BPC's opinion was sought
from all sides, and Steve Biko was consulted by people from far and wide
about what was happening in South African society.

The Banning of the BC Organisations

The Black Consciousness Movement never claimed responsibility for the
Soweto uprising, but acknowledged that its conscientisation process had
had an impact on young blacks, who were then ready to protest against the
government's imposition of Afrikaans as a medium of instruction in
schools.

The government's response to the march by schoolchildren shocked the
world. The killing of Hector Petersen and many others concretised in the
minds of black schoolchildren the ruthlessness of the system they were up
against. Defiance was the response of the youth and it was met with greater
ruthlessness. Stories of piles of children's bodies being seen at police stations began to spread in Soweto. Allegations of secret burials of children in
body bags abounded. Parents moved from one mortuary to another in
search of missing children – indeed, many have disappeared without trace
to this day. Mapetla Mohapi was killed in detention on 5 August 1976 after
a period of detention under Section 6 of the Terrorism Act at Kei Road
police station, just outside King William's Town. He was alleged to have
hanged himself with his jeans.

Political activists were detained in their hundreds under the newly
enacted Internal Security Act, which provided for preventative detention.
Many activities of the BCM were scaled down to a minimum until the end
of 1976. Most detainees were released in time for the New Year celebrations.

1977 was to see more repression. The King William's Town community
of activists was broken up: Thenjiwe Mtintso was banned and restricted to
Johannesburg at the time of her release in December 1976. Mamphela
Ramphele, Mxolisi Mvovo, and Malusi Mpumlwana were all banned in
April 1977 and restricted from participation in activities of BPC, SASO and
BCP.

Activists in other parts of the country were similarly affected. Hlaku
Rachidi, Tom Manthata, Sedupe Ramokgopha, and many others on the
Reef were banned. The whole BCM was ravaged by these actions, but most
activists kept contact with one another and continued to find ways of maintaining pressure on the system. The courts became an important site of
struggle, the tradition having been set by the much publicised SASO–BPC
trial of 1975–76. Trials also became an important meeting place for activists,
who used every excuse to call in their colleagues as witnesses.

Steve Biko intensified his efforts to forge black unity. He travelled far and
wide at great risk to meet important political actors. It was thus not surpris-

ing that his luck would run out on his way back from an unsuccessful trip to Cape Town where he had hoped to meet Neville Alexander, an important voice within the Unity Movement tradition.

The outrage following Steve Biko's death in September 1977 was enormous. The world was horrified as the story of his detention and torture unfolded. Yet the government reacted in a characteristic fashion: more repression. On 19 October 1977 all BCM organisations were banned, and many more activists were banned and restricted. Black South Africans were again left numb, but this time it was to be short-lived numbness. The spirit of defiance was too deeply implanted and widely spread to be crushed.

During the period of detention, many activists found themselves together in large prison cells and planned their next moves. Varied views were expressed. Some opted for the resuscitation of BCM-style organisations, while others argued that underground activity, using the structures of banned organisations, was a more appropriate response. It is thus not surprising that the 1980s saw the birth of the Azanian People's Organisation (AZAPO) as well as the revitalisation of underground activity.

Trade-union activity was heightened with the injection of leadership from former BCM and NUSAS activists. Cyril Ramaphosa, who took on the task of organising and running the National Union of Mineworkers, was the most notable amongst former activists in this area. The United Democratic Front (UDF), aimed at opposing the tricameral parliamentary system, represented the first bold step of open mass mobilisation after the repressive era of the 1960s and 1970s. Lessons had been learnt from the mistakes and triumphs of both decades.

The BCM can be said to have prepared the way for the bolder moves of the 1970s and 1980s, which culminated in the events of the 1990s. The impact of BCM goes beyond particular organisations. The psychological liberation brought about by the BC philosophy enabled blacks, particularly the young, to overcome their fear of the repressive system they were up against. Young blacks were able to stand up and be counted as people, often risking their lives in the process. They had ultimately found something worth dying for, and thus could live their lives more fully.

6

The Psychology of Liberation
C. D. T. SIBISI

Psychology, despite its claim to be a scientific study of human behaviour, has been widely employed to buttress the case for racism and exploitation. Both slavery and colonialism were justified by pseudo-scientific observations which held that blacks were morally and intellectually inferior. The capacity of their skulls was small, attesting to limited intellectual ability; their cultural development was limited; their moral development was arrested and they had a propensity to seek immediate gratification of (baser) instincts for food and sex, which posed a threat to civilised (white) society; and they lacked staying power and the capacity for sustained hard work, thus requiring supervision from those – whites – endowed with such virtues.

The work of these pseudo-scientists paralleled the efforts of those who sought, and found, biblical justification for slavery, racism and apartheid. Through selective observation and appropriate interpretation of the 'evidence' it is possible to obtain 'proof' of whatever theory is advanced. The theory is first advocated, and the evidence is then sought to support it, thus neatly reversing the normal scientific process of dispassionate observation giving rise to scientific laws and theories.

From the foregoing it would seem that psychology and liberation (in the South African context and from the perspective of Black Consciousness) are uneasy bedfellows; the task I have been set therefore seems particularly onerous. The discipline of psychology is not unique in this respect, however. Most scholars bring to the field their ingrained assumptions and prejudices, which colour their observations and theories.

There are innumerable standpoints from which one can approach the subject of the relationship between psychology and liberation or Black Consciousness. I shall advance an analysis of putative motivating factors on both sides of the 'great divide' of race in South Africa.

The principle of determinism is central to much of Western thought and science (and indeed to much of human thought and behaviour). It attributes causes to events. Things do not just happen by chance. They are caused to happen. The natural scientist may legitimately ask, 'What caused that object to move?' or more generally, 'What causes objects to move?' The psychologist may ask, 'Why does that person hold such views?' or more generally, 'Why do people hold views of a certain type?' The natural scientist may give simple answers: 'The application of a force causes objects to move.' The psychologist will give an answer that varies according to his or her standpoint – the views that people hold may be attributed to their genes, their childhood, the influence of peers and so on. This simplistic reductionism – the attempt to provide simple answers to complex questions – is a pitfall to be avoided, but I am afraid I may well succumb to it in the course of this chapter.

Of the numerous schools of psychology that may be utilised to examine the factors motivating the players in the South African drama, I have selected the psychoanalytic one. Freudian psychoanalysis and its derivatives have captivated the popular imagination probably more than any other school of psychology, notwithstanding the criticism levelled by Karl Popper, among others, that it fails to meet the scientific test. Psychoanalysis cannot be said to be a science, protested Karl Popper (1959), since it attempted to 'explain' everything. Practically anything in the variegated field of human feeling and behaviour is susceptible to psychoanalytic interpretation. Psychoanalysis does not generate hypotheses capable of refutation. It does not make specific predictions about human behaviour, so that, if the predicted behaviours do not occur, one can say that the theory has been tested and found wanting. What psychoanalysis does is to provide a *post hoc* explanation, whatever the situation.

The psychoanalytic schools perceive human beings as motivated by some fundamental drives (in this they are, of course, not unique). Preservation of the self and of the species is the goal towards which these innate drives work. The psychoanalytic schools also recognise the concept of the unconscious. There are actions and feelings which we may experience for reasons that are not apparent to us. There is a stratum of the mind which holds material that does not reach conscious awareness, and yet may profoundly affect conscious feeling and behaviour.

Freud, the father of the psychoanalytic movement, divided the mind, or psyche, into three parts: (i) The id is that part which contains our 'primitive' drives, wishes and desires. It develops early in life. Its contents are unconscious. The id is largely governed by the 'pleasure principle': it consists of material (drives) seeking gratification. (ii) The ego is that part of the psyche which is largely conscious, in touch with the real world. It is governed by the 'reality principle' and recognises that primitive instinctual drives run into conflict with the demands of society. (iii) The superego consists largely of conscious material. It develops later in life. It may be thought of as roughly corresponding to 'conscience', and contains society's highest moral principles and prohibitions.

Human beings are thus perceived as subject to conflicting influences – the ego has to reconcile the desires of the id with the prohibitions of the superego. Defence mechanisms are used to deal with primitive drives demanding gratification. Failure to do so is threatening to the ego and may be experienced as intense anxiety, guilt, or pain, or, in other words, leads to experiences of psychic ill-health. Defences against a threatening drive may involve repressing it, or keeping it repressed by developing contrary characteristics, described as reaction formation.

Thus an excessively puritanical person may be simply defending himself or herself against sexual impulses, and the person who crusades against violence in the media merely trying to deal with his or her own feelings of aggression. Reaction formation is often regarded as an inefficient defence mechanism, requiring much effort to maintain the repression and not always successfully at that. Sublimation is a defence mechanism whereby the energy associated with the primitive drive is diverted along socially approved lines, such as hard work. Displacement is a defence whereby the threatening impulse is attributed to others. Rationalisation involves seeking a 'logical' explanation for a base feeling or action.

Freud, and others after him, applied the foregoing concepts to an understanding of everyday life. Slips of the tongue, for instance, may represent unconscious material 'slipping through' and finding expression in speech. Much of social behaviour may represent the interplay of unconscious processes and defence mechanisms; for instance, many myths, rituals and folk-lores may represent society's attempts to deal with the instincts of sex, aggression and so on.

I should like now to return to the subjects of slavery, colonialism and racism, on which I touched earlier. The first two have a clear-cut economic imperative, benefiting the perpetrators in a material sense. The last, racism, makes sense if it is linked to the first two, providing a justification for them. We may look upon racism as an example of an ego defence mechanism on the part of the slave-owner or colonialist. There is a need to justify to the superego conduct (slavery or ruthless economic exploitation) that would normally give rise to intense shame and guilt. The mechanism of rationalisation is used to deny the humanity of the victim, or at least to belittle it, and thus provide a justification for untoward actions. The real motive for such actions – greed – is not acknowledged.

Another defence mechanism used is projection; the base instincts of the id are ascribed to the victim of racism (who, as observed earlier, is credited with a propensity for excessive and immediate gratification of drives for food or sex) and are thus not acknowledged in the self. This reassures the ego and reconciles it with the demands of the superego.

Such a formulation leads to three conclusions. Firstly, racism will arise where the victim of economic exploitation is readily identifiable (where he or she *looks* different). Secondly, there is clear economic benefit for the racist in the maintenance of the *status quo*. Thirdly, racism cannot be perpetrated by a group that is not economically dominant. This conclusion has been stated as an absolute by various people, such as Stokely Carmichael, defending black power against the charge that it was no more than black racism (see also Biko, 1978:97).

My analysis has similarities with Marxist theories which ascribe racism to economic exploitation. The latter, however, claim economic factors as the sole determinant of racism, and assert a congruence of interests between the oppressed white working class and the black struggle for emancipation. The formulation I have been propounding holds that, while economic factors are of cardinal importance, they are but part of a complex picture.

I should now like to look at the psychological factors at play among the oppressed in South Africa. The black response to racism is a complex one. Acceptance of the oppressor's viewpoint is but one aspect. Every black, from the cradle to the grave, is faced with evidence of his or her secondary status in society. This perception of one's worth is deeply painful to one's ego. A common response is the defence mechanism of denial, not of one's alleged inferiority, but of one's very blackness. Since all the symbols of success – material comforts, and scientific and literary achievements – are presented from a Eurocentric perspective, they are associated with whiteness. The superficial symbols of the denial of blackness are evident in the (formerly) widespread use of skin-lightening and hair-straightening agents by black women.

The defence mechanism of denial is usually regarded as inefficient and 'neurotic', because constant effort is required to protect the ego against anxiety, which is liable to break through. The further effort thus required entails the employment of yet further strategies to protect the threatened ego – projection (ascribing one's pain and predicament to persons and influences foreign to oneself), reaction formation (the blacks who are whiter than white) and identification with the aggressor. This last mechanism might be seen in the black official (the homeland leader or black security policeman) who diligently, and with genuine conviction, enforces apartheid laws; not all black officials in the service of apartheid are reluctant participants forced by economic necessity to play by the rules.

The defence mechanisms I have just referred to are 'neurotic' because they do not allow for the development of a healthy balanced ego, in touch with, and adapting in a healthy manner to, reality, and because they are not subject to conflicts with the id and superego. There is no 'healthy' way of adapting to apartheid or exploitation! Those who try to adapt end up being devoured, psychologically speaking; they must deal with the pain through means such as substance-abuse.

Black Consciousness was described by Steve Biko (1978) as an essentially 'inward-looking' movement; there is a preoccupation with the black psyche that forms the subject of much of Biko's writings. The term 'black' is stressed as a positive affirmation of one's worth, in contrast to the previously commonly used term 'non-white'. The powerful negative connotation of the latter term, which defines people in terms of their deviation from the 'ideal', epitomised by the white race, is stressed.

A brief overview of Biko's writings on black psychological liberation might stress the following. Firstly, black people, confronted daily with evidence of their subordinate position in South African society, come to believe in their inferiority. Secondly, the black people's culture has been denigrated (in particular by white missionaries) so they have developed a hatred for it. Thirdly, history is examined from the whites' perspective. Biko spoke eloquently about the 'emptiness of the past' and declared that 'a people without a positive history is like a vehicle without an engine'.

Biko suggested that these three issues need to be addressed as a matter of priority. He was not as explicit, however, in identifying the strategies to be deployed in addressing these problem areas. Having diagnosed the illness, he did not go on to prescribe a cure. The importance of self-reliance is implicit throughout most of Biko's earlier writings. The formation of exclusively black organisations, and the assumption of more visible black leadership roles, would, he believed, gradually result in the growth of a more positive self-image among blacks. The important role of religion in black society was recognised by Biko; he called for the creation of a black theology of liberation.

Biko was conscious of addressing himself largely to a small, unrepresentative segment of black society. He pointed out that the rural, 'traditional' African may have a different consciousness of the self, one largely unaffected by the influences that have impinged so greatly upon the more educated, Westernised urban dweller.

I would like to conclude this chapter by addressing some issues that may concern the inheritors of Biko's legacy in the evolving South Africa. Biko was concerned with political liberation, though the goal seemed distant during his time. Recent events in South Africa have changed expectations markedly from those of his day. Liberation in its widest sense may be seen in the present context to be a goal which is imminently achievable. Dealing with the psychological scars of apartheid, at both the individual and the collective level, will be part of the process.

The traumatic psychological effects of apartheid may be classified into two broad categories: those attributable directly to apartheid, and those resulting from the struggle against apartheid. The first category comprises the negative impact on black people's self-image, as well as the disruption of family life. The main onslaught against the black family has been the migrant labour system. This disruption has not only given rise to various stresses among those affected (manifesting, for instance, in episodic outbreaks of gruesome violence among inmates of mine compounds and the single-sex hostels for labourers forced to leave their families hundreds of miles away), but has also had negative effects upon children growing in unsettled environments, lacking the cultural anchor points provided by stable family life.

Several recent studies of family disruption have been conducted in the Western Cape (see Ramphele, 1989, 1990; Jones, 1990). Jones's study focussed particularly on children in the migrant labour hostels of Lwandle, Somerset West, and found evidence of severe child abuse, and insecurity amongst children caught up in a violent environment and lacking consistent parental love. Ramphele's study shows how social relationships are constrained by the limited space in which hostel dwellers in Cape Town find themselves. The question posed by these studies is the extent to which the scars arising out of legacy of the past can be healed by the mere abolition of apartheid. Similar effects to those of the migrant labour system have been produced by mass forced removals and the entire panoply of influx control (see Platzky and Walker, 1987).

The scars resulting from the struggle against apartheid are twofold. Firstly, there are the traumatic effects of violence, detention and torture at the hands of the security forces, and the random violence of their vigilante allies. The post-traumatic stress disorder is a well-recognised psychiatric syndrome attracting much attention in the West, but it undoubtedly has varied, culturally influenced manifestations that have not been adequately studied in South Africa – most poignantly among young children who develop mutism, and the 'frozen watchfulness' or the fearful vigilance of those who expect violence to be visited upon them at any moment, seen for instance among those who have witnessed the uniquely brutal atrocities of RENAMO in Mozambique.

Secondly, there are the brutalising effects upon those who have participated in various ways in the struggle, especially children who have committed acts of violence. Wilson and Ramphele's report to UNICEF detailed some of the salient features of this brutalisation amongst children in South Africa who have found themselves 'on the frontline' (Wilson & Ramphele, 1987). Of particular relevance to this chapter is their quotation of Jung's thoughts on the subject: 'The aspect of themselves, which human beings sacrifice in the attainment of a given objective in their lives, is reborn and returns, knife in hand, to sacrifice that which sacrificed it' (1989:270).

South Africans have yet to come to terms with the culture of violence that has become entrenched over the last few decades. Violence has been perpetrated by both the state and those opposing its policies, and both sides have been brutalised by it. The scars run deep, with serious implications for the future society.

Let us now return to the main theme of this chapter: liberation, the acquisition of liberty. The dictionary definition of 'liberty' is the power to determine one's destiny. It must be distinguished from emancipation, or the attainment of political, civil, or legal rights. Emancipation is but a stage on the path to liberty. Kwame Nkrumah's dictum 'Seek ye first the political kingdom and all else shall be given' has been proved hollow. It is, above all, economic power that guarantees true liberation. Groups that wield economic power can impose their will upon those that do not. The economically dominant Western countries (as well as the new economic powers of the Pacific Rim) are emerging as the main players on the world stage; lesser nations (in economic terms) are increasingly marginalised.

In the new South Africa, the economically dominant white group will continue to wield power, whatever political dispensation emerges. The empowerment of blacks will only be complete when they control a significant slice of the economic cake. Seizing it (by nationalisation) would alienate the dominant Western powers. *Realpolitik* dictates a strategy that has been used by others in similar circumstances. The transfer of a significant slice of the South African economic cake into Afrikaner hands in the first half of this century occurred as a result of factors not dissimilar to those which are operative in Black Consciousness ranks – namely, a sense of group pride and solidarity. The weapon of the boycott has demonstrated the economic power of blacks. This economic power, which proved effective when used in the negative mode (the boycott), may have a part to play in the economic empowerment and consequent liberation of all South Africa's people.

True liberation of both the oppressed and the oppressors in South Africa will entail a recognition by both parties of the full humanity of each individual, regardless of race, class or gender. It is a process requiring all South Africans to claim for themselves and to affirm for others nothing less than full humanity and dignity. Only when people are at peace with themselves, can they appreciate and live with the strengths and weaknesses of their fellow human beings. Psychological liberation, though not a sufficient condition, is a necessary one for the realisation of true liberty.

7

Towards the Armed Struggle*
KEITH MOKOAPE, THENJIWE MTINTSO & WELILE NHLAPO

> To take part in the African revolution it is not enough to write a revolutionary song; you must fashion the revolution with the people. And if you fashion it with the people, the songs will come by themselves and of themselves.
>
> In order to achieve real action you must yourself be a living part of Africa and of her thought; you must be an element of the popular energy which is entirely called forth for the freeing, the progress and the happiness of Africa.
>
> There is no place outside that fight for the artist or for the intellectual who is not himself concerned with, and completely at one with, the people in the great battle of Africa and of suffering humanity.

By 1972, these words of Sékou Touré, which Steve Biko frequently used, were beginning to translate themselves into action among black students. There had been walk-outs at black campuses sparked by the expulsion of Onkgopotse Tiro from the University of the North. There had also been a heated General Student Council meeting of the South African Students' Organisation (SASO) in July 1972; and elsewhere in the black communities outside the universities, the Black People's Convention (BPC) was taking root. Individually and collectively, Black Consciousness adherents were bracing themselves for confrontation with the South African regime.

Biko himself had, on many occasions, cautioned that students should not confuse their political awareness for that of the masses in general, and he made painstaking efforts to encourage students to study the history of the black struggle. The problem facing students was that reading material on the national liberation movements was scanty or unavailable because of censorship. The African National Congress (ANC), the Pan-Africanist Congress (PAC), the South African Communist Party (SACP), and the Unity Movement (NEUM) were all banned, and the leaders of these organisations

---

* This chapter reflects the experiences and views of some people who finally made their way to Umkhonto we Sizwe; in general BC activists moved in many directions and into many different organisations.

were either in prison or in exile. To overcome these obstacles, Biko organised youth leadership workshops and seminars, and encouraged participants to look incisively at the history of the people's political organisations. One advantage was that the early Black Consciousness Movement attracted students who had some links, direct or otherwise, with the main political groups of the pre-1960 national liberation movement. In addition, many political trials were taking place in the 1970s, and members of the BCM were encouraged to attend in solidarity with the accused, and because they were politicising forums. Biko personally encouraged the youth and students to follow these trials closely.

The cornerstone of Biko's thinking was that black people must look inwardly at themselves, reflect on their history, examine the reasons for past failures, and ask themselves, in the circumstances of the time, to use his phrase: 'What makes the black man fail to tick?' Biko maintained that black oppression in South Africa was twofold, psychological and physical – characterised in BC circles as 'Phase 1' and 'Phase 2'. He felt that the former (psychological oppression) 'is probably the one that creates mountains of obstacles in the normal course of emancipation of the black people'. As far as the latter (physical oppression) was concerned, students were becoming aware of the limitations of existing organisations, especially in so far as the armed struggle was concerned.

In BC circles, the questions relating to 'Phase 2' went largely unanswered, and it was often stated that when the time came 'the people will decide'. However, within informal sessions there was a strong recognition of the need for armed struggle. Yet even those who agreed that this was an absolute necessity, were still baffled by the 'how'. A number of case studies were examined privately, for example, those of Vietnam, Cuba, and Algeria. In addition, the contemporary struggles being waged by the PAIGC in Guinea-Bissau and Cape Verde, and by FRELIMO in Mozambique, were followed as closely as possible, as was the mobilisation by the people of Namibia against South Africa's illegal occupation.

Related to the above, the question of an organised movement of BC members into exile was firmly on the agenda by the mid-1970s. One of the issues frequently debated in this context was which organisation to join in exile. This was particularly pertinent after the repression following the 1972–3 student strikes at the universities.

Contact with the Liberation Movements

Although the motivation existed for a movement of students and youth *en masse* into exile, inside South Africa at this time individuals were seriously debating the question of 'what next?' In secret sessions, three options were discussed: (1) to continue with open mobilisation inside South Africa in the hope that 'approaches' would be made by the underground structures of the established political organisations; (2) to form a secret underground inside the country, to train and arm ourselves, and launch our own armed struggle from within the country; and (3) to go into exile and acquire some form of military training.

A small trickle of activists did leave the country at about this time, intent on reaching on-the-spot decisions once contact had been made with the exiled movement. Larger groups left after 1973 and settled in Botswana in a more organised manner, whereupon feelers were put out to the various liberation groups.

Unity Movement. Contact was made with two main factions based in Botswana and Zambia. Both dismissed the strategies of armed struggle as 'adventurism' and criticised an emphasis on underground organisation without a clear strategy for liberation. These two factions proved not useful. They were even sceptical about the BCM itself, and often attacked it as ideologically bankrupt.

African National Congress. The position of the ANC was that it could not accept for military training individuals who were not ANC members. The ANC agreed that it could accept into its ranks people who joined as individuals; but it could not enter into any alliance that had no principled basis. This proved a problem to the BC group.

Pan-Africanist Congress. Contact was made with two factions of the PAC, namely the Leballo and Ntantala groups. An agreement was reached with the latter whereby they would provide military training to any number of cadres as a basis for a future alliance. Indeed, arrangements were made through the Idi Amin regime in Uganda for 'scholarship' offers to be made, as a cover to enable recruits to leave and then to return to Botswana from Libya, where training was to take place.

Upon arrival in Libya, the recruits experienced numerous problems. They found that both factions of the PAC had recruits there, and this created enormous tension. In addition, the two factions of the Basutoland Congress Party also had trainees there, and strong animosity prevailed amongst them. The BC group faced a dilemma in their associations with all these factions. This caused suspicions on all sides. Their presence did not last for too long, however, as the PAC forced the Libyans to expel the BC group from the country because of their independence and influence over their cadres. Before their expulsion, a select group of BC activists had gone on for further training in Syria, under the auspices of the general command of the Popular Front for the Liberation of Palestine (PFLP). There, the BC component of the group did exceptionally well and participated independently in engagements alongside the Palestinians.

After their military training, and on their return to Botswana, the group faced new problems. First, the PAC had informed the Botswana government of the real purpose for which the groups had left the country. Second, the Soweto uprising of 1976 posed such a challenge that the debates on how to respond to the uprising produced divisions in the group. One tendency which developed strongly, particularly amongst those who had been trained militarily and could analyse developments from a more sober perspective, involved a shift to the ANC. This in fact did begin to happen, and it marked the beginning of the collapse of the group. Those who remained outside the ANC tried other arrangements with groupings like the Red Army in Europe and also some Palestinian radical groups, but these failed.

BC Organisations within South Africa

Inside the country in the mid-1970s, BC organisations remained highly active and kept up the momentum of their challenge to the regime. For example, after the Portuguese coup of April 1974, BC organisations based in Durban organised a mammoth pro-FRELIMO rally, which went ahead despite a government ban. In effect, the rally was an indirect endorsement of the strategy of armed struggle.

Internally, the June 1976 student uprising, brutally suppressed by the police, again raised the question of involvement in armed struggle, and individuals with strong BC connections began to link up to the struggle. For example, Mapetla Mohapi, the general secretary of SASO, was murdered in detention after he had been apprehended for having transported some students out of the country. This he had done despite an agreement within the inner circle of BC activists based in King William's Town that no assistance would be given to people leaving the country until a clear position was taken on which organisation to join in exile. The act of leaving the country was at that time automatically linked with the armed struggle.

The 1976 General Student Council saw a sizeable shift in BC ranks to the ANC. This was particularly strong among University of Natal (Black Section) students, some of whom had recently visited Swaziland where contacts was made with the ANC. Prior to this, in 1975, there had been an informal, clandestine meeting attended by some undelegated representatives from various organisations and areas. Steve Biko had felt that it was important at some level to brainstorm the issue of exile and the armed struggle. Of course, there was no unanimity on the question, but the discussion did underline the importance of unity between the ANC and PAC, which would enable the exiled movement to offer a political home and training facilities for the youth of the 1970s. Biko wrote that the BCM 'seeks to channel pent-up forces of the angry black masses to meaningful and directional opposition, basing its entire struggle on the realities of the situation'. By late 1976, Biko and close associates were involved in talks with the ANC, PAC, and some known figures of NEUM, discussing unity and the role of BC organisations, as well as the possibility of BC members joining some form of front in exile.

Can a Front Be Formed?

The message that came at the time from BC exiles, particularly in Botswana, was that the option of forming an 'own army' was fraught with enormous difficulties and frustrations. A courier sent to Botswana in 1976 reported that the Organisation of African Unity, the United Nations and the international community recognised only the ANC and PAC as representatives of the struggling people of South Africa. Even the Unity Movement did not receive international recognition, while Tsietsi Mashinini's group (former members of the Soweto Students' Representative Council, or SSRC, and their followers), which was attempting, with the assistance of some African governments, to form something like an army, was also having serious problems in obtaining international recognition and support.

Steve Biko felt that, in the light of this, and because of the militancy that was rapidly developing amongst the youth inside the country, it was better to investigate the possibilities of joining up with the existing forces in an organised manner. However, unity was a pre-condition.

The banning of BC organisations in 1977 and the murder of Steve Biko further fuelled the already tense situation within BC ranks. Frustration and anger at the vicious response of the regime to peaceful forms of struggle, and the limitations on the options for struggle, led to divisions within BC ranks as to which path to follow. Some urged that there was no longer any room for legal, above-board struggle, and that underground work and armed struggle were the only viable options. Others still called for caution and propagated the idea of forming new organisations with the same or similar aims.

Individual Initiatives Emerge

While these discussions were taking place, some BC individuals became active and began to transport people tirelessly and at great risk across the border to join MK, while even still claiming not to be supportive of the armed struggle or of the ANC. Other youths were naively and unknowingly carrying out missions arranged by organisations that they did not support. In the underground of that time, it was difficult to know who was who, and what forces were at play. At best, it can be argued, the youth were engaged in struggle. A small group within the SSRC was meanwhile carrying out its own version of underground and armed struggle. So-called 'sell-outs' were attacked, and houses burnt down. These youngsters were, in fact, receiving some arms and some sort of training from an unknown source. Their efforts were to collapse with the arrest of Paul 'Pa' Langa, who was sentenced to imprisonment on Robben Island.

By 1978, there was a definite parting of the ways amongst the former members of SASO, NAYO, SASM, BPC, and other organisations, as some opted to go into AZAPO and the Soweto Students' League (SSL), while others chose the underground, and still others left for exile. Within a year, however, the ranks of the exiles were joined by many of those who had opted to stay inside. Large numbers of these found themselves in Lesotho, which already had a strong ANC presence. By 1979, a former president, a former permanent organiser, and a former general secretary of SASO, as well as some former regional SASO leaders, were all in Lesotho.

By the 1980s, it is our estimate that more than 60 per cent of active members of BC organisations were to be found in the ranks of the ANC or MK. We would also argue that approximately 60 per cent of the youth who were not necessarily members of these organisations, were indirectly influenced by them and finally found themselves also in the ranks of the ANC or MK.

Conclusion

The creation of SASO, its ideology of Black Consciousness, and the subsequent proliferation of BC organisations radicalised the black youth of the 1970s. In their thousands, they joined the political struggle, and also injected a qualitatively new approach into the conduct of the armed struggle. It is to the eternal credit of Steve Biko that his colleagues never relented, but pursued with vigour the ideas which he formulated and they cherished. Today's imminent collapse of the racist regime owes much to Steve Biko's contribution.

8

The Continued Impact of
Black Consciousness
KOGILA MOODLEY

Internalised Colonialism and the Psychology of Liberation

In the late 1960s the idea of Black Consciousness heralded an era of alternative political awareness. This self-empowering, vibrant, reconstructionist world-view emphasised the potential role of black initiative and responsibility in articulating the power of the powerless. Between 1968 and 1976, Black Consciousness was one of the most important developments in South Africa, not only because of the self-confident protest and rebellion it unleashed, but 'because of the questions it posed about the nature of oppositional politics in South Africa and its relation to the nature of South African society' (Nolutshungu, 1982:147-148).

Black South Africa in the 1960s was ripe for an ideology of liberation. The oppression of apartheid society took place overtly and blatantly. With all opposition silenced and institutionalised racism triumphant, blacks were portrayed as innately inferior, accustomed to dehumanised living, sexually promiscuous, intellectually limited, and prone to violence. Blackness symbolised evil, demise, chaos, corruption and uncleanliness, in contrast to whiteness which equalled order, wealth, purity, goodness, cleanliness and the epitome of beauty. This stigmatisation was inevitably internalised by the victims themselves.

To be sure, the degree of self-doubt has always been lower in South Africa than among US blacks because of a variety of factors. Open collective discrimination allowed the cause of failure to be identified more easily than the informal discrimination hidden behind American laws of equality, which encourage individuals to search for causes of misery in themselves rather than in the system of social relations. Apartheid society also produced self-hate. Because of the limited range of opportunities available to them, blacks rationalised the *status quo* through belief in their own 'lacking abilities' – the victims blamed themselves. In addition to this self-hate, the fragmentation of the three black groups – Africans, Coloureds and Indians – through differential privileges and incorporation, reinforced an intra-black hierarchy which further emphasised what seemed to be the comparative success of the Indians, for example, as against the failure of Africans.

Thus Black Consciousness emanated from the differential material and political circumstances in which blacks were situated. Its prime movers in the early phase were relatively privileged medical students, not workers, who served as educated articulators of the plight of the underprivileged and politically excluded. Unlike the usual profile of medical students elsewhere, many of them came from working-class backgrounds and were not insulated from the harsh conditions of apartheid society.

Steve Biko, the best-known proponent of Black Consciousness, commented on the negative effects of the passive follower role blacks had played over the years in many spheres of South African life, as dulling their originality and imagination, 'where it takes a supreme effort to act logically even in order to follow one's beliefs and convictions' (Biko, 1988:32).

In the editorial introduction to the 1972 edition of *Black Viewpoint*, Biko referred to the great vacuum of black writing in the media. 'So many things are said so often to us, about us, and for us, but very seldom by us'. He also referred to the dependency created in blacks, as well as their depiction by the white press. He called for the deconstruction of the implicit interpretative connotations, underlying values, attitudes and interests of both the financial supporters and readership of the white press. Biko articulated a general insight into conquest, that defeat for the losers always means more than physical subjugation. It means, as two historians of the Soviet Union have described in other circumstances, 'that the conquerors write the history of the wars; the victors take possession of the past, establish their control over the collective memory' (M. Heller & A. Nekrich 1988:9). In short, the conquerors' definition of reality becomes the dominant explanation.

Rejection of Liberal Paternalism

The difficulty of working bilaterally with even the most sincere whites posed a moral dilemma for black students, who were the last to want themselves labelled 'racist'. Yet for Biko and others the need for exclusive black organisations was very clear, something Ben Khoapa referred to as the need for 'regroupment'. Blacks were considered an interest group, like workers in a trade union or teachers fighting their own battles. The collective segregation and oppression based on skin colour therefore provided an eminently logical basis for self-assertion and independent organisation. No longer would they allow themselves to be objectified in the negative image of 'non-whites'. Instead blacks reconstructed themselves as self-defining initiators. Gone were the days when they appealed to whites by persuading them that they too had civilised standards.

Black Consciousness was about pressuring whites through the will-power of the opponent (Adam, 1973:155). Accusations that this was a racist act were dismissed on the grounds that 'one cannot be a racist unless he [sic] has the power to subjugate' (Biko, 1988:39). Later, when Black Consciousness developed a more socialist tinge, the cooperation with white liberals was not rejected because of their race or their objective privilege, but because they were seen as representing a bourgeois class enemy. Collaboration with representatives of racial capitalism would amount to betrayal. 'Black Consciousness', writes the American historian George Fredrickson, 'had evolved from an effort to overcome a black sense of inferiority through independent, non-violent action into an explosive combination of race and class revolutionism' (1990:27). Whatever Fredrickson means by that phrase, Black Consciousness remained above all an awareness-raising movement rather than an organisation that practised revolutionary violence.

Redefinition of Blackness

Disillusionment with non-racial opposition organisations did not of course originate with the Black Consciousness Movement of the late 1960s. Its origins go back to the mid-1950s after the adoption of the Freedom Charter by the ANC gave rise to a split between the Charterists (ANC) and the Africanists who formed the PAC. The latter's definition of 'African' evolved into a broadly inclusive, subjective one, in that it included people of any group who considered themselves African, and who identified with Africa and its people rather than with exploiting settlers. By contrast, Black Consciousness utilised an objective definition of black to describe all those denied privileges by whites, as well as a subjective definition of those who consciously rejected white domination in all its forms. Even Bantustan leaders fell under the former category and were recognised as such for a while by SASO until the 1971 redefinition.[1]

What was distinctive about the movement was 'its originality in elaborating an ideology of hope rooted in a theology of liberation which emphasised the solidarity of the oppressed regardless of race' (Fatton, 1986:66). Unlike the PAC which, despite its stated goal of including all Africans, is perceived as narrowly Africanist, Black Consciousness as an ideology was genuinely inclusive. From its inception the Black Consciousness Movement sought to include Indians and Coloureds. In general it enjoyed greater appeal among activist Coloureds than Indians. Some Coloured students and clergy identified with its rejection of the label 'Coloured' in favour of an inclusive 'black' label that focussed on political oppression.

While the Black Consciousness movement had an appeal for this middle group through expressing political identification, Gerwel (1975) points out that it failed to provide the psychological identity they needed. Many Indians on the other hand, while prominent in the early membership of SASO, experienced in the movement a certain denial of self at the grass-

---

1 Biko emphasised two main features of the SASO definition of blackness. Firstly, that being black is a mental attitude and not just a matter of skin pigmentation. Secondly, merely describing oneself as black sets one on a road towards emancipation. Those collaborating with the system of oppression were deemed to have excluded themselves from this definition, and were labelled 'non-whites' (Biko, 1986:48).

roots level. They felt pressured to replace their cultural heritage with African symbols and were never accepted as authentically 'black' enough. Indeed, there were a few instances of Indians sympathetic to Black Consciousness, who are said to have given their children African names, as a way of identifying with the movement. However, these were exceptions – often alienated community members – rather than the precursors of a groundswell of Indian sentiment toward identification as blacks.

By transposing the label 'black', Black Consciousness transformed a white negative discourse about subordinate 'non-whites' into an inverted, positive discourse of resistance. Black Consciousness offered psychological support to an oppressed group by providing a model for positive identification. It sought to alter the contempt which the victims often felt for their own group. Despite the political motivation of movements such as Black Consciousness to provide an alternative to past descriptions, they have been criticised for implicitly accepting the legitimacy of colour as a marker. In doing so, it is argued, they also reinforced the accuracy of the dominant discourse of 'race' by which they have been signified and exteriorised as the 'Other' (Miles, 1989:73-76). On the other hand, Nolutshungu argues that 'the character of the state conditions not only the terms of domination and submission, but also the ideologies and political behaviour that challenge and reject it'. The very role that the state gives to national and racial domination and oppression calls forth 'alignments among the subject population that are focussed primarily on the terms of political domination rather than those of exploitation' (1982:147).

Ideological Influences and Biases

Notably lacking in the initial stages of the formulation of Black Consciousness was an economic perspective of the nature of exploitation. Conceptualisations of South Africa in class terms remained peripheral and there was no systematic analysis of what was later termed 'racial capitalism'. In part, this represented the rejection of Marxism as a white ideology and its association with the South African Communist Party. However, this omission also reflected the censorship of Marxist literature at the 'tribal' universities, as well as the exposure to existentialism, phenomenology and philosophical psychology which were popular among some of the European-oriented faculty. Hence the focus on values and essences, while the rejection of capitalism was couched in terms of dehumanisation and materialism, not commodity fetishism (Nolutshungu, 1982:155-157).

Barney Pityana stresses Black Consciousness inspirations as originating especially from Ethiopian religious movements, African religious political prophecy, struggles for land, the workers' struggles of the ICU, and both the Africanist and nationalist strands within the tradition of struggle. Philosophically, Black Consciousness was also broadly influenced by the writings of Senghor, Memmi, Fanon, Cleaver, Carmichael and Freire. They expressed the humiliation as well as the dignity of the colonised and the power of the powerless. Their main concerns dealt with the psychology of oppression and the exorcising of colonial humiliation. However, there is little evidence in the Black Consciousness literature that, for example, Fanon's central notion of the cleansing power of anti-colonial violence found resonance among South African activists. There was at the early stage rather a significant silence about the ANC's 'armed struggle' among Black Consciousness students.

Leaders made a clear distinction between their focus on Black Consciousness and the development of Black Power in the United States. Unlike the American version, Black Consciousness in South Africa had no need to become a revivalist movement, reconstructing a distant past and golden heritage, since African linguistic and cultural traditions continue as a way of life in this society. In the absence of the Afro-American trauma of slavery there was no need to search for putative roots. Blacks in the United States were already an enfranchised group, using Black Power to constitute themselves into a pressure group in a white majority society. In South Africa, Black Consciousness was seen as a tool to prepare people for equal participation in a transformed society reflecting the outlook of the majority (Motlhabi, 1984:115). Psychological liberation was sought through a return to African values of communalism, shared decision-making and more personal communication styles, in contrast to the impersonal individualism of white consumer society.

Although there was little of the hype surrounding 'Black is Beautiful' which characterised American black protest, Black Consciousness in South Africa was influenced by American trends. The movement raised consciousness about the extent to which blacks were bleaching, creaming and straightening their hair, at great cost, to fit unattainable white images of beauty. Above all, it restored to blacks their own sense of self-appreciation and self-acceptance. Indeed, in the early stages of the movement in Natal, there were reports that some African men had beaten African women who had straightened their hair, or used bleaching creams. One indicator of the success of Black Consciousness in this area was the vastly reduced advertising and sale of bleaching creams in South Africa.

However, despite the designation of the black world as 'communalistic' as opposed to the 'individualistic' orientation of the white world, the sexual division of labour within the Black Consciousness Movement closely resembled that of white society. Women were for the most part relegated to traditional women's domestic roles, responsible for child-care, moral education and socialisation in black cultural heritage, health, nutrition, and making of clothing. This view of women permeated women's self-defined roles, as is evident in the preamble to the constitution of the allied Black Women's Federation. It stated:

1. Black women are basically responsible for the survival and maintenance of their families and largely the socialisation of the youth for the transmission of the black cultural heritage.

2. The need to present a united front and redirect the status of motherhood towards the fulfilment of the black people's social, cultural, economic and political aspirations (*Black Review*, 1975–6:143).

The heavy use of the third person which prevails in the SASO policy manifesto of 1971 may well have reflected and reproduced standard English usage of 'he' and 'man' in what was viewed as their 'generic' sense. However, in contrast to the black cultural ideal of an inclusive communalism, the male is constructed as the empowered speaker and women, even when included as 'sister', are presented as the included 'other', powerless and voiceless (Driver, 1990). The ancillary role of women in the leadership of SASO further corroborates this tendency. Those women who were taken seriously were often in the position of honorary men, and a few of them were prominent in the Student Representative Councils and in campus activities. There may also have been structural factors that kept women from participating on a more equal basis, which raises questions about the fairness of attributing their under-representation in the movement to exclusionary practices.

Black Consciousness in Action

In its earlier phases, the movement was characterised by spontaneity and an easy evolution, without any rigidly worked-out plans of aims and directions. The style was informal, free of heavy organisational trappings.

What was distinctive about the movement at this point was its willingness to forgo the rhetoric-laden, sterile, non-compromise, traditional party lines of preceding organisations and for a while to liaise, for pragmatic reasons, with adversaries like Buthelezi. Indeed, Steve Biko and Buthelezi even shared a platform when the movement was bringing together an alliance of diverse black groups.[2] The same openness also manifested itself in the movement's seeking to establish a socialist dispensation, while striving for nationalist liberation. This unconventional mix of tendencies hampered fund-raising. To begin with, very few were willing to support Black Consciousness financially. Those who were willing to fund a nationalist cause would balk at supporting a movement with what they viewed as socialist sympathies. On the other hand, those who would support socialist initiatives would not do the same for one with a Black Consciousness emphasis. Given the choice between compromising principles and being funded, and being independent, principled, locally based but poorly supported, BC characteristically settled for the latter (Seleoane, 1989).

2 It should be borne in mind that Chief Buthelezi was seen by most people in the late sixties up to the early seventies as part of the liberation movement. His decision to join the Bantustan system was seen as a betrayal by SASO leadership who felt that his stature as an opponent of the system would give credibility to participation within the Bantustan system. The decision to share a platform with him indicated a realistic assessment of politics at the time and a hope that he could still be won over.

Conscientisation often took the form of light-hearted, satirical, humorous utterances. College campuses of the late 1960s were the base for frequently staged political theatre. For a while it amused even Afrikaner Nationalist staff members who seemed to rejoice at the way in which 'the natives' amused themselves, in images derived from their own lingo. The style of acting and diction was a refreshing variation from the previously stilted, imitative, colonial models of the 'Speech and Drama' genre. Afrikaner faculty at the tribal colleges loved this rejection of the British yoke and there was a self-congratulatory air about how well the colleges actually served people to express themselves. So it was very ironic that Black Consciousness was spawned in the very protected thought-streams of the government, whose aim was to ethnicise, depoliticise, fragment and render the opposition manageable.

However, the vehement reaction of the state followed this period of tolerance and even praise for the 'apartheid-like' student thinking. At a time when the state itself flaunted separatist black education, this movement which, on the surface, used the same symbols, nevertheless refashioned 'black identity' into a more inclusive category, through raising awareness about the structure of oppression. SASO emphasised black content in education and attempted to subvert the authority structure by divulging the relations of power and Eurocentric bias in institutional life. It problematised the process of education, demystifying the relationship between knowledge, control and hegemony. From the state's perspective, nothing could be worse than forces that usurped state idioms, and subverted its motives to challenge it.

The main tenets of the BC ideology permeated the thinking of a generation of students regardless of political persuasion. The initial analytical focus on 'culture', 'identity' and 'value systems' gradually shifted to define the struggle in terms of racism and capitalism. Under the influence of Nyerere's idea of self-reliance, various community projects explored ways in which blacks could become more self-supporting. In 1972 *Black Review* cited projects in operation throughout the country, mainly in rural and semi-rural areas in the Transvaal, Natal and Eastern Cape. Literacy campaigns, health projects, and home education schemes were meant to offer appropriate assistance. Popular short-term notions in the early 1960s of an imminent revolution were replaced with patient, disciplined preparation for the long march through the institutions. This called for a major shift from sheltered student politics to a broadened mobilisation of the workforce. It did not take long to discover that the intellectual bias of Black Consciousness impeded a major transformation as long as it did not reach workers effectively. Not only did this goal imply a modification of language, but a fundamental shift of concerns: building diminished self-images seemed peripheral, at best, to people whose lives were heavily burdened with the daily drudgery of earning a living.

The new project was severely hampered by the constraints of student life. Distances between campuses and townships, inadequate financial resources for travel and free time. So, too, was the marginal status of young students, who in the traditional scheme of things could hardly be considered leaders. All these constraints served to identify the need for an 'adult' branch of the growing movement (Gerhart, 1979:291-292).

Repression and Reconstruction

A series of industrial strikes throughout Durban during 1973, for which the Black Consciousness Movement was blamed but neither claimed nor disclaimed responsibility, ushered in a period of greater repression. BCM leaders were banned, activists were detained and many incidents of harassment occurred.

In the 1970s the Black Consciousness Movement was said to have been cocooned as an intellectual movement with little grassroots support, lacking a solid base in the organised trade-union movement. Some critics said the movement was heavy on 'moral purity' and faced the danger of stagnating at the level of black solidarity, without translating it into the 'politically possible' for 'political action' (Adam, 1973). Others expressed concern about whether the movement was forward-looking enough to prepare itself for a post-apartheid society (Turner, 1978).

In 1978, after the banning of seventeen Black Consciousness organisations, their successor, the Azanian People's Organisation (AZAPO), was formed. It included a class analysis in its policy and directed attention towards the political incorporation and involvement of the black working class. A focus on psychological liberation and 'blackness' gradually gave way to more talk of 'socialist', 'anti-capitalist' alternatives. AZAPO spokespersons refute charges that they are merely an intellectual movement. They affirm continued support from a wider base. Half of the 4 600 delegates to the Conference for a Democratic Future in Johannesburg in 1990, they claim, were AZAPO supporters.

In the end, Black Consciousness relies on the development of a 'fictive kinship' between all three 'non-white' groups who have experienced the shared indignity of oppression and material deprivation. At the psychological level this appealed to many in all groups. The effectiveness of Black Consciousness lies in the moral appeal it evokes. These feelings can be activated from time to time, but can they be sustained? One of the major obstacles to a consistent appeal can be found in the differential experience of apartheid. Material rewards co-opt and 'whiten', so does feared loss of 'cultural terrain'. For example, Indian traders in Durban, motivated by their relative material wealth, may not identify with other blacks, whereas an Indian labourer from Chatsworth may fear loss of a secure cultural base.

Black Consciousness in the Post-Apartheid Era

In the 1990s, analysts of black politics are puzzled by the disputes of the two anti-negotiation tendencies that seem ideologically so close. AZAPO and the PAC at the beginning of the 1990s appear to be further apart from each other, the more they were both marginalised by the opposition groups belonging to the Charterist power-sharing bloc. Thus journalist Patrick Laurence (*South African Foundation News*, January 1991) observes: 'Given the convergence between their ideological positions, including their insistence on black leadership and their commitment to socialism, AZAPO and PAC were strongly hostile to one another. AZAPO accused the PAC of intolerance, of forcing AZAPO members to wear their T-shirts inside out at a Sharpeville Day commemorative service instead of welcoming them as brothers-in-the-struggle, and of belatedly pressing for a constituent assembly, an idea first punted by AZAPO in 1984.'

Behind the petty quarrels, however, lies a class difference that often is overlooked. The PAC represents some of the least privileged and lesser educated members of the African subordinates. With a reservoir of Africanist sentiment in selected rural areas and among recent migrants, the social base of the PAC resembles that of Inkatha, rather than the more professionally led and urban-oriented ANC. AZAPO, on the other hand, has always comprised an even better educated, professional elite. AZAPO is particularly popular among university personnel, clergy, journalists and related professions. Given its sprinkling of Indians in prominent leadership positions, AZAPO was resented by Africanists just as, for similar reasons, the PAC initially objected to what it perceived as the inordinate influence of Indian and white communists in the ANC. Although the PAC has also prominent non-African members, it represents a much more down-to-earth articulation of diverse grassroots sentiments than the more intellectualising AZAPO grouping. In short, and with crude oversimplification, AZAPO comprises an intellectual elite in search of a constituency, while the PAC represents a potentially powerful army with disorganised and quarrelling generals.

In the 1990s the Black Consciousness Movement, though overshadowed by the ANC, continues to conscientise through community development programmes, health awareness projects and women's organisations. It has left the discourse in black politics with an indelible print although it is overshadowed by the publicity, diplomatic success and organisational clout of the ANC. Compared with the mass rallies of the ANC, AZAPO remains primarily an intellectual force. As opinion-makers in the universities, as clerics and, to a certain extent, as union leaders in NACTU, Black Consciousness lives on more as an alternative vision than an organisationally active political party.

Its success and failure lie in the extent to which Black Consciousness ideas have shaped the attitude of political actors, some of the organisational rivalries and even physical clashes between ANC and AZAPO supporters notwithstanding. The historic highpoint of the movement in the 1976 Soweto uprising was eclipsed by the subsequent rise of the Charterist hegemony, into which many of the exiled Black Consciousness supporters have been absorbed. Although the BCM continued organisationally as the third exiled liberation movement, separate from the ANC and PAC, without major sponsorship from abroad, many found their home in the ANC, which in turn benefited from the influx of committed students. Without this infusion of a new generation of young Black Consciousness radicals, the subsequent rise and renewal of the Charterist tradition would have been more difficult, and would have taken a different route. In shedding the internalised colonial mentality and liberal tutelage alike, Black Consciousness laid the ground for the self-confident challenge to the apartheid state, whether through refusals of co-optation or astute negotiations.

PART THREE

9

Empowerment and Symbols of Hope: Black Consciousness and Community Development
MAMPHELA RAMPHELE

The role of the Black Consciousness Movement in initiating, popularising and giving practical effect to community development as a deliberate strategy for empowerment in South Africa, has not yet been documented. Though Black Consciousness exponents did not invent community development in South Africa, they gave it a new focus as a strategy for liberation.[1] Central to the analysis in this chapter, therefore, is the relationship between community development and the liberation of oppressed people. The question of this relationship is of continuing relevance and importance: in the current South African context, it tends to be complicated by competing political interests, which see the allocation of resources for development purposes as a potential or real source of patronage. In the process of formulating in the 1970s a comprehensive development strategy, the relationship between development and liberation, and other critical questions were raised within the BCM. It is with the responses to these questions that this chapter is concerned.

International Context of Development

Black Consciousness activists were heavily influenced in their involvement in the field of community development by two main forces. Julius Nyerere, then president of Tanzania, was seen by many radical analysts as the inspiration and leading light in the quest by the poor for self-help and self-reliance (see Hyden, 1980:96-112). Of great significance in this respect was the Arusha Declaration of 1967, which committed Tanzania to *ujamaa* as a development philosophy. *Ujamaa* sought to utilise traditional structures of

1 At the same time the role played by other agencies in the development process over the years should not to be discounted. In particular the role of the South African Council of Churches, the Southern African Catholic Bishops' Conference and other church groups has been critical in intervening in the lives of poor people all over South Africa. Likewise, student and other welfare agencies, as well as various non-governmental organisations have played and continue to play a meaningful role in development work.

the 'economy of affection' for national development (Hyden, 1980:98 & 1983:8-25). Hyden defines 'the economy of affection' as 'denoting a network of support, communications and interaction among structurally defined groups connected by blood, kin, community and other affinities, for example, religion' (Hyden, 1983:8). Whilst hailed as a model for socialist development by many political economists and other analysts at the time, some critics saw it as a bid to achieve 'modernisation by traditionalisation'.

Black Consciousness exponents also found the notion of *ujamaa* attractive because of their own experiences of growing up in a culture where the idea and practice of *ubuntu* was central to social relations. They believed the person-centredness of this approach to life could be readily adapted and applied to a wider social structure to encompass elements of socialism. It was on this concept of *ubuntu* that the BPC's economic policy relied heavily in its formulation of what was referred to as 'black communalism' (*Black Review*, 1975–76:122-125). What BC activists did not examine, however, was the extent to which the 'economy of affection' or *ubuntu* translated into equitable social relations at a wider level beyond local affinity groups, a problem to which we shall return later in the chapter.

In addition to the Tanzanian model, Paolo Freire's conscientisation approach in Latin America was found to have great relevance for the problems BC leaders identified amongst black people in South Africa. The involvement of Anne Hope, a member of a lay Catholic sisterhood working on the Witwatersrand at that time, in leadership training for the BC during 1970–71, provided added impetus to this influence (Freire, 1972; see also Hope, Timmel & Hodzi, 1987).

It was inevitable that the BCM, with its emphasis on self-reliance, would become involved in the development debate which was in full swing globally in the wake of the heightened political consciousness of the late 1960s and 1970s. It was a period when the global economic order was being questioned by those experiencing poverty as well as those working with people who were poor. The reality of power differentials as determinants of access to economic resources was again under focus, both nationally and globally (see Fanon, 1963; Cabral, 1973; Reason & Rowan, 1981; Chambers, 1983).

Black South Africans, as traditional recipients of 'charity' handed out by the more privileged whites, were eager to hear Nyerere's call for freedom from dependency. In the South African context the negative impact of charity on blacks was critically analysed (Turner, 1972). Strategies were devised to redress the dependency situation which black South Africans found themselves in (see SPROCAS 2 report). These strategies form the core of this chapter.

From Hand-Outs to Development

In the period of political stagnation after the Sharpeville massacre in 1960, welfare organisations in South Africa were run mainly by whites and middle-class blacks. Among their concerns were child welfare, education scholarships, food parcels and care of the aged. Prominent organisations included the YWCA, Child Welfare Society, the South African Institute of Race Relations, Kupugani, ASSECA (the Association for the Educational and Cultural Advancement of the African People) and various church bodies.

The dual onslaught of political impotence, induced by state repression, and economic dependency, resulting from poverty and welfarism, wrought havoc on the self-image of black South Africans, who lost self-confidence as a people. Some even began to believe that they deserved the oppression they suffered because of innate inferiority (see Biko, 1986:27-32). A further complication was the growing distance between the poor and the black middle class, who modelled themselves on white liberals and thus perpetuated the myth of 'white' as the norm and 'black' as the aberration in all spheres of social relations.

In these circumstances students in SASO were anxious not only to examine critically the nature of social relations as they saw them at the time, but to get involved in practical programmes to redress the inequities of the past. This commitment stemmed from a number of considerations. Firstly, SASO promoted blackness as the primary social category, even before studenthood, and students were urged to pursue their responsibility for the liberation of blacks. Secondly, young activists recognised that their status as students accorded them privileges not available to the 'toiling black masses'. Students were thus urged to plough back their acquired skills into the community for the development of the poor. Thirdly, SASO's criticism of the failure of NUSAS to relate student activism to an ongoing commitment to liberation that stretched beyond the university in time and place, imposed a responsibility on SASO to create opportunities for black students to identify with the oppressed as a lifelong commitment.

At the same time, attempts were also made to engage groups such as ASSECA and the church to radicalise their approach to community development and organisational management. But an ASSECA conference held in Port Elizabeth in June 1971 demonstrated the difficulty of trying to convert people set in their own ways and fearful of change.[2]

It was SPROCAS (Special Project for Christian Action in Society) initiated by the Christian Institute and the South African Council of Churches that gave birth to the Black Community Programmes (BCP) under the directorship of a social worker, Bennie Khoapa, in 1971. BCP embodied the concern of Church leaders about the Church's need to commit itself to socio-economic transformation in South Africa. Within the Black Consciousness Movement BCP became the leader in the field of community development, but relied on the pathbreaking role of SASO for political direction.

---

2 The author was a participant, as one of six SASO activists, in a move to try to steer ASSECA towards a more radical perception of its role and that of its individual members. The response of ASSECA leaders was to debar us from the debate by evoking their standing rules for meetings.

Development Goals

Development is defined in this chapter as a process of empowerment which enables participants to assume greater control over their lives as individuals and as members of society. It is 'a process of capacity building and empowerment of people working for a preferred and shared future' (D. Marais, personal communication).

Goals of development for the BCM were articulated as the practical manifestations of the Black Consciousness philosophy, which not only called for a critical awareness of social relations amongst the oppressed, but for the need to translate that awareness into active programmes for liberation from white domination. Among the goals set for such programmes was the development of self-reliance in the black community. This implied that projects had to be initiated, directed, implemented and evaluated by blacks themselves. Moreover, through active involvement students were encouraged to seek a deeper commitment to development work as a career, while at the same time giving them practical training in fieldwork. This was seen as an important strategy to bridge the gap between the educated and uneducated in the black community. At the same time, through the active participation of professionals in development efforts, it was hoped that new models for professionalism would be developed, that moved beyond the elitism which was perceived as pervading the educated blacks at that time.

What is more, the types of projects undertaken were intended not just to meet the needs of the poor, but to establish models of development for the country as a whole. Projects covered the fields of health, education, leadership training, publications, home industries and child care. Finally, the projects themselves were seen as important affirmative statements to the oppressed people – a concrete way of saying that they mattered because they were people. It was argued that people who had known nothing but scorn and humiliation, needed symbols of hope to lift them out of despair and to empower them to liberate themselves.

Case Studies: The Trial Phase

New Farm Settlement Project

The period between 1969 and 1971 was marked by experimentation with community projects in and around Durban by students from the University of Natal (Black Section) (UNB). Projects ranged in type from assisting the impoverished squatters of New Farm, near Phoenix settlement, building more durable dwelling structures and providing clean water, to health work carried out on weekends at the Mahatma Gandhi Clinic in Phoenix.

The main feature of this period was the total lack of experience and knowledge about how to organise the student volunteers, train them in what they were to do, and help them plan their work, execute it and evaluate it on an ongoing basis. The work was thus characterised by enthusiasm by the active few, waning interest on the part of those more sceptical of the value of such involvement, and a measure of confusion on the part of the communities involved.

Malusi Mpumlwana, then chairperson of the University of Natal's SASO local committee, who was in charge of this project, carefully nurtured a working relationship between the students and the community. Among other things he encouraged those who enjoyed social drinking to socialise with the locals in their shebeens. A breakthrough seemed imminent when each household agreed to contribute R2 for the provision of clean tap water, and the SASO head office promised to subsidise whatever shortfall in funds the project encountered.

But matters went awry when a group of mainly young white activists, under the leadership of Richard Turner, a political scientist and lecturer at the University of Natal, entered the same community at about the same time. This created great confusion and disappointment in the ranks of SASO.

Turner was motivated by his commitment to a socialist future, and saw involvement in Phoenix as a practical way of engaging his students in the process of transformation. His group offered to provide all the money required for the clean water project, sapping the community's motivation for self-help which BCM activists had been at pains to nurture. It was as though the poverty of the New Farm residents offered a scarce resource, accessible to Natal University activists, for which they competed to test their ideals of community development. Needless to say, not much was practically achieved to alleviate the housing problems of the Phoenix community. On the contrary, it could be argued that more harm was done by raising the expectations of the residents, and dampening their own initiative in the task of upgrading their squatter settlement.

The involvement of the group of predominantly white activists in this project also reinforced BC fears of white domination. Their entry was seen as an example of the refusal by whites to accept that blacks could do things on their own. The disappointment was all the greater because Turner had up to that point been regarded by BC activists as one of the few white radicals who understood their views about white racism and economic domination.

Dududu Project

Dududu, a village on the South Coast of Natal, was later added to the list of SASO projects, but came under the control of the permanent organiser as a national project. Here the intention was to engage in integrated rural development. The project was to include a literacy campaign, a health facility for preventative health care, and agricultural support for the largely peasant community. A Mr Dlamini acted as the local contact person and project co-ordinator.

At the beginning of this project a reasonably careful assessment of needs, identification of priorities and formulation of appropriate strategies for action were undertaken. This approach was an outcome of the positive input of the leadership training programme which Anne Hope had conducted for some leading members of SASO. It also reflected the experience and lessons learnt from the mistakes of earlier projects.

There were, however, still many problems to be faced. Those involved did not anticipate the sheer effort required to consult adequately with the community. Transport costs and time involved were much higher than the limited student resources could carry. There was also inadequate recognition of the limited contribution which students could make, given their other commitments. Lack of continuity became a serious impediment to progress. A number of other problems arose which related to the assumption that 'the community' was a coherent entity, as well as to the existence or lack of credible leadership within the community, and the priorities set by the rural poor as against those of the activists. These will be dealt with later in the chapter.

Winterveld Project

During the university vacation of December 1971, a survey of Winterveld settlement area near Pretoria was undertaken as the basis for initiating an appropriate development programme for this vast area. It was the first major undertaking by SASO in this field, and I was asked to act as fieldwork leader. There were about twelve students involved in the project. We were hosted jointly by the local Catholic parish, with Father Clement Mokoka an enthusiastic supporter, and a sympathetic nursing sister, who was running a private clinic in Mabopane.[3]

We spent part of the fieldwork time assisting at the Mabopane private clinic, which provided ante-natal care and facilities for the delivery of expectant women. Our major task was, however, to get to know the area of Winterveld. Particular attention was paid to its geographic scope, population size, demographic details such as employment, education, and available amenities, common health problems, and quality and quantity of health-care facilities. We used an unstructured interview approach involving door-to-door calls in different areas to assess variations in the structure of dwellings, ownership patterns, relationship between owners and squatters, etc. We also visited the main activity areas – shops, clinics, informal markets, bus and taxi ranks – to get a feel of life in Winterveld.

The project afforded us a valuable educational opportunity. Firstly, the level of poverty we encountered was shocking, as was the enormity of the problems people had to grapple with. It put paid to the romanticism we as students had about poverty and people's responses to it. We had not bar-

3 This clinic was designated 'private' to distinguish it from government-run clinics in the area. In today's parlance it would be designated as a non-governmental clinic. It was also private in as far as it was being run by an individual and not a 'community'.

gained for 'the bitter fruits of powerlessness'[4] which pervade such poor environments. The majority of poor people we found in Winterveld were enveloped in apathy and despair.

Secondly, the level of exploitation of the poorest by the better-off people was far beyond what we had anticipated. For example, alternative healers of dubious qualifications were exploiting the ignorance and desperation of the poor with the connivance of some of the prominent medical practitioners in the area. We came across a homeopath who was running a health centre that included a maternity ward. He also treated children with various ailments including kwashiorkor (a protein-deficiency state). His explanation of the cause of kwashiorkor was that the children were possessed by a snake which inflated them with a bad spirit, making their bodies swell up. When questioned about his training for the work he was doing, he claimed that he had completed a degree in obstetrics at the University of the North. No such degree existed then or exists now at that university. His work in that community was afforded legal protection by a local general practitioner, in whose name his premises were registered.

Thirdly, we had to learn to cope with problems of human relations that resulted from the strain of young people being plunged into fieldwork such as this, without adequate support structures. Complaints ranged from inadequate food and money for personal needs, to boredom. As a team leader I was ill-prepared for the responsibility entailed. I was also personally in need of support, which was not forthcoming from the SASO head office. Sheer determination on the part of a few amongst us ensured the collection of adequate data, which later issued in a reasonable fieldwork report.

The Period of Maturation

With its entry into the development arena in 1971, BCP achieved a broader resource base, given its link to church groups that were well connected financially. The Christian Institute, and Beyers Naudé in particular, provided critical material and moral support. Furthermore, as it became established BCP provided opportunities for full-time employment for activists to grapple with issues of development and to utilise their greater access to skills and expertise more creatively. At the same time, BCP provided a more respectable umbrella under which newly qualified BC activists and university drop-outs could find a home and live out their ideals.

BCP acquired a national office in Durban, at 86 Beatrice Street, where SASO's national office was also located. It soon developed regional structures in response to the needs and projects in various parts of the country. The Eastern Cape office was set up in response to Steve Biko's banning and restriction to that area in 1973. Offices in the Transvaal and Natal followed

4 Wilson and Ramphele elaborate on this theme in their study of poverty in South Africa (1989:151-161). Bitter fruits of powerlessness include crime, alcohol abuse, broken families, etc.

in 1974 and 1975 respectively, but the Eastern Cape emerged as the dominant region in terms of projects and the calibre of staff it employed. A core of BC activists made the Eastern Cape region their base.

Major projects undertaken during the period of maturation included research and publications, leadership training, health and child care, women's programmes and home industries. These projects had varying degrees of success and impact on the wider South African society.

Research and Publications

Research and publications were deemed to be an important area, because of the total monopoly white people had over this field. Blacks were used mainly as objects of research, thus reinforcing their self-image as 'those acted upon' rather than as active agents of history. Research prevalent at the time, moreover, reflected paradigms which were largely unacceptable to BC activists. The dominant paradigms projected blacks as victims of racism and exploitation, while little attention was paid to the creativity and resilience which underpinned the strategies of survival blacks had elaborated over the years. Activists also expressed frustration about being written about without any attempt being made to draw blacks into the process of formulating the questions to be posed and responding to analyses of the results of such inquiries.

The few blacks who attempted creative writing at that time faced enormous obstacles. There was little support given to them at any level. The only outlet for prospective writers was to be attached to a white sponsor, which most people found humiliating. Publishers also shied away from black writers, who in their view did not represent good business. The threat of censorship was also a major disincentive for publishers. And so BC activists were determined to transform research and publication by and about black South Africans.

Black Review. The first task identified in the research field was to redefine the annual survey of major events in the country, which had until then been the preserve of the South African Institute of Race Relations. The major criticisms of the SAIRR's annual survey centred on both its focus and content. BC activists regarded the survey as a running commentary on the evils of apartheid and the extent to which blacks were victims of this evil. There was no attempt made to include reports of positive efforts by blacks to cope with their social disabilities, and the impression given was that of a totally powerless and hopeless people, a view that had the potential of becoming a self-fulfilling prophecy by reinforcing a sense of powerlessness within the black community.

Another criticism of the SAIRR's survey was that its portrayal of blacks as victims, aided and abetted by negative and sensationalist newspaper reportage in black dailies such as *Post* and the *World*, contributed in no small measure to the poor self-image blacks had of themselves. They were a people without any achievements, a community of failures who were noted for murder, rape, theft and family disorganisation. BC activists thus felt that there was a strong need to conduct research which would take seriously the problems of the black community, their survival strategies, as well as their own efforts to transform their life circumstances.

Black Review was initiated by Biko in 1972 in response to the need for an alternative approach. The task required a whole team of researchers, but was undertaken by him, as the only full-time staff member, with the assistance of volunteers, prominent among whom were Welile Nhlapo and Tomeka Mafole. Long nights and weekend work at the Beatrice Street offices of BCP were invested in this project. It was the sheer determination to succeed which kept those involved going.

Sources of data included newspaper reports, annual reports from organisations working within the black community, the *Government Gazette*, and interviews with community workers and leaders across the country. The end result was a magnificent publication in early 1973, which was officially billed as edited by Bennie Khoapa, for Biko's banning order earlier that year, which prohibited him from participating in publications of any kind, precluded BCP from acknowledging his editorship of *Black Review 1972*.

Subsequent issues were also shoestring budget affairs. The pace of restrictions under banning orders increased, leading to disruptions in editorial work: Mafika Gwala replaced Khoapa for the 1973 *Black Review*. Malusi Mpumlwana's term as editor was also short-lived, and he was replaced just before publication of the review by Thoko Mbanjwa for the 1974–75 issue. The last rescue editor was Asha Rambally for the 1976–77 issue, which had already been printed when Thoko Mbanjwa's restriction orders were served on her. The 1976–77 issue still bears evidence of the publisher's desperate attempts to blot out Thoko's name, so as to comply with the constraints of the restriction order.

BCP waged a continual struggle for the right to publish in the face of an increasingly repressive state. The main thrust of the strategy was to stay within the limits of the law, without showing respect for it. It was a survival strategy based on a constant evaluation of the tightrope the organisation was walking, whilst maintaining pressure all the time on the government to respond to the aspirations of black people in South Africa.

The impact of *Black Review* was immeasurable. Black organisations were inspired by it. It provided information about issues and the efforts of people across the length and breadth of South Africa which few had hitherto been aware of. Networking between community workers was thus facilitated. One of the lasting results of *Black Review* was the SAIRR's changed format and focus of its annual survey. Given the greater resources of the SAIRR, it is appropriate that only one such survey should be published in South Africa, but continued vigilance should inform the upgrading of both its quality and scope.

Black Viewpoint. The need for a forum for black people to express themselves on current and topical issues in the black community led to the launching of *Black Viewpoint* in 1972. The first issue was edited by Steve Biko, whilst subsequent ones were Bennie Khoapa's responsibility. *Black Viewpoint* was initially successful and BCP staff hoped that this success would open avenues for greater self-expression (*Black Review, 1975–76*:108). However, this initial success was not followed through, for a number of reasons. Firstly, the legacy of the educational system which blacks have been and continue to be subjected to does not encourage the development of creative writing skills. Secondly, those blacks who could write reasonably well had not had the opportunities to develop the skills of expressing themselves in the written form. The discipline required by the writing process frightened off many prospective authors as involving much of an effort. Thirdly, the few activists who were committed to the task of developing writing skills were overwhelmed by other demands on their time. One requires time and space for reflection and reading in order to write creatively, and these resources always tend to be in short supply amongst activists. Fourthly, greater value is placed by blacks on social interaction and the servicing of social networks than on reflective activity. This is also a result of the culture of survival which depends on strong social networks of support. Black intellectuals are often caught between the competing demands of social availability and academic life.

Black Perspectives was supposed to be a more scholarly publication catering for black academics and professionals. The main intention behind *Black Perspectives* was to encourage empirical research and publication on issues affecting the black community. Only one issue of *Black Perspectives* was published, in 1973. It also suffered the same fate as *Black Viewpoint* for more or less the same reasons.

Leadership Development

The programme for leadership development involved several levels of training and was undertaken as a joint venture by SASO and BCP. The initial group of SASO leaders trained by Anne Hope acted as a core of trainers; they also kept in contact with Anne Hope for regular review sessions. Moreover, weekend formation schools were held to train university students in various skills. In addition, an extensive training programme for youth leadership was undertaken to address the needs of high-school and township-based youth clubs in all the provinces of South Africa. The outcome of this drive was the formation of networks of youth organisations – namely, the Natal Youth Organisation (NYO), the Transvaal Youth Organisation (TRAYO), and the Border Youth Organisation (BYO) in the Eastern Cape, which all came together under a National Youth Organisation (NAYO). The equivalent umbrella body for high schools, the South African Students' Movement (SASM), comprised affiliated branches from high schools across the country. Training included organisational skills in both financial and human resource management. It was the youth involved in these leadership training programmes who spearheaded the revolt of 1976.

The increasing pace and intensity of repressive action by the state curtailed this leadership training programme: both the trainers, Biko and Nengwekhulu,[5] were banned early in 1973 and were thus unable to continue their task. It is not possible to speculate on the likely impact of a longer period of leadership training on the young people, nor on the role they could have played in shaping the history of South Africa.

Training was also provided for other activists. Such training was initially carried out through SASO formation schools. Training programmes were later extended to include BCP, which ran regular symposia and seminars, provided practical exposure to community development responsibilities, encouraged creative leadership and supportive peer review at staff meetings, as well as facilitating informal training and support. Practical skills in administration, organisational dynamics, social analysis and public speaking were the foci of BC leadership training programmes.

An important feature of the programmes for developing leadership skills was the high premium placed on diversity of opinions and political ideologies. Common purpose was defined as the total liberation of black people, but intense debates about appropriate strategies for attaining this liberation were encouraged at all levels. No one within the BC ranks claimed the monopoly over 'truth' with regard to strategies and tactics for liberation. Even at the level of local community projects, individuals were given the scope to experiment with different approaches, provided they took responsibility for the outcomes of their actions and were open to critical review by colleagues.

Health Projects

After the limited experimentation by BC students with health work it became quite clear that greater continuity was necessary if the BCM was to have any impact on the lives of the very poor in the field of health. There was also a desire by the BCM to establish models of health care which could be adapted by other non-governmental and governmental bodies.

Zanempilo Community Health Centre. The Zanempilo project was established in Zinyoka, ten kilometres outside King William's Town. The community centre was built with meagre resources in 1974 and opened for service in January 1975. The staff consisted of a medical officer, two nursing sisters, two assistant nurses, two cleaners, a cook, a bookkeeper, a gardener

5 Steve Biko and Harry Nengwekhulu were amongst the eight top leadership of SASO who were banned in 1973, following the Schlebusch Commission report, which ushered in a new wave of repression. NUSAS leadership was also similarly affected (see *Black Review, 1973*).

and a driver. I was responsible for the planning of the building, budgeting for and organising supplies, and other running costs, and was appointed the medical officer in charge with effect from 1 January 1975.

Because Zanempilo (The One Bringing Health) was the first major physical project of BCP, the pressure to make a success of it was considerable. The goals set were to provide affordable, accessible and appropriate health care for people in the rural districts of King William's Town. It could be said to have been one of the earliest primary health-care projects in South Africa. Services offered included consultations and treatment for various ailments; referrals to local hospitals for those requiring further management; ante-natal care and delivery of uncomplicated cases; clinic services for children under 5, including immunisations (which presented problems as the local authorities refused to provide us with free vaccines);[6] health-promotion services including education, nutritional counselling, home visits, etc.; out-station service to reach outlying areas in the district that had inadequate services; an ambulance service for the sick and expectant mothers, as well as for emergencies needing hospitalisation; and a 24-hour emergency service.

All of us involved in the project wanted to ensure that Zanempilo became not just a success as a place of healing, but also a concrete model of basic minimum facilities which black people regarded as acceptable for themselves. It was a symbolic statement of minimum demands for health services. Consequently much attention was devoted to providing and maintaining cleanliness inside and outside the premises, space and privacy for individuals, good quality food for in-patients, and reasonable wages for maintenance staff, as well as treating patients with respect for their dignity as people, and ensuring co-responsibility by all staff members in the execution and evaluation of the work of the centre.

Zanempilo quickly became 'a meeting place' for all activists in the area. It also served as a guest house for visitors from far and wide who came to see the project or to consult with Steve Biko over a range of issues. These visits increased as Biko's stature grew both nationally and internationally.

As the load of work increased, more staff and facilities were added. Because of the limitation of resources the work-load for individuals was often unrealistic. A second doctor, Seolo Solombela, joined the project in January 1976, to help me carry the impossible burden of running the health centre. I had also been given additional responsibilities of acting as a regional director for BCP in the Eastern Cape following the further restriction placed on Steve Biko at the end of 1975.

The project became a training centre for interested university students

6 The refusal by the local authorities to supply us with vaccines was the result of intervention by the Ciskei government, which saw our clinic as a competitor with their own health services. In an attempt to reduce our impact on 'their constituency' they set up a rival shanty clinic in the same village of Zinyoka. Needless to say, few people utilised that 'opposition clinic'.

during their vacations; they brought welcome relief for the overworked staff members. The demand for services provided at this centre expanded to include well-off people in the township, who saw it as a viable alternative to existing health services. This category of patients was charged on a sliding scale to provide needed funds for the project.

The success of Zanempilo prompted the BCP to establish a similar centre on Natal's South Coast near the old Adam's Mission, named Solempilo (Eye of Health). All the necessary administrative and public relations prerequisites for opening the centre had been finalised – staff appointments, purchases of supplies and discussions with the local community – when the banning of the BC organisations in 1977 put an end to the project. The equipment for this centre was confiscated at the Durban docks by security police, whilst the buildings were left to stand idle for many years after the bannings. The centre is currently being run as part of the KwaZulu Health Service.

Njwaxa Home Industry

A leather-goods home industry was started in 1974 in the village of Njwaxa, near Middledrift, in the Eastern Cape, by an Anglican monk, Father Timothy Stanton of the Community of the Resurrection. Father Stanton was based at the Federal Theological Seminary in Alice and regarded this industry as part of his ministry to the people of Njwaxa.

The main objective of the project was to create income-generating opportunities for the unemployed poor in Njwaxa. The initial focus was on producing small hand-made leather articles such as purses, tobacco pouches, and snuff-box carriers, using off-cuts from local manufacturers. Most of the producers were local women, working in a small mud house in the village. Finished products were sold on the local market, which showed a potential for expansion.

Malusi Mpumlwana, later to be joined by his sister Vuyo, was trained by a local shoe manufacturer to perfect the art of leather patchwork for the production of these articles, as well as nailbags, which became a popular item in the local market. Vuyo took over the management of the project for a period and then handed over to Mr Voti Samela, a trained leather tradesman in 1975.

With increasing demand, the home industry expanded and Mr Samela introduced a wider variety of goods: belts, handbags, saddles, cushions, sandals and fishing-rod holders. Machinery was bought to aid production. Soon some of the finishing tasks in the production line were given to unemployed women in Zinyoka, who worked on the premises of Zanempilo Community Health Centre on a piece-job basis. Marketing was also improved with the employment of Mxolisi Mvovo as a full-time salesman (see *Black Review*, 1974–75:120).

In 1977 further expansion necessitated the erection of a building, which was constructed by locals with money donated by the Organisation for

Inter-Church Co-operation (ICCO), a Dutch development aid agency. A corrugated-iron building was constructed on a concrete slab to provide an adequate, well-ventilated and safe working environment for the home industry. The success of this home industry rested on the good quality and simple design of the products and a good marketing strategy. However, the business had constant cash-flow problems.

In recognition of the constraints of this home industry, and with an eye to encouraging greater capacity-building, BCP decided to float a Section 21 company, the workers at the home industry to hold 49 per cent of the shares and BCP 51 per cent. It was envisaged that the resultant capital injection would hasten attainment of a break-even point, and that further growth in profits would be used to expand income-generating projects in the region and elsewhere in the country.

Njwaxa Home Industry also fell victim to the October 1977 bannings, which unleashed a vicious attack on all projects undertaken under the auspices of the BCP. The concrete slab on which the new building stood remains as a monument to the destruction wrought by a repressive state bent on the elimination of symbols of self-reliance and beacons of hope for a better future.

Other BCP Activities

Projects in other parts of South Africa were pursued with varying degrees of success. The Transkei region excelled in home industries for women's groups, which specialised in the production of items of clothing, both knitted and sewn. The region was to expand into other areas under the directorship of the Rev. M. Xundu, who joined the staff in 1977. An important project initiated during this period was an agricultural scheme on land along the Bashee River, acquired from King Sabata, which was intended as a model for rural development.

The Transvaal region, under Aubrey Mokoena as programme officer, and later under the directorship of Sedupe Ramokgopha, was involved in organising sewing groups for women, which had a special focus on dress design, adult educational work, artefact production and sales of items such as Christmas and commemorative cards (see *Black Review*, 1975–76:128-131). The education crisis which began in June 1976 challenged the Transvaal region to find creative solutions to the problem of children out of school. Various attempts were made in consultation and cooperation with the Black Parents' Association and concerned black teachers, but the problem was too great for any non-governmental organisation to have a significant impact. The bannings of 1977 also curtailed any further efforts.

BCP's presence in Cape Town was limited to a clothing factory; this was turned into a co-operative in which Peter Jones and others were involved. Financial and internal political conflicts (reflecting local political tensions) limited the growth of this venture.

Home industries were successful to the extent that they were productive, but financial viability remained elusive for many of them. The capital outlay required to establish going concerns was beyond the reach of BCP. This lack of capital constrained the home industries' capacity to develop into reliable suppliers of goods to the commercial markets which were opening up. There was also an insufficient base of marketing and purchasing skills within BCP to meet the challenges of operating viable commercial concerns.

A number of child-care projects were also undertaken during this period. The role of BCP was, however, limited to providing financial assistance to various community groups to start up and run their own projects. For example, the Ginsberg Crèche, in King William's Town, was resuscitated and became a viable community service as a result of BCP's intervention and injection of funds (see *Black Review*, 1975–76:128-130). The Ginsberg Educational Fund was a personal statement of thanks by Steve Biko to the people of Ginsberg township, his home base, for the scholarship they had given him to support his high-school education. In 1983 the Ginsberg Education Fund merged with similar ventures, Masifundise in the Western Cape and Ipopeng in the Tzaneen area, to form the Trust for Christian Outreach and Education, in which Malusi Mpumlwana was the leading light.

A successful consumer co-operative was also run in King William's Town. It involved a maximum of fifty families because of pressure on the local wholesaler from local traders to limit its growth, as it was seen as a competitor.

Zimèle Trust Fund

Zimele Trust Fund was set up to address the economic hardships and dependency problems affecting ex-political prisoners. Most ex-political prisoners were entirely dependent on the monthly stipend of some R30 which they received from the SACC Dependants' Conference. Many found themselves banished to remote areas on their release from long-term prison sentences, with little prospect for employment.

The objectives of Zimele were threefold. Firstly, it provided emotional and material support to ex-political prisoners at the time of their release. This took the form of a grant to purchase basic necessities such as clothes, essential furniture and food. Secondly, educational support in the form of bursaries was provided for their dependants. Thirdly, 'economic restabilisation' of ex-political prisoners was encouraged by supporting the establishment of home industries (*Black Review*, 1975–76:131-132).

The expectation was that a number of individual ex-political prisoners in a given locality would team up and initiate income-generating projects, pooling the skills they as individuals possessed to ensure self-sufficiency. Many such projects were initiated with varying degrees of success. They included carpentry, motor-repair services, housing construction and a variety of home industries.

The organisation's initial successes were shortlived. Its administrator, Mapetla Mohapi, died in detention on 5 August 1976. Subsequent work was plagued by repressive state action, which included the frequent arrest and detention of Mohapi's successor, Pumzile Majeke. The envisaged co-operative spirit amongst ex-political prisoners did not materialise. Individuals tended to want to work on their own for their own benefit, rather than teaming up with others. This was most disturbing to Zimele's trustees, who assumed that the high level of political sophistication among ex-political prisoners would translate into a willingness to work for the common good in a cooperative framework.

There were two main reasons for the failure of the intended co-operatives. Successful co-operatives, such as Mondragon in Spain, are based on relationships of trust between the members and strict guidelines for acceptable behaviour and co-responsibility of members. Ex-political prisoners did not necessarily trust one another, and in some cases there was open hostility based on personal and political differences. Secondly, the level of politicisation and sophistication varied widely among the ex-prisoners. Some had been imprisoned for merely having been at the scene of some political conflict without necessarily having been involved in any major political programme.

With the 1977 bannings of all BCM organisations, the intended expansion nationwide from the initial focus in the Eastern Cape never came about.

Evaluating BC Community Development

How did the BCM fare in pursuit of its goals as set out at the beginning of this chapter – developing self-reliance in the black community, encouraging students to realise a greater commitment to development work, creating new models for professionalism and service provision, and empowering the poor?

Self-reliance

The notion of self-reliance is open to many interpretations. During the period under review, BC activists used it to denote the capacity for blacks to initiate, control, evaluate and interpret development efforts relevant to their own needs. Self-reliance was perceived as a pillar of empowerment for people who had hitherto relied on others to do things for them. To restore a sense of independence it was deemed essential to promote black leadership and control over the allocation of resources within the black community.

In spite of its limited resources, SASO succeeded in popularising self-reliance as a viable liberation strategy. The initiative taken in launching a new student organisation, training leadership, and formulating and enunciating the Black Consciousness philosophy, was living testimony that self-reliance was a feasible strategy and objective. The successful experimentation with some of the practical applications of the Black Consciousness philosophy was also an achievement not to be devalued.

The success of BCP as a development agency witnessed to the maturity which the BCM attained as a liberation movement in South Africa in the 1970s. Former SASO activists found a home in BCP to live out their commitment. The limited training in formal skills of most BC activists did not dampen their enthusiasm to experiment and succeed with new approaches to community development. For example, few if any of those involved in publications such as *Black Review*, had any practical training for this enormous task, yet the determination to succeed ensured success. This venture in a sense illustrated the importance of believing in oneself and the impact of self-confidence on achievement-orientated behaviour. The same lack of expertise was evident in the field of community health care, where likewise the sheer determination to succeed ensured success.

A distinction needs to be drawn between self-reliance and insulating oneself from important sources of information and resources for the successful implementation of whatever task one has at hand. The latter tendency ultimately leads to atrophy because of the lack of any cross-fertilisation of ideas and strategies. Self-reliant development does not preclude creative and enriching interaction with other people in the same or allied fields of interest. BC activists of the 1970s opted for creative interaction with a wide spectrum of people nationally and internationally, without regard to race, colour or creed.

Self-help

The concept of self-help raises a number of questions. Is it realistic to expect people who are struggling with mere survival to help themselves in a sustainable process of development? Is it reasonable to expect people who need to muster every ounce of energy at their disposal to apply themselves voluntarily to communal development? Is it not being overly optimistic to expect the poor to lift themselves up by their own boot-straps? These questions have to be addressed before any successful development programme can be tackled.

The idea of pulling oneself up by one's own boot-straps presupposes that one has boots to wear in the first instance. For that 50 per cent of the total South African population found in 1980 to be living below subsistence or the minimum living level (MLL), boots are in short supply. This is particularly the case for those Africans in the reserves or homelands, of whom 81 per cent were living in dire poverty in 1980 (Wilson & Ramphele, 1989:17).

Extreme poverty creates a dilemma for activists opposed to creating or perpetuating dependency when they come to choose effective intervention strategies in situations of need. One can opt for the route labelled 'the Grahamstown syndrome'[7] by Sally Damana, a social worker, who describes hand-outs and the widespread begging of the poor in this town as

---

7 'The Grahamstown syndrome' is a concept coined by Sally Damana, a local social worker, describing the dependency relationship between poor Grahamstown blacks and their better-off white co-residents, who give hand-outs on a regular basis to blacks (Damana, 1984:5).

demeaning for all involved. In her experience, the relationship between poor blacks and better-off whites nurtures an entitlement mentality amongst the former, which becomes an impediment to any development process. An alternative strategy for intervening in the lives of people living in extreme poverty is that of respectful poor relief. This takes the form of emergency relief in situations such as drought, unemployment and illness, that enables those so assisted to develop the energy to help themselves (see Wilson & Ramphele, 1989:261-263).

BC activists found the distinction between these two approaches blurred and the contradictions of the real world rather bewildering. It did not fit in with our ideals and romantic notions of the capacity of poor people to be active agents of history.

Furthermore, self-help at a community level presupposes a degree of social coherence that enables individuals to identify 'self' with 'community'. Such assumptions of coherence have been shown in many instances to be fallacious. For example, in Tanzania, Nyerere mistook the 'economy of affection' that allowed villagers to cooperate around particular tasks such as hoeing and reaping (*ujima* or *letsema*), for people's readiness for a life of communal ownership and working together for the common good (*ujamaa*). The consequences of Nyerere's error are still evident in Tanzania. Peasants exercised their power by simply withdrawing from prescribed communal efforts and thus brought the national economy to a standstill.

BC activists were influenced by their admiration for what Nyerere preached and saw Tanzania as an important model for development strategies in South Africa. They committed the same error in their approach to community organising. Projects were planned on the basis of the willingness of 'the community' to work together for the common good, without due regard to the internal differentiation within various 'communities' and the ability of some blacks to exploit other blacks. The fact that black people were discriminated against as a group was regarded as a sufficient condition for their capacity and desire to identify with one another for the common good.

Such naiveté was in a sense an inevitable consequence of the very analysis underpinning the BC philosophy. 'The overall analysis, therefore, based on Hegelian theory of dialectic materialism, is as follows: That since the thesis is a white racism there can only be one valid anti-thesis, i.e. black unity to counterbalance the scale' (Biko, 1986:51). The general validity of this analysis was, however, challenged by the complexities of social relations. Steve Biko was later to acknowledge that there were some blacks who should be seen as 'non-whites', because of their failure to identify with the aspirations of the black community (Biko, 1986:48).

SASO thus failed to comprehend, analyse and tackle the contradictions resulting from internal differences amongst blacks that occurred along the lines of class, gender, age and geographic location. Instead, Black Consciousness exponents opted for the simplistic excommunication of those blacks who failed to act for the common good in solidarity with others –

they were banished to the realm of 'non-whites'. A deeper examination of the limitation of their philosophical standpoint was not undertaken.

Similar errors of analysis continue today to plague community organisers in their development efforts countrywide. 'The people' or the 'democratic masses' are examples of other romantic phrases in current usage, applied in various circumstances to invoke the illusive coherence of 'the community', without any real underpinning on the ground (see Thornton & Ramphele, 1988:29-39).

What is more, voluntary work presupposes the availability of leisure time, and so the preponderance of upper- and middle-class people in voluntary organisations is not accidental. Voluntary service was popularised among blacks in South Africa by early missionaries in particular and has had a significant bearing on approaches to community development in the country. That one has to be able to afford the time to pursue such communal activities is generally ignored. This is not to deny that some individuals who are unemployed or are motivated by goodwill would gladly involve themselves in voluntary efforts. However, the question of the sustainability of such efforts still remains (see Ramphele, 1990:1-15).[8]

Another dilemma for community workers relates to the fact that the poor are often inconspicuous, inarticulate and unorganised. In consulting with 'the community' their voice is hardly ever heard (see Chambers, 1983:18), hence their priorities for action rarely become the priorities of community developers. The problem of the 'invisibility' and 'inaudibility' of the poor is further complicated in rural areas by gender inequalities. The majority of the poor are women, who feel even less able to express themselves. They are also often morally pressurised to accept responsibility for communal voluntary work as an extension of their nurturing roles in the domestic sphere.

The outcome of the inadequate attention by the BCM to differentials of power amongst blacks was the predictable dominance of committee structures at community level by the educated, by males and those who were articulate. The poor and the women voted with their feet, and did not show up for voluntary activities beyond the initial stages.

Community participation, a pet phrase in development circles, was constrained by the failure of BC activists to take seriously the issues I have raised above. There was also insufficient understanding of the different levels of participation possible in different socio-economic circumstances. Morley distinguishes between two types: direct and indirect participation (Morley, 1983:85-86). Direct participation entails contribution in material terms to a development project at hand. Many people are able to engage in

8 My experience in working with hostel dwellers in the Western Cape makes me sceptical of voluntary efforts in the long term. In a recent article I examine the shift from voluntarism to demands for pay over the duration of a participatory research project (Ramphele, 1990).

this form of participation, for even the least educated and poor can contribute their labour if they see it as advantageous to do so. Indirect participation, on the other hand, entails involvement in the whole process of development: planning, execution, evaluation and replanning. This form of participation brings about growth in the persons involved and their empowerment (Morley, 1983:86).

Few projects undertaken by BC activists managed to attain indirect participation by the majority of the communities they worked in. A major reason for this failure was the limited life-span of the organisations espousing Black Consciousness. The BCM development efforts I have described were spread over no more than three years, too short a period for any visible results to emerge. It is, however, important to note that some of the individuals initially involved in the BCM projects have been personally empowered, and some have gone on to become leaders in their own localities. Accurate assessment of the full impact of the process of empowerment would require a more systematic study of project participants, which is beyond the present brief.

Black Consciousness managed to attain unprecedented success in empowering activists in its ranks at all levels. Most of these individuals attained total psychological liberation and realised the meaning of being active agents in history. The impact of this success also had a multiplier effect on the wider black community. Nothing succeeds like success.

Developing Models for a New Professionalism

The success of the BCM in developing new role models depended on the success of its leadership training programme as well as on the outcome of the initial projects undertaken. Developing role models was by far one of the most successful aspects of Black Consciousness during the 1970s. Indeed the mushrooming of community development organisations in the 1970s and their continued popularity to date are partly attributable to the impact of the BCM's development thrust.

There were two main obstacles to be overcome in the process. The first was the 'Kupugani mentality' (dependency and hand-outs) of the 1960s that had taken root amongst many community workers, including professionals. Setting up alternative models of community development required a lot of effort on the part of those committed to such ideals. A significant shift in the paradigm has since occurred. Most community workers today profess a commitment to development work which empowers people.

The second obstacle was the criticism from those claiming to offer a more radical analysis of social relations in South Africa, who accused Black Consciousness exponents of delaying the revolution by providing outlets for poor people's frustrations in community development projects. They argued that people had to be left as they were in their poverty so that they could build up sufficient anger against the system and eventually revolt, even though none of the radicals could point to an example anywhere in the world of desperately poor people having successfully led a revolution. Theirs was a romanticisation of 'the poor' which bore no relation to the interests of poor people themselves. It is ironical that most of these radicals condemned others to hunger and sickness from the comfort of their privileged positions.

A more refined argument advanced by other detractors of development was that non-governmental organisations let the government off the hook by providing services and other developmental inputs for needy communities. Such criticism had validity with respect to those community workers who saw themselves as an alternative source of welfare services. In the South African context such a prospect is precluded by the sheer enormity of the task. For example, attempts by community groups to set up alternative educational structures after 1976 failed for precisely that reason. Those involved underestimated the enormity of such a task and the huge resources which would be required.

BCP projects were never intended to replace government-provided services, but were aimed at creating practical models in critical areas to challenge the government to meet its responsibilities. The existence of concrete models was also intended to provide black people with visible standards of services which would enable them to make demands on those in authority to provide similar or better-quality care. Through playing an advocacy role for the most powerless amongst the poor, these models also enhanced the chances of poor people gaining access to existing government services.

Working in an environment that focussed on people as important in their own right also created opportunities for the emergence of a new professionalism – a person-centred approach. This approach affected most of those involved and forged a sense of commitment to and respect for people beyond their usefulness in a material or political sense. The notion of using people as political fodder was discouraged.

Person-centred professionalism involved significant sacrifices. There were limited material rewards for this kind of work in a concrete immediate sense. The 24-hour, seven-day, and year-round service was sustained by nothing more than the support one got from fellow activists. These sacrifices were even more remarkable given the poor family circumstances of most of the activists involved.

There were, however, many non-material rewards, such as recognition by one's peers, as well as by those in leadership, which sustained one. In addition, personal qualities of those involved were nurtured actively through an organised process of empowering individuals to extend their horizons and perceive themselves as active agents in history. The lived experience within organisations like BCP encouraged staff participation at all levels. Many of those involved experienced significant personal growth, which made their sacrifices worthwhile.

However, the limitations imposed on the development of new models of professionalism by inadequate funding were considerable. Commitment to the struggle was no substitute for the need for material rewards. Resource constraints in particular hampered the involvement of many black students from poor home circumstances, most of whom had studied with the assistance of loans which needed to be repaid. Their families also expected a return for the sacrifices they had made to put their children through university education. In the end only the zealots remained committed to working in these organisations on a full-time basis. And because of the limited number of posts available, enormous work-loads were placed on these individuals. Exhausting work-schedules bore negative consequences. With little time for reading and reflection, the danger of repeating the same mistakes became real. Moreover, inadequate attention was paid to the evaluation of work done. This was compounded by (state-enforced) isolation from people doing similar work in other parts of the world.

In addition, people tended to seek relief in wild parties from the stress they were working under. This was not only detrimental to health in the short term, but bred bad habits which had long-term lifestyle implications. Alcohol-abuse and chain-smoking were particularly negative features of such a lifestyle.

However, the commitment of BC activists set an example for professionals working in other organisations. The SACC, for example, changed the approach of its Dependants' Conference completely in response to the work of Zimele Trust Fund. From being mainly a hand-out programme it became more involved with empowering ex-political prisoners. Another example of the BCM's impact was a visit by officials of the Department of Health and Welfare to Zanempilo Community Health Centre in 1976 to assess whether it could be used as a model for government health centres.

The Role of Development Aid

In the early part of the period under review – from 1970 to 1977 – there was a universal reluctance on the part of funding agencies to support black initiatives. The only notable exceptions were IUEF (International University Exchange Fund) and WUS (World University Service).[9] Conventional wisdom then was that South Africa had the economic resources to support all its citizens, and thus the international community had no obligation to support non-governmental efforts here. There were also racist undertones in the choices of the type of involvement some donor agencies made. European and North American philanthropic organisations favoured support for groups such as the SAIRR, but refused to support black organisations. Their choice was a statement that they could entrust their aid to whites doing things for blacks, but not to blacks themselves. When confronted with the racist connotations of their selective support, some of the donors argued that their aid had better security in white hands against interference by a repressive government, than would be the case in black hands. These arguments had some validity, but their proponents ignored

9 It was thus logical for the South African government to plant a spy in IUEF (Craig Williamson) to monitor this important source of support.

the protective impact which support from powerful international donors could have had on beleaguered black organisations.

In spite of inadequate support, the performance of the BCM was impressive and attracted many visitors and supporters. Local church groups such as the Christian Institute, and international bodies such as ICCO in the Netherlands, as well as individual donors, provided the necessary lifeline to keep the projects afloat.

It is interesting to note the radical change that overcame the funding situation after 1976. Millions of US dollars have been pouring into South Africa for development aid from many sources since the late 1970s. The South African business sector has also begun to make its contribution to black development through various agencies, notably the Urban Foundation. The development circuit is well established in South Africa, marked by development-related conferences, books and other publications, streams of overseas visitors, and trips abroad for South African activists.

What accounts for this upsurge in international and national interest in development work? There are several possible explanations. Firstly, black anger manifest in the Soweto uprising shocked South Africa and the world out of their complacency. Something had to be done. Two notable local responses by individuals in the private sector were the launching of Women for Peace and the Urban Foundation. Secondly, the USA, having emerged from the civil rights era, was more responsive to the plight of black South Africans and felt less vulnerable to public criticism of its own racism at home. The USA government and other agencies also responded to pressure from African-Americans who identified with the struggles against apartheid.

Other Western countries such as Europe and Britain also felt the need to express their moral outrage at the situation in South Africa. Some of these countries had just emerged from bitter independence struggles in their former colonial domains and were in a stronger moral position to add their voice to denouncing apartheid.

Thirdly, the possibility of change from white domination to majority rule was seen as real by the international community. Some of the great powers, notably the USA with its strategy of 'managing development' (see Gendzier, 1985), felt the need to establish a foothold in order to monitor and influence the direction of change in South Africa.

It is perhaps true to say that South Africa has become a huge industry in international development terms. The participants in this industry trade on the notion of 'victims of apartheid'. People's careers depend on their ability to play an advocacy role on behalf of the victims. The victim image is, however, ultimately disempowering. Whatever short-term gains are made out of this 'victimology', disempowered people will need to be weaned from the resultant dependency. It also appears that too much dependence is placed by most political actors in South Africa on the goodwill of the international community to support transformation in South African social relations.

One of the legacies of this development industry is the system of patronage which permeates the non-governmental organisational sector. The ability to negotiate the political minefield connected with this industry determines the success or failure of funding proposals. Political organisations, including the government, are eager to control the development process in the socio-economic arena. Given the demands made on organisations to fit into the requirements of this industry, individual activists are stressed beyond the limits of human endurance. For example, the need to attend to the string of overseas visitors to successful projects and prominent political actors consumes enormous energy and ultimately undermines the effectiveness of those involved.

The consequences of this massive international interest are many. Now there is money desperately chasing projects. Funding agencies have fallen over one another in their keenness to be seen to be supportive of 'the struggle'. Some are content to dump money on projects that may not need it, if only because it is expedient to be seen to have donated money to the right people and organisations.

The stress under which activists work has the potential of creating a generation of people with a 'culture of entitlement'. It is only human for one to demand something in return for so much effort expended in the struggle for justice. Manifestations of this culture of entitlement include arrogance, failure to conduct oneself in a courteous way as an official of a public organisation, and making demands on public resources without putting enough into those organisations in return.

Conversations with individual members of some of the organisations caught in this development circuit indicate that they are experiencing serious problems already in this area. For example, huge telephone bills and travel expenses are incurred by NGOs out of proportion to their work output.[10] The inordinate time people in many organisations spend away from their work-desks is also a concern. Servicing 'the South African industry' also subtracts from productivity at the grassroots level, when community workers' time and energy are put under strain.

What is more, the potential for corrupt practices is also real. Corruption is already a major problem in South Africa and is prevalent in most government structures, at a central, local and homeland level. Can South Africa afford another 'gravy train' in addition to those created by apartheid?

Conclusion

The BCM was an important trendsetter in the field of community development. Many lessons can be learned from the successes and failures of the 1970s. Paramount amongst these is the importance of determined effort

---

10 The *Cape Times* reported on concern expressed about the misappropriation of funds within the Centre for Development Studies (CDS) based at the University of the Western Cape. The CDS trustees subsequently promised to investigate the matter (*Cape Times*, 7 June 1990).

and its rewards. Furthermore, the lessons of the 1970s underline the importance of individuals in shaping history. A few dedicated individuals made it possible for the BC philosophy to become a way of life in large parts of South Africa.

Thirdly, one cannot stress too much the need for analyses which take into consideration the complexities of a given situation. A serious and costly error of the BCM was its failure to recognise that not all black people are necessarily committed to liberation and that the poor are not inherently egalitarian. There are differentials of power along lines of class, gender, age and geographic location that need to be taken seriously in development strategies.

Fourthly, development work is about the empowerment of people to take greater control over their lives. Symbols of development are important in alleviating misery and creating hope where there is despair. But these are but tools of development and should not be seen as ends in themselves. True empowerment occurs when individuals and communities are able to take control over their lives and effectively participate in decision-making processes which lead to outcomes that affect them.

Finally, the importance of uprooting poverty through development has finally been recognised by the South African government. The launching of the Independent Development Trust (IDT) in 1990, with an initial capital of two billion rands from the government, marks the beginning of an important era in South Africa. Judicious utilisation of both local and international aid, combined with the vibrancy and energy evident in the non-governmental sector, could result in significant development, which is essential for the fundamental transformation of social relations in South Africa.

10

The Impact of Black Consciousness on Culture
MBULELO VIZIKHUNGO MZAMANE

Black Consciousness Cultural Regeneration

Black Consciousness and the literature and cultural output it inspired emerged in the midst of the political and cultural repression of the sixties, which followed Sharpeville. The majority of writers of the Black Consciousness era began their work in a near vacuum, with few works in circulation by older writers on which they could model their own writings. They had no surviving tradition of their own which they could follow. A great deal of the literature written in the indigenous languages for schools under the Bantu Education system was unacceptable to them as it tended to reinforce apartheid and inculcate attitudes of inferiority and dependence. It helped propagate the government myth that Africans would 'develop along their own lines', in the impoverished reserves called Bantustans. It encouraged Africans to renounce their claim to the rest of the land and the wealth they had helped to generate in industry, mining and commerce. This was equally true of such internationally acclaimed white South African liberal authors as Alan Paton in *Cry, the Beloved Country*. In an interview he gave to Bernth Lindfors at the University of Texas, Austin, on 20 March 1979, Richard Rive summed up in the following terms the position the new writers found themselves in:

> Black writers in South Africa today haven't got much of a precedent to fall back on, because most of the older writers have been banned, so that the young people have no access to them. There is a big gap in South African literature between 1963 and 1971. The new generation really doesn't know much about us, and they don't know much of the writing that is going on outside (Rive, 1980:57).

When the new writers emerged, the Sophiatown renaissance in Johannesburg had died with the destruction of Sophiatown between 1955 and 1958. In Cape Town, the District Six school was equally under siege, with blacks of mixed ancestry facing similar removals. Ezekiel Mphahlele, who had been the literary editor of *Drum* since 1956, left for Nigeria on an exit permit in 1959. Nat Nakasa, the founding editor of *Classic*, mentioned in its first issue in 1963 other writers who had already left South Africa: Alfred Hutchinson, Arthur Maimane, Todd Matshikiza, Lewis Nkosi and Bloke Modisane. In an article published in 1980, Lionel Abrahams stated that in a *Government Gazette* of 1966 there were forty-six exiles listed whose work could neither be read nor quoted as they had been banned under the Suppression of Communism Act (1980:46). Kelwyn Sole estimated that 'by the mid-sixties at least 15 black writers [had] gone into exile in various ways, some of them after incarceration in jail' (1979:164). In addition to the writers already mentioned, Sole's list included Mazisi Kunene, Bessie Head, Arthur Nortje, Keorapetse Kgositsile, Cosmo Pieterse, Dennis Brutus and Alex La Guma. But Sole's list did not include Peter Abrahams, Africa's first exiled writer; Noni Jabavu, author of *Drawn in Colour* (1960) and *The Ochre People* (1963), and the first significant African woman writer in English; A. C. Jordan, whose Xhosa classic *Inqgumbo Yeminyanya* (The Wrath of the Ancestors) was published in 1940; Jordan Ngubane, whose Zulu novel, *Uvalo Lwezinhlonzi* (Frowns Which Strike Terror), appeared in 1957; Sam Guma, Daniel Kunene and Gideon Mangoaele, all of them academics and authors; and the poet, academic and literary critic Vernon February, who left in 1963. When the new writers started, few of them were aware of their predecessors.

In 1961 *King Kong*, a musical play devised by Harry Bloom, left for London with most of South Africa's top African entertainers. Among the musicians and actors who left and did not return to South Africa were Todd Matshikiza, author of *Chocolates for My Wife* (1961) and composer of the musical score for *King Kong*; Miriam Makeba, who was the leading lady in the play; members of South Africa's leading music groups, the Manhattan Brothers, the African Inkspots and others; Hugh Masekela, Caiphus Semenya and Jonas Gwangwa, who settled in America and formed their own band called The Union of South Africa; Letta Mbulu, who married Caiphus Semenya; and Alton Khumalo, who later worked with Athol Fugard before forming his own group in London, Temba Productions. As repression had intensified in South Africa after Sharpeville, these actors and musicians stayed on in London, or settled in America. Over the next five years other actors, dancers and musicians who left South Africa with productions such as *Sponono* (a play based on Alan Paton's story dealing with an African boy in a Johannesburg reformatory, which was taken to New York in 1964) decided to settle abroad.

This large-scale emigration of actors and musicians paralleled the drainage of intellectuals, writers and politicians. At the same time as government action after Sharpeville was stifling political and literary expression, voluntary exile was also taking its toll in all other spheres. Before the rise of the writers and artists of the Black Consciousness era, most of whom had been in their early teens during the Sharpeville crisis, there was as much stagnation on the cultural scene in South Africa as there was on the political front.

Not everybody left. A small but distinguished group of artists kept an unfolding culture of liberation alive. They include the pianist from District Six, Dollar Brand (Abdullah Ibrahim), who was also at the head of the new wave of poetry; Kippie Moeketsi, a saxophonist living in Soweto who used to record with Dollar Brand and had also been involved with *King Kong*; Mackay Davashe, another Soweto saxophonist and the band leader in *King Kong*; Mankunku Ngozi, the saxophonist from Langa who achieved instant fame with his composition *Yakhal' inkomo* (The Cow Bellows), which gave Mongane Serote's first collection of poetry its title; the Malombo Jazzmakers from Mamelodi, who came to prominence when they won the 1964 jazz festival in Soweto and whose music combined jazz or *mbaqanga* with traditional Venda and Pedi rhythms and tunes, music reaching back to a cultural heritage and fusing its traditional elements with Western and other influences; jazz singers Abigail Kubheka and Sophie Mgcina, who had both been to London with *King Kong*; the musicians Gideon Nxumalo, Early Mabuza, Elijah Nkonyane and Tshukudu, all four of whom together with Mackay Davashe are the subject of Sipho Sepamla's poem 'Encore: The Quintette' in *Hurry Up to It*, recollections from a period when Sepamla was himself a jazz impresario; and Dumile Feni, a sculptor from New Brighton in Port Elizabeth whose work is the subject of Serote's short story 'When Rebecca Fell', which appears in Mothobi Mutloatse's *Forced Landing*.

The continued presence of these artists, writers and musicians made possible the cultural renaissance, the retrieval of black culture, and the assertion of black identity, which are celebrated by Serote in his poem 'Hell, Well Heaven' from *Yakhal' inkomo*. The rhythm of the new poetry derived as much from jazz as from the African beat which was resuscitated and made popular by the Malombo Jazzmakers, Dollar Brand and others. The African drum-beat became a prominent feature in the poetry recitals organised by Black Consciousness cultural activists such as Dashiki, Mdali, Mihloti, TECON (Theatre Council of Natal) and Joinery.

Despite the fact that the majority of writers and artists of the Black Consciousness era were unfamiliar with the work of their predecessors, they emerged as their spiritual heirs. In the literary sphere, this was achieved through the mediation of the few established writers such as Richard Rive and James Matthews who stayed on in South Africa. Although the early work of Matthews and Rive, published in *Quartet* in 1963, and Rive's collection of short stories, *African Songs*, issued in the same year, as well as his novel *Emergency*, which came out the following year, had all been banned, these writers were still well known to their people, who mixed with them every day. Moreover, their new work continued to circulate in South Africa, unlike the exiled writers who could only be read outside. Rive's stories trickled out more slowly after his earlier books had been banned but his critical articles continued to pour out in literary magazines such as *Contrast*. Matthews, who had lived in Alexandra and District Six, was consulted by many aspiring younger writers. With the publication of *Cry Rage* in 1972, he effectively switched from the short story medium to poetry. In 1974

Matthews established the Black Publishing House in Athlone and became the first black person to venture into publishing in this way. In the same year he published *Black Voices Shout!*, an anthology of Black Consciousness poems, and a collection of his short stories, *The Park and Other Stories*, which included some stories from *Quartet* and others written in the 1950s.

Casey Motsisi and Stanley Motjuwadi, both of whom had emerged towards the end of the Sophiatown renaissance, also bridged the gap between the evolving writers and their exiled predecessors. Both were journalists who provided some degree of continuity with the past. Their imaginative writing and articles appeared regularly in *Drum* and *Classic* and, later, in the *World* and *Weekend World*. Casey Motsisi, best known as a columnist from 1958 to 1977 in both *Drum* and the *World*, in which he provided witty and entertaining sketches of township life, published his poem 'The Efficacy of Prayer' in 1963 in the first issue of *Classic* and subsequently, ten years later, in Royston's anthology, *To Whom It May Concern*. Motjuwadi wrote a weekly column for the Johannesburg *Rand Daily Mail* and eventually became the editor of *Drum*, the magazine that had nurtured many of the writers who emerged in the 1950s. During his brief period in 1968 as a member of *Classic*'s editorial board, he wrote poetry for the magazine, subsequently appearing in *Playboy* magazine and Royston's anthology. The literary revival of the Black Consciousness era was to a degree made possible through the inspiration and example of these writers. However, they were primarily authors of prose, despite the occasional poems they produced. The new poets who still wrote in English had to teach themselves to write English poetry and struggled to learn the craft, without reference to any African poetic tradition in English. A resistance to writing in an African language also resulted from the imposition of the vernacular by the Department of Bantu Education on pupils at school. A marked contradiction in the literary revival ushered in by Black Consciousness lay, in fact, in the neglect of the African languages, although the poets who wrote in English were also to dip into the resources of orature as in *izibongo*, *maboko* or *lithothokiso*.

The literary revival after 1967 was greatly facilitated by the availability of a number of literary magazines, some of them under African control. *Classic*, initiated under the editorship of Nat Nakasa, had become the forum for both the more established, and a new crop of, writers. It was already in its fourth year when in 1967 it published Dollar Brand's poems, which inaugurated the poetic renaissance of the Black Consciousness era. Other magazines and periodicals emerged. The *SASO Newsletter*, which first appeared in 1970, accepted a certain amount of poetry which projected an African image. When *Classic* ceased publication in 1971, it was replaced by *New Classic* in 1975. *Donga* appeared in July 1976 but was banned in March 1978, after eight issues, and replaced by *Inspan*. *Staffrider*, the most representative literary magazine of writers of the Soweto era, the high-water mark of the Black Consciousness period, first came out in March 1978. It was followed by *Wietie* in 1980, edited by two poets of the new generation, Fhazel Johennesse and Christopher van Wyk. It appeared under the auspices of a new publishing company they were trying to form called SABLE (South African Black Literature) Books. Blacks were on the editorial boards of all these magazines. Several other magazines, edited by whites, regularly published work by writers from all the ranks of the racially oppressed. This gave added impetus to creative writing within those communities. *The Purple Renoster* was founded by Lionel Abrahams in 1956 and continued in existence until 1972. Lionel Abrahams and two of his colleagues, Robert Royston and Eva Bezwoda, were also responsible for the publication of Oswald Mbuyiseni Mtshali's collection of poems, *Sounds of a Cowhide Drum* (1971), and Mongane Wally Serote's *Yakhal' inkomo* (1972), under a new company they called Purple Renoster Publications.

Other magazines to promote the work of the new writers were *Contrast*, founded by Jack Cope in 1960; *New Coin*, which first came out in 1965 and was followed by *Ophir* and *Bolt*; and *Izwi*, which appeared in twenty issues between October 1971 and December 1974. In the case of many of these white-controlled publications, it is true that relations were sometimes strained between the white editors and their black contributors who privately resented the idea of whites having to dictate terms all the time. But on the whole these editors (and some white publishers, including Ravan and Ad Donker) were willing to take the risk of incurring the displeasure of the government censors. They did not always stick to unexciting and innocuous work devoid of radical political content – what Nadine Gordimer has described as 'safe biography with a collector's' piece savour of Africana of the good old kind; carefully vetted anthologies; safari adventure' (1968:73).

Poets of the Black Consciousness revival period after 1967 largely stopped writing for a predominantly non-black or non-South African audience, as poets such as Dennis Brutus and Arthur Nortje had been compelled to do by the protest tradition, censorship, and the fact of exile. Protest literature is writing by the underprivileged and exploited which is primarily addressed to those who wield political and economic power, or are close to the seats of such power, in an attempt to elicit their sympathy and support against discriminatory laws and practices; while the 'liberal tradition' is an expression used to describe literature written by whites appealing to Christian liberal humanistic ideals in race relations. Protest had imposed on those writers working within its tradition the burden of writing for an essentially white readership. However, the writings of the Black Consciousness generation were addressed directly and primarily to the downtrodden and oppressed. Their aim was to liberate their people as much from white oppression as from their own selves: from the self-inflicted pain and suffering, and the senseless and devastating violence of the townships. Their audience and preoccupations affected their language and other stylistic features of their poems. Amongst their targeted township audiences many had probably not had the benefit of more than four years of formal schooling, although they would have acquired some speaking knowledge of English and Afrikaans from the factories, or wherever they were employed. Because most employers in South Africa are white, anyone who expects to find employment must learn to speak a European language. Many township residents could therefore follow the simple English in which the new poetry was written – although one could still hear hecklers from the audience shouting *'Khulumani isiZulu nina ... Buang SeSotho'* ('Speak in Zulu ... Speak in SeSotho'). Public poetry readings, which attracted moderately large crowds, were reported in the press. At every conceivable occasion organised by advocates of Black Consciousness, poetry was performed in the manner of *izibongo*: at funerals and memorial services, at public performances and private houses, and at labour-union meetings. These public meetings grew in popularity after the June 1976 student and worker uprising.

Two theories have been advanced to account for the popularity of poetry among writers of the Black Consciousness era. One was advanced by Nadine Gordimer, who argues that, in the light of censorship after Sharpeville, 'black writers have had to look for survival away from the explicit if not to the cryptic then to the implicit; and in their case they have turned instinctively to poetry' (1973:52). Their need for self-expression amidst repression, she says, led them to adopt a form of expression less vulnerable than the explicit medium of prose, which had been heavily censored earlier. The second theory was expressed by Richard Rive, who did not subscribe to the argument that the reason poetry became a popular medium was that by its very nature it is cerebral and, therefore, more difficult for the censors to fathom; he pointed out that the poetry of some of the leading literary figures of the Black Consciousness cultural renaissance, such as James Matthews, was straightforward, explicit and more prosaic than poetic. His own explanation was that it was possibly because of the success of the poetry of Oswald Mtshali, who chose poetry in a form that started off the new wave, 'that we have had a wave of poets writing' (Rive, 1980:63).

Sepamla endorsed Rive's opinion and attributed the upsurge of poetry among the new generation to the fact that many aspiring writers who rubbed shoulders in the townships with Mtshali and Serote were seized by a desire to emulate them as the only role models they had. He acknowledged that 'those fellows were a great inspiration, because a lot of the people who are writing today saw them; talked to them; they know their experiences and they know how they translated their experiences into poetry,' he says. 'And I think that the writing that is being done today is an extension of what those guys started' (Sepamla, 1977:92). He adds that few writers in the early years of the renaissance had the time or inclination to write lengthy prose, and so they chose to say what they had to say through the most cryptic medium at their disposal.

There were other factors responsible for the upsurge of poetry during the years after Sharpeville: the existing outlets for publication tended to favour poetry; the tradition of orature, which never completely died out, even in the cities; and, above all, the impetus derived from Black Consciousness.

Black Consciousness and the cultural renaissance it fostered illustrate the adage that when people live under conditions of severe repression, with no attention paid by the rulers to their political voice, culture often becomes an important medium for expressing their desire to transcend their oppressive situation. The last three decades in South Africa have been remarkable in this regard. Writers and artists of Black Consciousness persuasion carried a similar responsibility to the role that the labour movement and the church have had to play at different times in our unfolding history, a role which filled the gap left by the more conventional, extra-parliamentary political formations. The legacy of Steve Biko and Black Consciousness lies in the way culture came to take on the burden of articulating African political aspirations after the African National Congress and the Pan-Africanist Congress had been outlawed in 1960; it also lies in the manner in which culture came to be utilised in prosecuting the liberation struggle. This must not be construed to mean, however, that the genesis of our liberation culture was Black Consciousness, for this was but a continuation of earlier traditions. Indeed, it may be argued that Black Consciousness, which came to exercise considerable hegemony in the 1970s, was largely superseded in the 1980s by another political expression which was not itself devoid of elements of its predecessors. All of this is dialectical, for these stages build on one another. In our unfolding culture of liberation, therefore, the beginnings of this process predated the late 1960s, although from the late 1960s it became sustained and moved with greater intensity for a number of historical reasons.

Operating in a different and more vicious political climate, Black Consciousness adopted a different approach, that of mobilising and strengthening the inner resources of the downtrodden and oppressed. It realised that a demoralised people with no confidence or pride in their forebears, capabilities or achievements could never carry out a successful revolution. The founding members of Black Consciousness advocated withdrawal from unnecessary collaboration which could perpetuate dependence upon whites, but only as a strategy in order to achieve self-sufficiency and solidarity. In a climate where overt extra-parliamentary opposition attracted swift and brutal retribution, the need for less overtly political expression meant that Black Consciousness paid more attention to historical, cultural and artistic issues. In this regard, Black Consciousness realised, more than any other group, the essentially political importance of the cultural struggle. It was active in all the arts, but in none more effectively than theatre, which included poetry performances. Black Consciousness emphasised the educational function of cultural and artistic activity and exploited the political resources of art, theatre, music, dance and culture in general.

Until the late 1960s not many of the performing arts that had evolved in South Africa had been politically relevant, in the sense that they either contributed directly to the analysis of the repressive system or advocated political action against the regime. In spite of a widespread tradition of 'sketches', consisting of skits on every conceivable subject and speaking directly to the affected community, it was really only with the rise of Black Consciousness that systematic and coordinated efforts to promote popular consciousness through theatre, and to promote self-respect and self-reliance among the deprived and underprivileged, began to take root. By the mid-1970s these efforts had spread from the urban areas to some of the rural communities, to which, by then, many of the leaders of Black Consciousness had been banished.

Ambiguity, Commitment and Reaction in Theatre

There were several reasons why theatre, including poetry performances, became a crucial area of political activity in the 1970s. Robert Kavanagh argues that conventional political action, under the banner of the ANC or PAC, was illegal and dangerous; the press and broadcasting were in the hands of the white establishment; publishing was, by and large, a white monopoly and vulnerable to censorship; film was beyond the reach of fledgling political artists in the townships. Kavanagh points out the many advantages of theatre: it was cheap, mobile, simple to present, and difficult to supervise, censor or outlaw. He does not point out, however, that such theatre as emerged already had a tradition, which derived from ancient performance practices in the community, such as the traditions of story-telling (as in *intsomi, inganekwane, tsomo*), heroic poetry (as in *izibongo, maboko, lithothokiso*), song and dance in ritual and other ceremonies, and sketches. Theatre, like graffiti, was the one medium left to the people to use to conscientise, educate, unify and mobilise the rank and file.

Shanti, a play by Mthuli Shezi, expressed solidarity between men and women, and among oppressed groups, irrespective of their racial categorisation by the apartheid state, whose purpose was divide-and-rule. The play extended the definition of Pan-Africanism, in line with Black Consciousness ideology, to include blacks of mixed and Asian ancestry, all of whom were victims of the same oppressive system. Fatima Dike, in such plays as *The Sacrifice of Kreli* and *The First South African*, emerged in the 1970s, after Shezi's death, as the first major African woman playwright in English.

The thin body of published playscripts belies the rich theatrical tradition of the black community, especially among the women. In this tradition, women take part in dance, music and songs for religious and agricultural festivals and celebrations of birth, death and marriage, as well as the everyday songs that accompany all aspects of work and play. Through their responsibility for educating the young, women largely developed the African story-telling tradition of *intsomi, inganekwane* or *tsomo*. Such orature constitutes a direct vehicle for ethical teaching. More indirectly, orature expresses the shared attitudes and beliefs of the community – through songs for grinding grain, songs for entertaining children and songs the children themselves sing for their mothers going off to the day's work.

Such performing arts have survived conquest. Evidence of their resurgence, adaptation and transformation abounds in South African women's culture. Although not directly influenced by Black Consciousness, whose legacy in promoting women's culture was minimal, the women of the squatter communities of Crossroads in the 1970s used the tradition of sketches to enact their plight and depict forced removals, separation of families, police brutality and their own epic struggles. Thus women in South Africa, in unscripted productions such as this guerrilla theatre from the squatter settlements such as Crossroads, or in formal dramatic terms at the Space Theatre in Cape Town or the Market Theatre in Johannesburg, have been quick to exploit the political resources of theatre, in the manner of Black Consciousness activists, to place women's issues on top of the agenda of the liberation movement.

A contrast with Black Consciousness or radical theatre was provided by Gibson Kente's township plays of the 1960s and 1970s. In its non-radical or ambiguous phase, as in Gibson Kente's early plays, township theatre was both urban and commercial by nature. The range of themes which characterised this theatre includes education, adultery, promiscuity, rape, religion, crime, drinking, the corruption and cruelty of the authorities and, occasionally, working conditions. Although many of the plays projected an apolitical message and proposed non-radical solutions to society's ills – usually some humanitarian, moral solution – the issues they dealt with were, however, an accurate reflection of the quality of life led by the urban majority. This is not to say that traditional culture was no longer relevant and that these plays did not reflect it; for example, a stock scene would still be the visit to the *isangoma* or *inyanga* (diviner or herbalist) in moments of crises. But a marked characteristic of such theatre was its truly eclectic nature. Zionist (independent African Christian) music, dance and lifestyle permeate these plays, as they do township life. Wakes, weddings and funerals retain certain traditional characteristics overlaid by new and often perverse ways. All over the Witwatersrand, and further afield in such townships as New Brighton (Port Elizabeth), theatre groups sprang up and toured other urban centres (Kavanagh, 1981:ix-xxxi).

By the mid-1970s, as Kente sensed the changing political pulse of the youth in the townships who formed the bulk of his audiences, his plays turned radical. The lead had had been set by the success of such Black Consciousness productions as *Shanti* by Mthuli Shezi and *Give Us This Day* by the Rev. Mzwandile Maqina (the latter was to become a reactionary leader of amaAfrika, a pro-apartheid vigilante group based in the Eastern Cape). Using the popular formula of the period, usually depicting some disgruntled student activists, in quick succession Kente wrote his political plays, *How Long, I Believe* and *Too Late*, all of which carried a message of defiance and anger to the urban masses. The accumulated effect of such theatre activity played an important part in preparing youth groups and the workers for the struggle that was precipitated when, on 16 June 1976, police shot demonstrating African students in Soweto.

For Kente, however, the radicalisation of township theatre by proponents of Black Consciousness did not derive from any deep political convictions and was little more than a formula for producing box office hits. By the end of the 1980s, this mood had swung, and sensing a new and more prosperous audience among white theatre-goers, he turned in a decidedly reactionary direction, as reflected in his entry from the 1987 Grahamstown National Arts Festival. *Sekunjalo* (The Time Has Come), which was a success at the festival, is Kente's dramatic monument to his own disaffection, ambition and opportunism.

In its ambiguous and radical phases, nonetheless, Gibson Kente's theatre forms a valid basis for popular theatre such as Black Consciousness cultural activists themselves used to conscientise their communities. Its accessibility makes it a potent weapon in mass education. It shares some common features with Poor Theatre, which evolved in Latin America and is increasingly used in formal and non-formal education (Freire, 1970), in adult literacy, health and agricultural campaigns; in the promotion of participatory democracy; and in encouraging collaborative effort in problemsolving as well as in mass mobilisation for a variety of other purposes.

Influences came from other parts of Africa: the University of Dar es Salaam led the field in community theatre, and in Nigeria, Wole Soyinka devised a 'guerrilla' theatre, modelled to some degree on Hubert Ogunde's Yoruba Travelling Theatre, which employed any available open space to enact drama based on contemporary issues, such as the corruption which beset the implementation of the Green Revolution in Nigeria under the Shagari regime. Two other moderately successful programmes are to be found in the Samaru Project in Zaria, Nigeria, and Badzanani Theatre in Botswana. The struggles of the people of Mozambique, Eritrea and Palestine continue to validate culture as a weapon of struggle, and these examples were not lost on cultural workers in South Africa.

The legacy of Black Consciousness in this regard thus lies in its promotion of 'alternative' theatre in South Africa in the work of playwrights such as Matsemela Manaka, Maishe Maponya, Gcina Mhlope, John Ledwaba, Mbongeni Ngema and Percy Mtwa. This 'alternative' theatre has taken a distinct turn, away from establishment theatre. More and more, theatre practices evolved in Africa, the Middle East, Eastern Europe and Latin America are taking root in South African theatre, and people are discarding cultural imperialism, along with alien and alienating cultural modes that have hitherto dominated their cultural practices. At the head of this movement to decolonise the African mind and radicalise culture stood Black Consciousness.

From Imbongi to Worker Poet

In the African community, poetry as an element of theatre plays a different role from that in the white communities of South Africa, especially the English-speaking section. André Brink has argued that English-speakers in

South Africa, 'having lost their political power and much of their economic power after a century and a half of uncontested domination, find in poetry a – relatively harmless – domain within which the old muscles may now be flexed in a literary manner in order to maintain an illusion of power.' For African writers, however, he says, poetry is exactly the opposite: 'an instrument of liberation, a new language which exhilaratingly gives shape and meaning to black aspirations and awareness and an experience of unity that transcends all vernacular divisions. It is a means of ... confronting political power' (*Weekly Mail*, 10-16 July 1987). Poetry is not, however, a 'new language' to the African, and the *izibongo (maboko, lithothokiso)* is the highest verbal art form among the Southern *abantu*. With less exaggeration and more penetrating insight, Jeremy Cronin draws the link between popular culture and mass struggle, between people's poetry and people's power, in the context of the trade-union movement in South Africa. We were once taught to think of poetry as obscure and elite, he says. However, in the last three decades since the rise of Black Consciousness, poetry has been marching in the front ranks of the mass struggles that have rolled through our land. Cronin argues, in slightly limited fashion, that it was the township student and youth organisations that began to integrate militant oral poetry into their activities after 1976. In fact, the trend goes back a decade earlier to the rise of Black Consciousness and the cultural renaissance it fostered among groups such as Dashiki, Mihloti, PET (People's Experimental Theatre) and TECON (Theatre Council of Natal), and harks back further to ancient African traditions. What is qualitatively new, however, is the way in which performance poetry has also taken root within the trade-union movement. In particular, it is the traditional art form of *izibongo* that we find in evidence in the labour movement: 'The poet draws from what Amilcar Cabral described as "the great reservoir" of the liberation struggle, the centuries-old people's cultural traditions' (*Weekly Mail*, 18-19 March 1987).

The vitally important role played by poetry in pre-colonial African society is being re-enacted in the altogether different context of the African labour movement and political struggle in South Africa today. In traditional African communities, the performance of poetry was a significant ritual element in education and government, at dances, feasts, festivals, weddings, circumcision schools, funerals and other social, ceremonial and religious events. The reasons are not hard to find (NELM, 1987):

> In oral culture, the word is sound, and discourse – partly for mnemonic reasons – naturally lends itself to poetic organisation. Thought typically finds expression in heavily rhythmic, balanced patterns, in repetitions and antithesis, in alliterations and assonances, in proverbial and other formulaic expressions. The traditional community's history, values, beliefs and aspirations were recorded not in books but in its oral tradition of songs, folk tales and epic narratives.

With the advent of literacy in South Africa, orature was for a long time relegated to the margins of literary, cultural and political respectability. It survived, however, in the rural areas and in such urban adaptations as the work songs chanted by black labour gangs – such as *'Shosholoza'* and the work chant *'Abelungu ngo-damn'* ('God damn whites'). Generally speaking, however, African poetry bowed before the supremacy of print and the influence of Western models to express itself in an art form written and read by individuals. It did, however, remain more determinedly public, more social and political, in its characteristic concerns, than its white South African counterpart.

Informed by the ideology of Black Consciousness, the new poetry of the late 1960s and early 1970s was initially characterised by bitter ironic depictions of ghetto life and injustice – as in the poetry of the five leading authors from the Black Consciousness era: Oswald Mtshali, Mongane Serote, Mandla Langa, Mafika Gwala and Sipho Sepamla. As the 1970s wore on, and particularly after the Soweto revolt of 1976, increased use was made of rhetorical devices derived from orature, in order to articulate a growing political militancy. South African poets began to assert their identity by recovering a sense of cultural continuity with the heroic, pre-colonial past – a continuity long effaced by the discourse of white supremacy – while at the same time valorising the township 'subculture' of their experience. Mothobi Mutloatse, a poet, short-story writer and anthologist who emerged in the heady days of Black Consciousness, described this process in his introduction to his epoch-making anthology, *Forced Landing* (published abroad as *Africa South: Contemporary Writings*), as a concerted attempt to nationalise the English language and its literary conventions in the service of the populist cause. The process culminated in the publication in 1979 of Ingoapele Madingoane's 'contemporary epic', *Africa, My Beginning*.

Significantly, before its appearance in print, Madingoane's work had already achieved great popularity at township performances, organised by such pioneering Black Consciousness groups as Mihloti and Mdali (Music, Drama, Arts and Literature Institute) – the acronym also means 'Creator' in Nguni – to both of which Madingoane belonged and whose genesis from the late 1960s Molefe Pheto describes in his prison memoirs, *And Night Fell*.

For Africans, poetry has once again become an important means of popular communication. Since 1976, after the Soweto revolt, it has become customary for poetry to be performed at political meetings, funerals, trade-union rallies and other occasions providing for an affirmation of group identity and solidarity of purpose. In this resurgence of orature, heroic poetry, or *izibongo*, has enjoyed a particularly vital renaissance in the context of the labour movement. This revitalisation is reflected in the publication in 1986 of *Black Mamba Rising*, a collection of *izibongo* by worker poets Alfred Temba Qabula, Mi S'dumo Hlatshwayo and Nise Malange. The poems were originally performed at trade union meetings in the Durban district. Qabula's celebrated 'Praise Poem for FOSATU' (Federation of royal *izibongo* by apostrophising the organisation as the 'Black Forest' (*Hlathi' limnyama*) in which its members seek refuge, a familiar praise name for both King Cetshwayo and the veteran ICU official A. W. G. Champion. In the labour movement of the 1980s in South Africa, '*izibongo* of this sort are a unique tool in raising workers' consciousness of their union and its role in their lives as workers. Yet they are also quite clearly an expression of an old and tenacious art form with its roots deep in social and political awareness' (NELM, 1987).

Such poetry, like drama and the new prose fiction, has carved a role for itself in our unfolding culture of liberation. Mi Hlatshwayo, as COSATU's Cultural Coordinator, states that 'Creativity without a base, without direction, is easily manoeuvred into commercial art' (*Weekly Mail*, 17-23 July 1987). It was Black Consciousness that first provided a base and outlined direction for the new writers' movement in its post-Soweto formation. The new man and woman in South Africa were determined not to be manipulated and exploited again. In a 1985 manifesto, the Durban Workers' Cultural Local declared:

> We have been culturally exploited time and time again: We have been singing, parading, boxing, acting and writing within a system we did not control. So far, black workers have been feeding their creativity into a culture machine to make profits for others. Worker-creators are promised heaven on earth and hoards of gold – from penny-whistle bands to *mbaqanga* musicians, from soccer players to talent actors ... they were taken from us, from their communities, to be chewed up in the machine's teeth. Then ... they were spat out – an empty husk, hoboes for us to nurse them. This makes us say it is time to begin controlling our creativity.

Black Consciousness sought to correct the Eurocentric assumption that literature could not exist without writing (an assumption which had led early ethnographers to ignore the role of orature in their accounts of African society). Black Consciousness realised the folly of ignoring the resources of orature in raising consciousness, transmitting values and re-integrating the African majority with their culture and history.

From Protest to Challenge in Recent African Fiction

Black Consciousness fiction, largely unheralded in the early days, suddenly came of age after Soweto. In the 1970s, the tradition of short fiction, one of the finest anywhere in the world, was preserved in the work of Ahmed Essop, Mtutuzeli Matshoba, Mothobi Mutloatse, Miriam Tlali, Achmat Dangor, and the finest practitioner of the craft yet to emerge, Njabulo Ndebele, winner of the 1984 Noma Award for his collection, *Fools and Other Stories*. A qualitative leap in fiction was made, however, with the emergence of the 'Soweto novel'. As the culture of liberation continued to unfold, the 1980s produced a radical shift in South African fiction from protest to revolt. It is a literature of empowerment. Now more than ever, the literature is concerned with the shifting balance of power.

The novel since Soweto is not just concerned with depicting the courageous acts of the youth, but with also reflecting the upsurge of guerrilla activities and revolutionary actions. In Mongane Serote's *To Every Birth Its Blood* and Sipho Sepamla's *A Ride on the Whirlwind* the revolt itself does not receive the comprehensive treatment that it does in the present author's *The Children of Soweto* and in Miriam Tlali's *Amandla*. Serote and Sepamla are more concerned with showing the links between revolt and the liberation movement, and the way these associations gradually fused into organised guerrilla struggle far beyond the usual character of 'riots'. We obtain from all these novels a comprehensive coverage of the nature, the character and the essence of the revolt. The sum total of the picture adds up to a documentation of African experience in the period.

The 'Soweto novel' has a structural complexity which its immediate predecessor lacks, as represented in Miriam Tlali's *Muriel at Metropolitan*, Ahmed Essop's *The Visitation* and Sipho Sepamla's *The Root is One*, and contains a number of innovations and modifications. In both character and situation there is a deliberate turn away from ambiguity and subtlety to direct confrontation and radical action. Events in the novels jump into one another; the numerous characters fuse and separate; the time sequence varies with each episode and point of view, so that the work becomes loose and variegated. These general assumptions are not absolute because each has its peculiarities. *The Children of Soweto* is a 'trilogy' only in the sense of an escalating crisis, but does not retain the same characters in all three parts. *To Every Birth Its Blood* begins with a linear plot, which suddenly becomes more complex as other characters and points of view come into prominence and the tempo of events is heightened. Subsequently, the political direction the events ultimately take and the development of the characters determine the structure of the novels. In other words, the Soweto novel is structurally situational.

There are no heroes, in the classical sense, in these novels. Although we meet flesh and blood characters with real desires and distinctive eccentricities, their individualism is submerged beneath the collective predicament. The epistemology of the individual gives way to the political ethics of the greatest good for the vast majority; the private world of the individual, without necessarily being desecrated, ceases to be as important to explore as public conduct and accountability in the arena of struggle. The effect is to downplay charismatic leadership and emphasise interdependence and organisation in which all have a role. The characters, however, are not stereotypes but credible individuals with different levels of personal integrity and intellectual insights. Nonetheless, their private lives are never allowed to cloud the collective predicament or to assert themselves too much over the collective aspirations of the communities in which they live. The community as a whole is the hero in these novels. Collective concerns triumph over purely personal aspirations. Thus the social environment itself, in as far as it determines our being and consciousness, becomes the central protagonist in the unfolding events.

Mike Kirkwood, former director of Ravan Press, the publishers who blazed the trail of liberation literature in South Africa, views the new writers as the story-tellers in orature come to life; he says that he finds it difficult as he reads their work not to see the authors in front of him:

> It is the polar opposite of James Joyce paring his fingernails behind the complete and self-sufficient art-work. The Soweto writers carry the function of the story-teller into the midst of the fractured lives of the prisoners of apartheid. They are the sympathetic listeners who tell the stories of others, but sometimes they will advise, and maybe at the crucial juncture they will act. They look for the continuities hidden under the oppressed face of the land. (Personal communication)

Their work, which raises several generic expectations, can fully be appreciated in the context of the unfolding culture of liberation in South Africa, especially as advanced by BC and the cultural renaissance it fostered.

Conclusion

Black Consciousness barely had a decade to organise and infiltrate the community before it was banned in 1977; and even before then, its leaders had been banned and restricted to their homes, banished to remote areas of the country, imprisoned on Robben Island, or exiled. Against the spate of repression unleashed by the state, its accomplishments were truly remarkable in creating the possibility of a black identity which ignored the apartheid definition of blacks and kept alive the spirit of resistance. Black Consciousness was counter-hegemonic in its thrust and set itself the task of counteracting the cultural imperialism that had sapped the spirit and being of the racially oppressed. Its tool was culture itself, understood by Black Consciousness proponents as the ensemble of meaningful practices and uniformities of behaviour through which self-defining groups within or across social classes express themselves, and as the process which informs the way meanings and definitions are socially constructed and historically transformed by the actors themselves. Black Consciousness quickly came to grips with the fact that cultures are distinguished from one another by their differing responses to the same social, material and environmental conditions; and that culture is not a static or even a necessarily coherent phenomenon but is subject to change, fragmentation and reformulation. Black Consciousness operated from an instinctive knowledge that culture is both adaptive, offering ways of coping and making sense, and strategic, capable of being mobilised for political, economic and social ends. Black Consciousness understood that just as culture can be oppressive, it can also be liberating. Such an understanding of the function of culture in society is necessary in our appreciation of the political importance of the cultural struggle which Black Consciousness writers and artists excelled in.

11

Steve Biko, Black Consciousness and Black Theology
DWIGHT HOPKINS

Steve Biko, martyred by apartheid, has left an enduring legacy to the struggle for a full and liberated humanity in South Africa. Indeed, Biko's historic bequest to the poor in his own country has profound lessons for those throughout the world who dare to make their marginalised voices heard over against oppressive principalities and powers. Though most noted for his insightful analyses of politics, race and cultural relations in South Africa, Biko also maintained definite views on theology. This chapter will elaborate Biko's developing positions on Black Consciousness and Black Theology in South Africa.

Biko was a 'theologian' from and with the masses of black people. He never became bogged down with strict doctrinal or theological categories of thought or elaborated long-winded treatises. Quite the opposite, as we will see, he involved himself in theological issues pertaining to the very life and death of his community. For him, experience of and talk about God arose from one's practical activities amongst the suffering victims of apartheid and their movement towards liberation. As he argued: 'Black theology therefore is a situational interpretation of Christianity. It seeks to relate the present-day black man to God within the given context of the black man's suffering and his attempts to get out of it' (1986:59). In short, Biko began to radically reinterpret old Christian concepts from the perspective of Black Consciousness.

Christian Churches in South Africa

It is no accident that Biko used the politics and culture of Black Consciousness to analyse the connection between apartheid and Christianity. In fact, the white church's understanding of black–white relations in South Africa had a great impact on the institutionalisation of the apartheid system. Specifically, the NGK (the largest of the three white Dutch Reformed churches) had already established the dynamics of apartheid within its own communion, prior to the National Party assuming state power in 1948, having created three subservient 'daughter' churches for Indians, Coloureds and Africans. The 'daughter' churches were segregated along racial lines in order to keep them apart from the white 'mother' NGK. When the National Party won power in 1948, the official NGK newspaper, *Die Kerkbode*, stated: 'As a church we have always worked purposefully for the separation of the races. In this regard apartheid can rightfully be called a church policy' (Villa-Vicencio, 1983). Thus, prior to the political establishment of apartheid on a nation-wide basis, there existed a white Christian theology with specific principles, policies, and practices. Furthermore, the NGK drew on a heretical interpretation of Scripture to sustain its racist internal divisions. For instance, in one of its official declarations, it claimed: 'Ethnic diversity [read 'apartheid'] is in its very origin in accordance with the will of God for this dispensation' (De Gruchy, 1979:71). And once the National Party put apartheid in place, the white church justified this racist system theoretically and theologically. The liberal English-speaking churches, too, though opposed to apartheid, were likewise guilty of discriminating against blacks and privileging whites within their own communions. Biko, as a result, knew that to attack apartheid politically and culturally, one also had to attack the white Christian churches theologically.

But from Biko's vantage point, however, black Christians could not wholeheartedly fight against the sins of the white church because they, in fact, had accepted and internalised white dogma. Biko commented: 'Because the white Christian missionary described black people as thieves, lazy, sex-hungry, etc., our black churches through our ministers see the vices of poverty, unemployment, overcrowding, lack of schooling and migratory labour, not as manifestations of the cruelty and injustice which we are subjected to by the white man, but inevitable proof that, after all, the white man was right when he described us as savages' (1986:57).

Hence the problem with the black churches was that they had uncritically swallowed the racist doctrines of white Christian missionaries. In particular, black churches embraced a false notion of sin as primarily drinking, smoking, stealing, etc. And by directing the attention of black Christians to these petty sins – what Biko termed 'petty morals' – white theology prevented them from comprehending a larger perspective on sin. In the South African reality, sin comprised a system of evil, a structural matrix in which whites lorded themselves above the black majority. Because black Christians regurgitated the confused notion of petty sins, and not the more correct appraisal of systemic and structural sins, they gave support to apartheid, instead of witnessing and struggling against it.

In addition to the corrosive presence of white theology in black churches, Biko also raised concern about the debilitating control of white Christian leadership. White Christians monopolised positions of leadership in the mainstream churches whose members were overwhelmingly black. Excluding the Dutch Reformed churches, Biko asserted, blacks comprised 70–90 per cent of lay persons, while at the same time 70–90 per cent of the leadership of these very same churches was white. Obviously, white leadership in the churches posed a fundamental problem for the masses of blacks struggling for justice and peace on earth. Just as the broader South African society discriminated against blacks and privileged whites, so did the churches mirror this repugnant, unchristian reality. The basic issue was one of authority, who controlled the resources, who made the decisions, who had power over worship and liturgy, and who defined the content and curriculum of religious education. Because of the teachings and practices of the white leadership, Biko concluded that the church had become 'extremely irrelevant'.

What Is to Be Done?

As an authentic 'theologian', one whose faith manifested itself in the struggle for social transformation and justice, Biko responded to the state of the church in South Africa in several ways. First, he believed that the black God had to speak in the black churches, and thus present the word of faith to all South Africa. 'If the white God has been doing the talking all along,' Biko wrote, 'at some stage the black God will have to raise His voice and make Himself heard over and above noises from His counterpart' (1986:30). To Biko, the Christian church in South Africa reflected the interests and practices of a demonic white God. This 'divinity' operated on the assumption of white superiority over black inferiority. Indeed, this white God had created white South Africans naturally and morally more advanced than the immoral and heathen black person. Furthermore, from the perspective of white Christians, this white God had 'divinely appointed' whites to lead blacks on earth (1986:24).

In contrast, the black God, the true Christian God, would realise God's will for justice through all those who struggled with the black majority for a full, God-ordained humanity. Black Consciousness, in Biko's theology, sought to provide a positive expression for the pains, suffering and anger of the black majority in order to realise God's will for liberation. Consequently, Black Consciousness – God's positive will to end apartheid and forge a new humanity – needed to replace white theology and a white God with black theology and the black God in the South African churches.

In one sense, Biko specifies the literal nature of God as black. In this manner, he criticises the cultural inferiority of blacks who fail to perceive an ebony divinity that looks like them. If the Christian God is black, then black people should be proud of their physical features, values and traditions. From a slightly different perspective, Biko also underscores the political nature of a black God. A black God speaks to the urgency of organising politically for revolutionary change against the evil structures of the racist, capitalist system which is apartheid. The will of the black God, the word of God, has to be heard anew both culturally and politically.

Second, for Biko, black theology (that is, Black Consciousness in Christianity) necessitated a new interpretation of the Bible. The white God proclaimed Christian Scripture to support the maintenance of apartheid. The white God employed the Bible as a weapon to keep black people down. For example, white Christians used Romans 13:1 ('Let every person be subject to the governing authorities. For there is no authority except from God, and those that exist have been instituted by God') to force the black majority to obey the apartheid state. The white leadership in the churches taught a biblical interpretation calling for adherence to all government laws regardless of the ethical consequences of right or wrong. Why? Because, in the image of the white God, all governments are ordained by God.

Not so! claimed Biko from his faith commitment and reading of the Bible. 'Obviously', he stated, 'the only path open for us now is to redefine the message in the Bible and to make it relevant to the struggling masses.' How would a new hermeneutic result? Biko replied: 'The Bible must not be seen to preach that all authority is divinely instituted. It must rather preach that it is a sin to allow oneself to be oppressed' (1986:31). Biko called for viewing Christian Scripture with new eyes, seeing the world through new lenses. To avoid a misleading understanding of Romans 13, Biko argued for coupling this scriptural reference with such passages as Revelations 13 (where evil 'beasts' can also claim authoritative legitimacy in the name of absolute power), Luke 4:18ff (where Jesus defines his singular mission for liberation of the oppressed), and Matthew 25:31ff (where Jesus grants eternal life only to those who concretely and materially aid the poor, the hungry, the homeless, the naked, the imprisoned). And so Biko challenged black Christians, and all Christian churches, to creatively craft a new biblical hermeneutic from the perspective of the poor in society. Christian scriptural tradition must tie spiritual salvation with systemic material freedom. 'This is', Biko believed, 'the message implicit in "black theology"' (1986:31).

Third, Biko spoke to the issue of God's relationship to the creation of black humanity. What does Black Consciousness have to say about who created black South Africans and how they were created? Were black South Africans an offspring of the apartheid system and its concomitant white theology, white God, and white interpretation of the Bible? Quite the contrary, Black Consciousness 'is a manifestation of a new realisation that by seeking to run away from themselves and to emulate the white man, blacks are insulting the intelligence of whoever created them black.' Here Biko suggests that no adherent of Black Consciousness and free humanity can achieve liberation by aping white values, language and culture, and still claim a created nature from God. Either whites created blacks (exemplified by those blacks whose way of life is more white than white) or the Creator fashioned black life. Biko continues on this theme of the black created nature: 'Black Consciousness ... takes cognizance of the deliberateness of God's plan in creating black people black' (1986:49). This indicates at least two highly subversive implications for South African Christians. Firstly, blacks need to realise and recognise that there exists an authority higher than white churches and white church leadership. If black Christians were to submit to such an interpretation of a higher divine authority, then they would be compelled not to prostrate themselves before the apartheid structures. Obviously, this has ramifications for Christian witness and action.

Does the higher authority mandate obedience to apartheid or overthrowing it?

Another subversive implication relates closely to the first. If God produced black humanity and not whites, then to be a black Christian means witnessing so as to fulfil God's intentional will for black humanity. In other words, black South Africans do not result from a whimsical accident of nature or an unconscious act on God's part. Instead, God moulded black humanity with the 'deliberateness of God's plan'. Therefore, in order to conform to God's will for black humanity, black Christians should live their lives fully and fight to create a new society on earth where they could be a free humanity, foreshadowing the liberated nature of God's kingdom. Accordingly, the movement for liberation offers a glimpse of the full reality of God's kingdom or just society to come. To know who your Creator is empowers you to fight false advocates of your creation.

Fourth, Steve Biko presented a radical re-imaging of Jesus. In his words, 'Black Theology seeks to depict Jesus as a fighting God who saw the exchange of Roman money – the oppressor's coinage – in His father's temple as so sacrilegious that it merited a violent reaction from Him – the Son of Man' (1986:31-2). Jesus was a militant fighter who dedicated his life to defending the interests of his 'father's temple'. God's spirit to uplift the poor and expropriate the rich possessed Jesus to such an extent that he deemed the rich money-changers as sacrilegious. Jesus felt compelled to use defensive force against those who violated the plight of the poor in his 'father's temple'. God's kingdom, embodied in Jesus, vilified and condemned the rich rulers' subjugation of the poor and weak, those without power.

For Biko, Jesus lived not like a passive sheep who turned the other cheek. No, Jesus lived on earth with deep concern for the wretched of the earth, even when this required him to defend his people. In the face of a fundamentally demonic system, Jesus chose sides in a militant, uncompromising way. Jesus opted for certain sectors of society. Biko relates: 'Here then we have the case for Black Theology ... it seeks to relate God and Christ once more to the black man and his daily problems' (1986:94). Confronted with the kingdom of evil, Biko discovered a fighting God in Jesus Christ whose mission sided with the daily tribulations of the black poor and the world's poor.

Fifth, Steve Biko answered the theological question: What does it mean to be human? He argued that South African Christians should incorporate lessons from African cultural and religious traditions into present-day Christian heritage. However, to be human in Western culture, in Biko's interpretation, meant being a cut-throat individualist who viewed the community as a stepping-stone to one's next level of personal accomplishment. Capitalism, the epitome of such a human configuration, fostered, encouraged and preached the survival of the fittest individual at the expense of the collective's survival and well-being. In contrast, Biko advocated that Christians accept traditional African religious values: 'We believe in the inherent goodness of man. We enjoy man for himself. We regard our living together not as an unfortunate mishap warranting endless competition among us but as a deliberate act of God to make us a community of brothers and sisters jointly involved in the quest for a composite answer to the varied problems of life.'

African traditions encouraged their adherents to revere the individual-in-community because neighbourliness resulted from a deliberate act of God. Therefore you exist because I exist, and the individual exists for the prosperity of the community. The community exists for the nurturing of individuals. 'Hence', Biko resumes, 'in all we do we always place man first and hence all our action is usually joint community-oriented action rather than the individualism which is the hallmark of the capitalist approach' (1986:42).

Furthermore, Biko's indictment of the 'capitalist approach' to collective human relations confirmed his black theological understanding of a political economy based on traditional African expectations. More explicitly, the very nature of capitalist political economics breeds an inherent exploitation of people. Here people relate to one another for the primary purpose of utility and not for communal activity. Thus Black Theology calls on the South African churches to alter their theological anthropology by rooting out capitalism. Theology is not unrelated to political and economic structures. On the contrary, a black theological understanding of what it is to be human materialises only in a society where capitalist social relations have been abolished.

Finally, Biko entertained the issue of who does theology? He began by criticising the 'tendency by Christians to make interpretation of religion a specialist job'. The doing of theology, therefore, is a vibrant process crafted not by 'erudite' academic scholars or the 'esoteric' knowledge of priests. Theology flows from the human struggle of people organising for life. Furthering his argument, Biko writes: 'Young people nowadays would like to feel that they can interpret Christianity and extract from it messages relevant to them and their situation without being stopped by orthodox limitations' (1986:58). Hence doing theology means that (a) black theology and all Christian theology come from below and not from above; (b) the masses of unlettered people, and not abstract systematisers, do theology; and (c) consequently, theology is a popular activity bubbling forth out of the variegated, creative culture and politics of the folk.

Steve Biko employed Black Consciousness in the realm of Christianity and honed a Black Theology for the liberation movement in South Africa. The ideas of Steve Biko shed a new perspective on Christian discourse and practice in his native land. During his life he called on black religious leaders within the struggle against apartheid to adopt a true understanding of authentic Christianity. 'It is the duty, therefore, of all black priests and ministers of religion to save Christianity by adopting Black Theology's approach and thereby once more uniting the black man with his God' (1986:94). To be called to the leadership of Christ's church required a witness in the tradition of Black Theology.

Moreover, not only did the limited presence of Black Theology in the churches retard Christian participation in the movement for justice, but the victory of the entire liberation process hinged on the existence of a black theological faith. Biko's insight shines with clarity when he categorically writes: 'No nation can win a battle without faith, and if our faith in our God is spoilt by our having to see Him through the eyes of the same people we are fighting against, then there obviously begins to be something wrong in that relationship' (1986:60).

Steve Biko grasped the pivotal role for Black Consciousness and Black Theology in attaining victory. Thus he grounded Christianity and the entire black community's quest for a true humanity in a visionary faith for the poor.

12

Revolution Within the Law?

N. BARNEY PITYANA

The South African justice system poses a dilemma for those concerned about human rights. That court proceedings bear all the hallmarks of proper and correct legal procedures as practised in any other civilised country in the world is well attested. Yet it is common knowledge that that system has administered some of the most repressive and racist legislation imaginable. In political cases investigation has been in the hands of an elite security police force effectively outside legal controls. The rule of law has been systematically eroded throughout the apartheid years. Yet South Africa continues to enjoy the reputation of having an impartial and independent judiciary. Many eminent international jurists, church dignitaries, human rights experts and scholars have expressed admiration for the legal procedures of the South African judicial system. An observer at the Biko inquest was Sir David Napley, then president of the Law Society of England and Wales. In his report he expressed admiration for the fairness and the correct procedures applied during the proceedings. An unjust political system seemed to be well served by an independent legal profession.

But there have been dissenting voices. Professor Charles-Albert Morand, of the Faculty of Law, University of Geneva, observed the trial of the SASO–BPC Nine at Pretoria in 1975 on behalf of the International Commission of Jurists. In his report, dated 16 December 1975, he said:

> The legal system of South Africa is characterised by the coexistence of two kinds of laws and procedures which are in strong contrast with each other. The criminal procedure governing public trials is largely governed by Anglo-Saxon traditions. It can be considered as perfectly correct from the point of view of the rights of the accused. On the other hand, the laws to be enforced are of an extreme severity in that they provide for very heavy penalties ... for activities which in states under the rule of law are considered as harmless and belonging to the sphere of political opinion or of free expression. The measures which can be taken in the phase of preliminary investigation, including detention without trial for an indefinite period and solitary confine-

ment for periods of several months, constitute typical violations of personal freedoms.

This is a perceptive comment. Its value is in seeing the processes of justice holistically; that investigation and trial have to be examined together in order to make a judgment about the justice or otherwise of the processes of law.

This chapter examines the contradictions inherent in any struggle for liberation within a repressive political system and a judicial system which serves that political system and yet regards itself as impartial, unaware of its limitations. Black Consciousness believed that radical political activity could still be undertaken within the constraints of the legal and political structures of apartheid. That could be done, it was felt, by pushing to the limit the bounds of possibility. It was a strategy that relied on the possibilities of mass conscientisation in order to confront and undermine the system. What it aspired to was no less than a revolution.[1] What it shared with other liberation movements was a commitment to radical change. Where it differed was in exploiting what it believed were possibilities as a prelude to more radical mass action. We shall analyse the adequacy or otherwise of this strategy for change. What are its achievements and what contributions has it made to the liberatory struggle in South Africa today?

The Structures of Injustice

Can there be a credible coexistence between an unjust legislative system and a just execution of the law? The underlying principle of government in South Africa is the sovereignty of the legislature. The judiciary is then subordinate to the legislature. Its interpretative functions and its role in the evolution of the body of law, are circumscribed. The judiciary and its preoccupations have been shielded from public scrutiny both by the phobia about security and by the resultant oppressive legislation. Given a policy of statutory intervention in the judicial process that operates to the extent that legislation reads like administrative instructions, judicial officers are in a sense reduced to mere administrative functionaries.

Few would deny that the judicial system in South Africa has served the interests of the apartheid state. If that is the case, then the Black Consciousness strategy should have taken account of the courts as part of an intricate web of injustice in society. Somehow, the Black Consciousness activists had some ambivalence about the implications of such a strategy. I have some vivid memories of law school where it was drummed into us that what was more fundamental was not 'rights' but duties, which were constructed on the basis of loyalty to the state. Universal principles like human rights and the rule of law were relativised.

In South Africa there has been a strong emphasis on the sovereignty of the legislative arm of government. This has given rise to an elaborate secu-

1 See Dr Sam Nolutshungu's analysis of the revolutionary claims of Black Consciousness in his book *Changing South Africa*.

rity machinery to enforce the wishes of the regime. That enforcement has also taken place through parliamentary commissions of enquiry like the Schlebusch and Eloff Commissions of the 1970s. Executive action has been just as easily resorted to, especially in such a way as to exclude the judicial process. As a unitary state South Africa has a strong central government. This leads inexorably to central control and the imposition of the diktat of government on all branches of the administration. There may be in principle a separation of powers, but the executive wields power and the legislature rubberstamps. This process has gone on for a long time because there has not been any credible opposition within the parliamentary system, and popular opposition has been ruthlessly suppressed.

The legal system is also very tightly controlled from the centre. While the judiciary is appointed after consultation with the Bar Councils, there has been persistent criticism of political appointments right from the time when the High Court of Parliament Bill was enacted in order to overturn the opinion of the highest court in the land.

The lower courts are served by civil servants employed as magistrates and prosecutors. In past years they have had to carry the great burden of political cases, and their powers of sentence have been increased. At the same time the burden on the Supreme Courts has increased and, hence, the work of reviewing the decisions of the magistrates' courts can only be done in a perfunctory manner.

In security-related cases, the security police have enjoyed wide powers of arrest and detention without trial. They could cause banning orders to be issued on the basis of reports they submitted to the Ministry of Justice; these reports were provided, invariably, by informers paid from the public purse to spy on others and to produce incriminating reports. Once people were banned, the security police considered themselves to have a right which overrode all other legal considerations, from invasion of privacy to gratuitous violence. Harassment and intimidation were their stock-in-trade tools of enforcement.

The government's predilection for security and law and order rather than justice and the due legal process can best be illustrated by reference to parliamentary debates. On 2 March 1973, the Minister of Justice banned eight leaders of NUSAS and eight leaders from Black Consciousness organisations. Six months earlier the prime minister had instituted a parliamentary commission of enquiry (called the Schlebusch, later the Le Grange, Commission). This Commission was to investigate the activities of certain organisations, among them NUSAS. On 27 February, the prime minister tabled the report in parliament. In it the Commission recommended the establishment of a permanent Commission on Security and, secondly, that urgent action be taken against certain student leaders. Amazingly, while the black student organisations were not under scrutiny (or certainly none that was admitted in parliament), their leaders were subjected to arbitrary action without even the excuse of an inquiry. No reference was made in parliament to the impending action against the leaders of SASO and BPC.

On 8 March, Mrs Helen Suzman obtained parliamentary time to discuss the bannings. She enquired as to why the black leaders and their organisations had not been referred to the Commission. In reply to an Opposition MP's statement that 'We believe that the foundation upon which the whole fabric of our society rests is in freedom, the dignity and integrity of the individual ... that freedom exercised within the law', the prime minister interjected: 'And the other side of the coin is the security of the state' (*Hansard*, Col. 2266). But there was consensus within parliament that law and order was supreme, even if there were differences about the extent to which the state could use arbitrary powers to enforce it. The Opposition, significantly enough, argued for the use of the courts to enforce 'law and order'. But the Minister of Justice refused the judicial option arguing that 'you cannot fight everything in the courts. There are other methods ... as long as we stay within the law ... we are taking preventative measures in regard to these so that worse things should not happen' (Col. 2270). Pressed further, the Minister gave the ultimate reply: 'It will give them a platform.' To which the Leader of the Opposition protested: 'A platform for what? Is it a platform to spread doctrines for which they can be punished?' (Col. 2274).

This turned out to be less a debate about civil liberties in South Africa and about the use of arbitrary executive action than about the appropriateness of one method of control over another. According to Steve Biko, what the Ministers were in fact saying was that they reserved the right to choose the moment to act. Explaining a banning order to Donald Woods, Steve Biko is reported to have said: 'It isn't a preventative measure. It's a way of punishing people the state cannot punish under normal law. Many of the banning restrictions are designed simply to inconvenience and exasperate' (Woods, 1978:83). Biko added that the banning orders were designed to criminalise ordinary human behaviour and to harass people.

The question of the independence and role of the judiciary in South Africa became a public issue when raised by the academic lawyers Professor A. S. Mathews and Dr Barend van Niekerk in the early 1970s. They argued that in a situation where human rights were consistently violated, judges had to be impartial. Arguing the case against the death penalty, Dr Van Niekerk took the argument further. He contended that the judges should refuse to enforce unjust laws. He was duly charged with incitement and, as per *S. v. Van Niekerk* (1972), the court ruled that it was unlawful to call on judges to refuse to enforce the law 'because this amounts to an exhortation to the judiciary to refuse to carry out its duty to apply the law'. Commenting on the implications of the judgment in an article in the *Sunday Times* (11 June 1972), Professor John Dugard of Witwatersrand University observed that 'It will come as a shock to a naturalist lawyer who contends that when a law sinks below a minimum standard of justice it should not be enforced on the ground that it ceased to be law.'

In the past thirty-five years South Africa has seen the erosion of the power and influence of the judiciary in favour of the executive. This ascendancy coincided with the period of the most intense repression in the history of the country, when apparently the executive entrusted the security of the state to the police and not to the judiciary. Moreover, 'the judiciary has assisted informally in its own loss of influence, particularly with respect to rights of detainees. Notwithstanding the extension of the powers of the executive, the higher courts have still maintained an ability to control executive excesses but ... generally tended to interpret such choices in favour of the state rather than of the individual's rights' (Foster, 1987:154).

Black Consciousness Falls Foul of the Law

There was a conviction within the Black Consciousness Movement that in the period after the banning of the major political movements, the ANC and PAC, oppositional political ground had been yielded to opportunists in the homelands, community councils and other government-created institutions as well as to white liberals, who arrogated to themselves the right to speak on behalf of the oppressed. In the face of widespread resignation and despair that nothing else was possible, Black Consciousness sought to demonstrate that in matters of liberation there are always possibilities. There was no glossing over the fact that risks had to be taken, but it was argued that risks could be taken within the law.

At the Pretoria SASO–BPC trial (1975–76) there was a strong defence line that Black Consciousness had never engaged in any subversive activity as a matter of conviction and strategy. Steve Biko, then honorary president of the Black People's Convention, appearing as a defence witness, stated that 'BPC operated within the law... It was non-violent... Confrontation would be self-destructive.' What that meant was that BPC had no programme of action that included violence as a method. It certainly did not mean that BPC was an organisation based on the principles of pacifism nor that under attack or provocation defence was not considered legitimate. What SASO and BPC had to contend with was the fact that a totalitarian system would not tolerate any challenges, let alone free thinking

But the reason that such naiveté could be sustained was the widespread belief that South African law did not proscribe thoughts but actions. Arguing for the dismissal of the prosecution's case, defence counsel Roy Allaway SC said that it was not illegal to seek to bring about a complete change in the constitutional structure of the country. 'The Terrorism Act', he argued, 'is aimed at violence, not words.' To express one's philosophy as 'an attitude of the mind, a way of life', as Black Consciousness did, did not, therefore, warrant the attention of the security police. The Pretoria judgment was to prove this assumption wrong.

The government was at first ambivalent about SASO. The new student organisation attacked the liberal establishment in the country and seemed, superficially at least, to echo some apartheid principles. Even as late as June 1972, government Ministers, while acknowledging that SASO was behind the widespread student uprisings on campuses up and down the country since the expulsion of Onkgopotse Tiro from the University of the

North (see *Hansard*, 5 June 1972, Cols. 8705-8716), would not take any action against SASO as an organisation. Rather than addressing 'the menace' caused by SASO, the Minister of Police was content to direct his ire at NUSAS: 'Of course, SASO is to a large extent behind the unrest amongst the nonwhite students...,' he told parliament. 'Although SASO had already intimated that it was an exclusively black organisation, NUSAS did everything in its power in an attempt to retain the favour of the nonwhite students as well,' he complained (Col. 8710).

Whilst the Ministers were taking that cautious approach, other agents of repression were already at work. Black activists were expelled from universities and colleges and victimised at work, mainly because of the interventions of the security police. Some were interrogated and the premises in which the affiliated organisations operated came under surveillance. Landlords were harassed by the police for harbouring subversive organisations. In 1972 serious questions were raised within SASO about its moderate policy, challenging the movement to a more confrontational style. Elements of the radical wing left in protest, joining the liberation movement and, once suitably trained, the ranks of the active combatants. When Mthuli Shezi, a former SRC president of the University of Zululand, was pushed in front of an oncoming train at Germiston in 1972, it was clear that the forces of repression were stepping up their campaign.

These developments posed a deep dilemma for a movement whose *raison d'être* was to press against the bounds of possibility within the law. That dilemma was resolved elliptically when 1973 ushered in an era of naked repression. It began, ominously enough, with the banning of eight leaders of Black Consciousness organisations on 2 March. In the months that followed there was a rapid turn of events: some activists were convicted of writing poetry which 'promoted feelings of racial hostility'; the highest-ranking official of BPC to be jailed was Mosibudi Mangena, the national organiser, who spent five years on Robben Island allegedly for incitement. Mapetla Mohapi was murdered while in police custody in East London in 1976. With the brutal murder of Steve Biko in police custody in 1977, the police overreached themselves, and the only option left for them was to ban the organisations. That they did on 19 October 1977.

Such a catalogue of repression did mean that the organisations and their members had to adjust to the new realities. But they refused to be defeated; instead they continued to live and work as fully as they dared, despite the legal constraints; testing, challenging and even redefining the rules of the state's deadly legal game. Personal coping mechanisms against the extensive detentions and widespread torture and violence became necessary. Strategies for sustaining organisational capacity in the face of police vigilance became essential. Yet during that time, Black Consciousness organisations continued to grow, and the leadership gained enormously in stature and popular respect. Many of those who were banned were never idle. They generally defied the banning orders or continued the principle of testing the limits of possibility. Besides covert political activities, many responded to community needs where they were living and provided leadership in places where they might otherwise have been occasional visitors. Community projects sprang up, providing much-needed jobs and local leadership. The period of bannings was a very creative one.

However, banning orders were but one aspect of the repressive machinery. Detention without trial became widespread. In the course of detention, many were severely assaulted and tortured. Simon Farisani, a former president of the BPC, Dean and Vice-Bishop of the Northern Province of the Lutheran Church, was detained three times. On all those occasions he was brutally treated. At one stage he says that he despaired of life and prayed what might have been his last words: 'Lord, ... if I must die, let it be; but one thing I ask of you, let not the hope for freedom die in my people. Amen' (1988:43). It seems that many comrades were emotionally sustained by their faith and a sense of humour. In reading Farisani's recollections both in his *Diary from a South African Prison* and in his subsequent book of poems *Justice in my Tears*, one is carried away by his sense of humour which enabled him to laugh at the foolishness of humanity. His commitment was never diminished.

Black Consciousness activists had to display this air of superiority: it thoroughly unnerved 'the system', because an encounter with a self-confident, articulate and fearless black person was not part of the police's experience. So, from time to time, it was proper to sit them down and give them a lecture about history, the law or politics. To demand that they produce a warrant – to search or to arrest – wasn't so much to give legitimacy to their operations as to buy time, assert one's authority or to maintain control of one's circumstances. Farisani was under arrest when he demanded a warrant. The security police treated his demand contemptuously: 'For a moment I gathered enough courage to use one of the few rights left to the black person ... the right to ask, "But you have not shown me your search warrants?"' Then he comments: 'Even to question, I discovered to my dismay, was not a right but a privilege, a white-given privilege. You are surely not pretending not to know us and our powers?' But, unperturbed, he soon had his own back. To the demand that he should open the door to his office, he handed them the keys and said: 'You yourselves open it. I have no need to go into the office. You have a need. That is your work, your job, your call. It's your mission, not mine. I am not opening. God forbid that I shall participate in the raid of a church office' (1987:20).

The refusal to be an accomplice in one's own oppression was also the motivating factor behind Mamphela Ramphele's dramatic return to King William's Town in 1976 from banishment in Tzaneen. After she had been delivered to her place of banishment, she discovered that the banning order contained material errors: her names were wrongly spelt and her identity number was wrong. So, after seeking legal advice, she decided that the banning order was invalid and drove back to King William's Town.

In his prison writings Antonio Gramsci emphasised the fact that activists have to be disciplined. That they should never seek martyrdom or undue

publicity by playing into the hands of their enemies, was a cardinal principle. And so he insisted on his legal rights in prison but 'would never do
anything that might cast the slightest doubt on his stance as an uncompromising and combative opponent' (Fiori, 1990:220). As if to underline this
point, Gramsci says in a letter to his mother: 'My morale is very high ... I
have no desire to be either a martyr or a hero. I believe I am simply an
average man who happens to have deeply rooted convictions, and I will
not give them up for anything in the world' (226). It can be said that
activists in South Africa had to learn to live by Gramsci's philosophy.

The SASO–BPC Trial, 1975–76

In this section I analyse the celebrated SASO–BPC trial, where it was
widely believed that Black Consciousness itself was on trial. This analysis
will amplify the operations of repressive 'justice' but will also help us to
examine the strategies of Black Consciousness within an obvious situation
of injustice, as appears in the evidence. Of particular interest for the purpose of this study is the testimony of Steve Biko. Biko was seen as
giving an authoritative view and vision of Black Consciousness. But I
intend to do more than just dwelling on past case history. By reference to
the trial of Antonio Gramsci I hope to set the struggles of the Black Consciousness militants in a more general context.

What is the function of the courts for the victims of a political system?
They expect neither fairness nor justice; they are not there by choice yet
they need to let their convictions be known. An understandable restraint,
however, is the fact that as accused, the activists are in a weak position.
They are not in control of their circumstances. How can the courts be made
to serve the cause of struggle? Biko made just this point in response to
Donald Woods: 'The verdict does not matter. The magistrate will white-
wash the Security Police. The system won't convict the system. But what
matters is the evidence – the facts must be published; the Security Police
methods must be exposed in public' (1978:89).

There are others as well who attach value to the legal process, not because
of what it hides but what can be said in public: banned people can be quoted,
the police can be interrogated in cross-examination, their sadism and foolishness exposed. What was a criminal trial becomes a political trial. Mandela
and his co-accused used the Rivonia Trial in a similar way as a platform for
expressing their political views, and for speaking to their followers and to the
international world outside the court. Biko's evidence at the SASO–BPC trial
reinforced this tradition. In spite of being in the dock he spoke from a position of strength, using history as his point of reference, and thereby brought
out the force and passion of what Black Consciousness was about.

> We certainly don't envisage failure. We certainly don't have an alterna-
> tive. We have analysed history ... the logical direction is that even-
> tually any white society in this country is going to have to accommo-
> date black thinking. We are mere agents in that history. There are

alternatives. On the one hand we have groups that are known in this country who have opted for another way of operation, who have opted for violence. We know that the ANC and PAC have done this, but we don't believe it is the only alternative. We believe there is a way of getting to where we want to go through peaceful means. And the very fact that we decided to form an aboveboard movement implies that we accepted certain legal limitations to our operations. We accepted that we were going to take this particular course. We know that the road to that particular truth is fraught with danger. Some of us get banned like I am. Others get arrested, like these men here. But inevitably the process drives towards what we believe history also drives to, an attainment of a situation where whites have to listen' (Woods, 1978:142).

Biko's bargaining from a position of strength, the Hegelian thesis–antithesis, was of special interest to the prosecution because the Hegelian principle was considered to be the centrepiece of revolutionary strategy. But court scenes are never the best places to propound philosophical statements of profound significance. Black Consciousness philosophy echoes the commonsense approach of Marxist social analysis. At the heart of the Black Consciousness strategy was what Gramsci called 'the acceptance by the ruled of a "conception of the world" which belongs to the rulers' (Fiori, 1990:238). But more significantly, Gramsci takes the Hegelian concept to its logical conclusion. The trouble with Biko's analysis is that he was inclined to stop at the Hegelian level. His historical analysis lacked the force of the Marxist historical materialism. Gramsci says, 'the antithesis has to posit itself as the radical antagonist of the thesis and tend towards its complete destruction in order to take its place. The synthesis is indeed the overcoming, the resolution of this conflict; but no one can say *a priori* what of the original thesis will be conserved in this synthesis' (1990:240). Some have said that Black Consciousness in praxis might have come out as much more of a revolutionary movement if this analysis had been incorporated into its strategy.

The SASO–BPC trialists went further than simply using the dock as a public platform: they challenged the very judicial process. Indeed, the SASO–BPC trial has taken its place in South Africa's legal history. The accused were described in press reports as militant and uncompromising. They sang and shouted, made Black Power salutes and resisted the orders of the police. There were several occasions when there were scuffles. It was obvious that this was a different brand of accused before the apartheid courts. Some would not plead to the charges as put and insisted on making statements instead of a plea. They were charged with conspiring to transform the state by unconstitutional, violent or revolutionary means; conspiring to condition the black people for violent revolution and conspiring to create feeling of hostility between the races. The judge interrupted Saths Cooper's statement, protesting that 'I don't want to know if this is a travesty of justice and the rest. I want to know whether you plead guilty or not guilty.' When the other accused persisted in making statements as well, the judge turned to defence counsel and threatened to curb the proceedings. Allaway replied: 'I have never faced a similar situation. But as I read the law, the accused are entitled to offer explanations about their attitude to the charges they face.'

Judge Boshoff accused defence counsel of hedging and time-wasting. He made a point of interrupting their cross-examination of witnesses and he would not allow counsel to lead evidence on the treatment the accused received while in police custody. For him, once the police had denied the accusations, there was no point in persisting with that line of questioning. It is no wonder then that the judge was accused of bias by the accused. But their application for him to recuse himself was refused.

Although the accused never expected any justice from the court, they appeared to be satisfied that they were able to make a political demonstration. The security police produced a letter in court written by Saths Cooper, one of the accused, to friends in the Black Allied Workers' Union in Durban. The letter was written while Cooper was on trial. It read: 'On our second court appearance we shook the daylights out of the system by our attitude and conduct.'

In South Africa, how can a state whose policies arouse racial hatred through apartheid then charge the victims with propagating racial hostility? How can a system that perpetrates violence judge the victims who take defensive action? That was the challenge which caused the court some discomfort. But the questions do not address the deeper issue about the structural relations of dominance and exclusion which apartheid imposes.

Gramsci and his comrades appeared before a Special Tribunal for the Defence of the State. This was to be a show-trial which, according to Gramsci's biographer Giuseppe Fiori, was 'framed by every sort of Fascist pomp and circumstance' (1990:229). Gramsci admitted his activities within the Communist Party, but he averred that these were open and in the exercise of his public duty as a deputy. But, he went on, 'All dictatorships of a military sort end sooner or later by being overthrown in war.' When the prosecutor kept interrupting his statement, he shouted back at him: 'You will lead Italy to ruin, then it is we communists who will have to save her' (230). But it was Terracini, Gramsci's co-accused, who made a statement on behalf of all the accused just before sentence was passed. In delivering it he was interrupted by the president of the court who wanted to stop him. At one stage the president said: 'Leave politics out of this, keep to the substance of the matter in hand.' Terracini concluded: 'Your Honour, it is a political forecast which I would like to make: we are about to be found guilty and condemned for exciting class hatred and inciting civil war. But tomorrow, nobody who reads the list of ferocious sentences waiting to be delivered will see these proceedings as other than an episode of civil war and a formidable act of incitement to hatred among social classes' (232). The parallels with the SASO–BPC trial in Pretoria are all too obvious. The social context is not dissimilar.

Mr Justice Boshoff, delivering a lengthy and closely argued judgment, found all accused guilty on the alternative charges of conspiracy to cause feelings of racial hatred. He ruled that Black Consciousness was not a revolutionary doctrine. Commentators thought that the judgment determined the parameters of legitimate political activity. The judge maintained that 'In our country we have democratic norms, and freedom of speech and assembly play an important part in our party system, which is based on opposing views and consequent dispute of ideas.'

The judge then refused a defence application for leave to appeal, arguing that 'I am not satisfied that there is a reasonable prospect that the court of appeal would take a different view...' The same judge also turned down another application for 'special entry' on the basis of administrative irregularities in his conduct of the case. He considered this application as 'not made in good faith and was frivolous and absurd'. How does it come about that the same judge was expected to judge against himself?

Confident as the judge was that he could not have erred in his judgment, there are suggestions that other courts of equal status might have come to a different decision. In two cases on Section 1 of the General Law Amendment Act 94 of 1974 (the clause is also enshrined in the Terrorism Act), the question of intention in political cases was refined. The first one was a Natal case (*S. v. Kubheka*, 1974(3) 443) where Mr Justice Leon found that 'for the state to succeed in a prosecution of this kind, it is not sufficient to show that the appellants possessed a constructive intention to promote feelings of hostility, but it was necessary for the state to go further and show that the appellants possessed the actual intention of promoting such hostility'.

And in a case subsequent to the Pretoria judgment, that of *S. v. Mbilini and Others* 1978(3), the court ruled that 'it is not an offence under the section to do an act which is calculated to or does cause hostility between different race groups unless it is proved that there was also the intention to cause or promote such hostility'. On the nature of the intention required, Mr Justice Addleson had this to say:

> While it must be proved that the accused had the required intent, such intent need not be his principal or only aim in publishing the statements in question. Where the enquiry as to his intention is based on the necessary inferences to be drawn from the contents of the publication, a court must bear in mind that the main contention may, on the one hand, negate any further intention to promote feelings of hostility while, on the other hand, the principal intention may be such that it can only be achieved by promoting such feelings of hostility. Between these two extremes will often lie situations where it is the intention of the accused to promote feelings of hostility as well as to achieve some other aim. In every case where there is no evidence of his state of mind, the test still remains whether it is a necessary inference from the contents of the publication that the accused intended to arouse feelings of hostility between two groups.

My contention is simply that Judge Boshoff should have allowed for the possibility that another court might have found differently from him. Secondly, he might have said that to have had to make a finding on the basis of circumstantial evidence, another opinion should have been sought to test his inferences.

Conclusions

Since 2 February 1990, of course, South Africa has been promoting itself as a reformist state. The government under State President F. W. de Klerk is committed to putting behind its apartheid past. Thus a programme for the release of political prisoners and the return of exiles is under way; the process of negotiating a future constitution is in the offing while talks about the removal of obstacles to negotiations are in process between the government and the African National Congress. The government's Law Commission has been outlining principles for the administration of justice in a democratic South Africa, including human rights and the rule of law, a bill of rights and all forms of civil liberties. In his 1 February 1991 address to parliament, De Klerk went further than previously and called on the nation to affirm certain basic common principles.

Should these developments be sustained, and especially if they should be enshrined in any future constitution, then South Africa can joyfully put behind its shameful past. Those who will work on a new constitution need to ensure that there is a genuine separation of powers; that the power of the executive is limited; that the repressive security laws, a legacy of apartheid, are repealed; that the police be decentralised and accountable to locally elected political leadership. Should these provisions be enacted, they would go a long way towards restoring confidence in the system of justice in a democratic South Africa.

The lesson from the experience of the Black Consciousness Movement, therefore, has to be that no authentic revolutionary struggle, even in the qualified sense that BC stalwarts gave to the term, can take place without risking contravention of the law. If this had been built into the strategy of the movement, then the conduct of its liberatory activities might have taken a different shape. In this, Black Consciousness displayed a naiveté and innocence born out of an inadequate theoretical basis for its political activities. Black Consciousness, as such, was not a political philosophy or ideology but a strategy for action. Having said that, it must be conceded that once the apartheid system declared that it would do everything to destroy Black Consciousness, BC activists developed a capacity to make political statements through challenges and responses to the legal constraints under which they were bound. By learning through experience, Black Consciousness has given South Africa a legacy of political sophistication, community organising and sacrifice which soon became necessary qualities in the political turmoil of the era immediately subsequent to the banning of the BC organisations on 19 October 1977.

PART FOUR

13

The Dynamics of Gender Within Black Consciousness Organisations:
A Personal View
MAMPHELA RAMPHELE

Personal accounts of journeys on life's path have often been used to examine issues which are close to the bone for individuals, groups, and even
nations. A number of survivors of Nazi concentration camps and Stalin's
gulags have enriched humanity by telling their stories as they were – ordinary human experiences of suffering, pain and joy – without the masks of
ideological positions.

I have chosen a similar approach to deal with issues of gender within the
Black Consciousness fold, where I cut my political teeth in the late 1960s
and early 1970s. I shall present my personal account of a journey which has
led to my political and social growth as an individual, as a way of
analysing the politics of gender within the wider liberation movement, of
which the Black Consciousness thrust was only a part.

Major themes in the analysis will include the debate around the importance of gender, in addition to race and class, as a differential of power. I
will also deal in general with the constraints on the participation of women
in public and political processes in general, and in particular their under-
representation in leadership roles. Finally, I comment upon the practice of
sexism within liberation organisations, and its specific manifestation within
BC organisations.

Women and Black Consciousness

I was introduced to student politics by Vuyelwa Mashalaba, an attractive,
articulate, and confident woman who was in her second year at the University of Natal Medical School in 1968. I had joined her class as a new arrival
at the school earlier that year, having done my pre-medical courses at the
University College of the North. We also shared the same residential block
in Alan Taylor Residence and became close friends.

Student politics on campus at that time were dominated by male students, with Steve Biko as one of the leading lights. We attended many
meetings on campus where the need for a Black Consciousness approach
was debated and articulated eloquently. Vuyelwa was the only woman

who participated in those debates, while the rest of us watched silently though with interest.

The thrust of the emergent Black Consciousness politics was on the need of the oppressed, defined as those not classified as 'white', to liberate themselves from the oppressor, defined as those classified 'white' (Biko, 1986:48-53). Central to this approach was an understanding of racism as the dividing line between South Africans, as well as the barrier to access by those not 'white' to the country's resources. Women were thus involved in the movement because they were black. Gender as a political issue was not raised at all.

The socio-demography of women attracted to the BC philosophy in its initial stages shaped in an important way the nature of their participation and the impact they had on gender dynamics within the movement. In the early period, 1969–1977, most adherents were university students: their preponderance was an inevitable result of BC having started as a student movement. It was university students who formulated, articulated and popularised the Black Consciousness philosophy. It could be argued that it was our privileged position in society which gave us the space to play this important role. Experiences in other countries, such as Guinea-Bissau, also provide evidence of the tendency for intellectuals to play historically significant roles in initiating and articulating shifts in the perceptions of oppressed people (see Cabral, 1973).

A second feature of the early participants in BCM activities was the predominance of medical students, due mainly to Steve Biko's own location at Natal Medical School. It could also be argued that there was greater political space for black students at the University of Natal than at the 'ethnic' university colleges, which were under closer control by the government and where the risks attached to political involvement by black students were perceived to be greater than at Natal (see Biko, 1986:6-7). Medical students could thus be seen as representing an elite within a relatively privileged category of blacks.

High-school students and township youth groups became involved in the movement as Black Consciousness spread outside the universities. Their involvement resulted in the formation of the South African Students' Movement (SASM) and the National Youth Organisation (NAYO), with local, regional and provincial formations. These organisations were the direct outcome of a leadership training campaign by SASO and the Black Community Programmes (BCP) between 1971 and 1973. Those involved were predominantly urban-based young people.

A third category of women participants comprised professionals: nurses, particularly in the Natal region, social workers, teachers, ministers' wives (the women's wing of the Inter-Denominational African Ministers' Association of South Africa), medical doctors and so on. The involvement of professional women was at its peak in the years 1973–77. Professionals got involved both in their individual capacities and through membership of associations which identified themselves with the BCM.

Ordinary women became involved through a number of routes: firstly, as participants in community projects run by BC operatives, such as health care and literacy projects, and secondly, as members of self-help groups like Zenzele, Parent–Teacher Associations and YWCA, which had some sympathies with the BC. Thirdly, women became involved by association with their male 'significant others', as wives, girlfriends, sisters, mothers and aunts. A strong urban bias within the BCM persisted even at this stage, except in those rural areas where development projects were in progress.

The recognition by the BC leadership that a greater effort needed to be made to mobilise women's active participation led to the launching of the Black Women's Federation (BWF) in Durban in December 1975. The BWF acted as a national umbrella body for organisations of women from all walks of life. A total of 210 women attended the launching conference (see *Black Review*, 1975–76:109). People such as Fatima Meer, Winnie Mandela, Deborah Matshoba, Nomsisi Kraai, Oshadi Phakathi, Jeanne Noel and other prominent mature women from established groups such as YWCA, Zenzele and church bodies were key participants in this conference.

The thrust of the BWF reflected its aim of mobilising women as a political force in the process of liberation. This commitment was encapsulated in the expressed need for a united front 'to redirect the status of motherhood towards the fulfilment of black people's social, cultural, economic and political aspirations' (*Black Review*, 1975–76:109). There is no evidence to suggest that the BWF was concerned with the special problems women experienced as a result of sexism both in the private and in the public sphere. Women were important as wives, mothers, girlfriends and sisters, in fighting a common struggle against a common enemy – namely, white racism. Scant regard was given to their position as individuals in their own right.

Generally speaking, black women in leadership positions in the early 1970s tended to be courageous, articulate people, who took on a host of responsibilities. They had to face the problem of resistance to their active participation by their 'significant others' at home, as well as the danger of taking on a repressive political system and government. This was brought rudely home when most of the women named above who participated in launching of the BWF were detained in the crackdown of 1976 (see *Black Review*, 1975–76:109).

Yet it must also be acknowledged that where women of ability made themselves available for leadership and other meaningful roles, they made important contributions and were accepted fully as colleagues by men. For, example, Mrs M. Kgware, the first president of the Black People's Convention (BPC), was treated with respect by all. Her maturity and ability to reach out to both young and old were particularly appreciated.

Though women's involvement in the BCM was largely limited to urban, young and relatively privileged people, the massive crackdown of 1976–79 forced many women who had hitherto stayed out of active political life, to reassess their positions in the light of the loss of life, detentions and threats of further action. Very few black people, especially in the urban areas, were left personally unaffected by the government's repression.

In general, the BC Movement had a significantly positive impact on black women in South Africa. The assertion that 'Black is Beautiful' spoke to many blacks, whose self-doubt and depreciation of their blackness had dominated their lives. Black women, like women all over the world, are subject to scrutiny by society, which seeks to define their body image (see Brittan & Maynard, 1984). The assertion that 'Black is Beautiful' liberated black women from being defined in terms dictated by the dominant white culture.

For the first time many black women could fall in love with their dark complexions, kinky hair, bulging hips and particular dress style. They found new pride in themselves as they were. They were no longer 'nonwhites', but blacks with an authentic self, appreciated on their own terms. The skin-lightening creams, hot-oil combs, wigs and other trappings of the earlier period lost their grip on many women.

The reconstruction of blacks 'in their own image', as it were, permeated all levels of society and had a decided impact on the new-found positive self-image amongst blacks. At a more particular level, it could be argued that black women within BC ranks benefited as people, because they also became more liberated as individuals. Having experienced being assertive as blacks, women claimed greater psychological space in which to assert themselves in both public and personal relationships. Black women also benefited from the intellectual stimulation they received in the course of their activism.

Sadly, this impact did not penetrate all strata of society. Those in rural areas, the poor and those in the Western Cape exposed to the extra burdens of the Coloured Labour Preference policy which privileged 'coloureds' above 'Africans', remain vulnerable to an inferiority complex. The material benefits of being 'slightly coloured', compared to being proudly African, are too real for those at the lower socio-economic strata to ignore.

A Personal Journey

Initiation into a 'Man's World'

My involvement deepened after SASO was launched in 1969 at a conference held at the University College of the North, where Steve Biko was elected its first president. Vuyelwa Mashalaba, Thembi Nkabinde (née Sibisi) from the University College of Zululand, and Manana Kgware were the only women participants at that conference. I got to know Steve Biko well during that year, having been introduced to him by Vuyelwa Mashalaba. As my interest in SASO grew, so too did my participation in student politics increase.

It became clear to me then that my participation in student politics required self-confidence, eloquence and dedication to endless meetings and discussions. I found myself wanting at all those levels, and decided to confine myself to playing a supportive role to those in the forefront.

A combination of closer relationships with SASO activists and the effectiveness of leadership-training workshops ('formation schools') increased my self-confidence and skills as a public speaker by the end of 1969. It was an informal process of capacity-building within a network of friendships and a comradeship which merged work and play. I also read a lot of the literature which was circulating secretly within a circle of friends; this expanded my own horizons and helped me examine social relations in a challenging manner. Fanon, Césaire, the Black Panthers, Martin Luther King and Malcolm X were the popular authors, orators and heroes of the time.

The socialisation I underwent at that time also included learning to survive in a male-dominated environment without falling prey to it. One had to be able to stand up to intimidation by men who were used to having their way. The following incident indicates some of the problem areas.

Disaffiliation from the largely white National Union of South African Students (NUSAS) was a hotly debated issue on Natal Medical campus. Ben Ngubane, a respected senior student leader, had been the most formidable opponent of such a move. He thus felt personally defeated when the motion of disaffiliation was finally carried at the University of Natal (Black Section). I put my foot in it by making reference to the motion during a social evening. He promptly told me to shut up, because I understood little about politics, and that he would not tolerate any disrespect from little girls like me. What a shock! Steve Biko defused the situation in some way, but the basic issue of little girls challenging seniors was left unchallenged.

I soon learnt to be aggressive towards men who undermined women, both at the social and at the political levels. Socially one had to cope with being regarded as available to men, because one was single. One was also constantly told and reminded that one was an exception to the male assumption that beauty and brains do not combine. One fell prey to the flattery implicit in such remarks and began to see oneself as being different from other women.

A major part of the process of being socialised into activist ranks was becoming 'one of the boys'. Late nights, alcohol consumption and smoking became part of life. An interesting aspect of this lifestyle was that the same men one socialised with took a dim view of women being seen doing the same things as them publicly, particularly smoking. This disapproval also had a pragmatic side in a social milieu which was highly intolerant of women smoking in public. The following incident illustrates the point.

Fort Hare had been a very difficult campus to get on board the SASO ship, because of its history of non-racial politics and the divisions among students around the issue of whether or not to compromise on the request by the university authorities that the SRC constitution gain its approval. Barney Pityana and Steve Biko did a lot of preparatory work and finally shifted opinion-makers towards accepting the launch of a local SASO branch. Vuyelwa Mashalaba, a member of the SASO national executive committee, was sent to address the student body in preparation for the launch. Her public smoking during the meeting left the students horrified! How could they be associated with an organisation that had such women in leadership positions? It took some skilful smoothing of ruffled feathers by Pityana to get the launch back on track.

One has thus to judge BC male activists as products of their environment. They had to be sensitive to the feelings of people on a wide range of issues, including sexism, if they were to influence public opinion.

There was an interesting disjuncture between the genuine comradeship one experienced within the movement, and the sexism which reared its head at many levels. For example, the responsibility for catering, cleaning-up and other entertainment functions tended to fall on women participants, be it at national conferences, formation schools, workshops or elsewhere. In those cases where the top leadership was sensitive to gender discrimination and allocated duties regardless of gender, males feigned incompetence, and women would then have to take over the entire nurturing responsibility, thus positively reinforcing the feigned incompetence of the men. On one occasion when Barney Pityana and I were responsible for a formation school, we confronted the men and insisted on their rightful share in domestic chores. But in general, sexist practices and division of labour along gender lines were never systematically challenged within Black Consciousness ranks.

Interestingly enough, Desmond Tutu, then recently appointed general secretary of the South African Council of Churches, remarked during a visit to Zanempilo Community Health Centre on the absurdity of holding on to notions of traditional gender roles. A lively debate followed after supper, with Tutu relating his experiences in London and the joy of participating in all the domestic chores, including nappy washing! That was a difficult one to swallow for a community so used to traditional gender roles. He had few, if any, converts by the time he left the following morning.

It was not just a matter of men being reluctant to share in domestic chores; we as women activists were also uncomfortable about fundamental change in stereotypical gender roles. I remember arguing one day with Father Aelred Stubbs, a member of the Community of Resurrection who used to visit Zanempilo quite often to see Steve Biko, about his insistence on helping me wash up after supper. Although I resented the fact that my peers would not lend me a hand, I felt uncomfortable about a man nearly old enough to be my father, washing up with me. It was as if I was being disrespectful towards him by allowing him to help me. But he just pressed on regardless of my protests.

Honorary Male Status

Over time women evolved survival strategies in the male-dominated political sphere. I was one of a group of women within the Black Consciousness ranks who became assertive, to the point of arrogance. We learnt to be tough, insistent, persistent and to hold our own in public and private debates. At the 1972 SASO conference in Hammanskraal three of us made our mark: Nomsisi Kraai, Deborah Matshoba and myself. We overcame the trivialisation of our concerns by male colleagues and broke the monopoly over the interpretation of standing rules and procedures of meetings, and thus entered the world of political discourse which had been until then inaccessible to us.

An interesting symbolic manifestation of our new-found liberty was our disregard of hitherto important taboos: women were not permitted to smoke in public, or participate in parties where alcohol was drunk and political discussions took place. These parties dragged on into the small hours of the morning. We also freed ourselves from the stigma attached to meaningful platonic relationships with male colleagues, without being seen as 'available'. We strove to prove that we were as good as any man in as far as that was biologically possible.

It was thus inevitable that we were treated as, and accepted the role of, honorary men. We had, after all, entered the domain generally regarded as the preserve of men and were treated accordingly. We also saw ourselves as exceptions to the rules governing conventional gender relationships. We were thus in a similar position to other women in history, such as Simone de Beauvoir, Rosa Luxemburg, women fighting wars of liberation as active combatants, and many others (see also Koestler, 1964). Roger, describing the position of women such as ourselves in the House of Commons, refers to them as 'matter out of space' (Roger, 1981). It is not infrequent for such women not only to revere their unique positions, but in some ways to look down upon those women filling traditional roles. We, too, looked down upon women who played traditional roles within activist ranks as well as more widely within the student world.

The honorary male status came with special benefits, such as the ability to say 'no' to men's demands for catering services during meetings, which often led to one missing out on important discussions; and the right to break taboos, such as deference to men in regard to preferential seating arrangements and special privileges with regard to food, particularly meat, of which men tend to be given liberal portions of the best cuts. An example of this was the custom of excluding women from the communal eating of delicacies such as stewed sheep's head and trotters. This exclusion bore no relation to the cash contributions women made towards buying the slaughtered sheep. At the Zanempilo Health Centre, where I was the medical officer in charge, I confronted the men who objected to my participation in communal eating, by saying that the only remedy they had was to withdraw to protect their honour, because I was determined to exercise my right to participate. The men relented.

It should, however, be noted that these challenges to male privilege did not represent a systematic departure from traditional gender relationships, but only served to undermine this tradition for the benefit of those who were prepared to take risks in challenging sexism at a personal level. Interpersonal relationships remained largely unchanged, with the man as the dominant partner, and many women remained trapped in unsatisfactory relationships that violated their dignity as people.

Feminism, which was then sweeping through the USA, had very little impact within BC ranks or on my own personal journey at that stage. This was partly because of lack of access to the relevant literature, on account of censorship, but also because feminism was seen as irrelevant to the needs of blacks in South Africa. The feminist movement was dismissed as a 'bra-burning' indulgence of bored, rich white Americans. My own path towards liberation as a woman would take a different route.

Tensions and Ambivalences

My appointment in 1975 as the medical officer in charge of Zanempilo Community Health Centre in Zinyoka, outside King William's Town, enhanced my honorary male status. Medical professionals wield enormous power in most societies. There was also the added scarcity value in being a medical officer in a population where few blacks, let alone black women, ever attain such qualifications. I also derived power from control over the health centre as a resource for activists. This power increased with my appointment as BPC regional director at the beginning of 1976.

My position of power was particularly useful in dealing with security police. In spite of themselves, they showed deference to my status as a medical doctor. When I admitted Steve Biko to Zanempilo Health Centre for pneumonia at the beginning of 1976, they resented the fact that they could not keep an eye on him in the protected environment of the clinic, and moreover could do nothing about it. Captain Schoeman was to have his own come-back in April 1977 when he served a banishment order on me and packed me off to Tzaneen in the northern Transvaal. His parting shot was, 'Goodbye, Dr Ramphele, you bitch!'

Other people also responded to me as an unusual phenomenon. Donald Woods, then editor of the *Daily Dispatch* in East London, describes our first meeting thus: 'I was unprepared for the attractive young black woman in blue jeans and a white sweater who strode aggressively into the office and introduced herself in a loud voice as Dr Ramphele' (Woods, 1980:251). The perception of aggressiveness has to be placed in the context of his own admission that he had expected 'an Uncle Tom figure to walk deferentially into my office' (Woods, 1980:251). I was so different from what he expected me to be like, and my questioning of his wisdom in ignoring Black Consciousness leaders and their viewpoints in his newspaper was such a fundamental challenge to his world-view, that it is no wonder that he depicted me as 'the kgokgo'[1] he had always feared.

In spite of all this power, there were many ambivalences about control of the Zanempilo Centre and lines of authority and responsibility. Steve Biko

---

1 A word used in many African languages to depict a mythical fearsome creature which attacks disobedient children.

remained a leader within BCP and of the community of activists even though he had no official position, a situation I accepted with relief because I was already overloaded with my health-care responsibilities. I saw myself as a caretaker director, and expected Biko to continue to play an active role in coordinating the non-health programmes of BCP.

It should also be borne in mind that the authority structure within BCP was participatory and thus no strict hierarchies existed. The benefits of such a structure were numerous, and the sharing of responsibility was real. There were, however, the practicalities such as the need to curb spending and to keep within the limited means afforded by our small budget, and to submit regular reports to head-office, which someone had to take responsibility for.

Ambivalences arising from blurred lines of authority and responsibility created tensions at times. For instance, there was an assumption that I was to be protected from knowledge about certain activities deemed to be sensitive by Biko.[2] These related to his efforts to facilitate greater unity in the liberation struggle, particularly bringing the ANC and PAC closer together. For example, I would expect staff members to prepare and present reports at regional board meetings, only to discover on the morning of the meeting that a head of a section had been sent by Biko on a mission to another part of the country. My irritation was not only on account of the disruption of meetings, but also the effect this lack of consultation had on undermining my ability to function as an effective director.

There was also an interesting tendency for some women colleagues to undermine my authority. This was particularly problematic in the Transkei area before the Rev. M. Xundu took office as regional director. Mrs N. Ndamse, old enough to be my mother, found it difficult to accept my authority. Tensions were heightened around matters requiring political judgment, because of our disparate political views on the status of Transkei as an 'independent' state. The problem of women undermining other women has been identified as one of the barriers to fundamental change in gender relationships. In the health sphere in particular, nurses have been found in some studies to respond more to doctors' orders issued by men than by women (Boston Women's Collective, 1984). Fortunately in my case, the nurses I worked with were marvellous in cooperating with me in running Zanempilo Community Centre efficiently.

Daring to Travel the Risky Path

Suffering is like fire; one either gets consumed or strengthened by it.[3] The repression following June 1976, and the subsequent banning of all organi-

2 Steve Biko was motivated to protect me by a number of considerations: the centrality of my role in ensuring continuity of BCP projects; the fact that I was a woman and therefore vulnerable in a situation of torture designed to extract information; and also that it made sense to limit the number of people involved in such sensitive activities to a minimum.

3 I am indebted to Francis Wilson for this metaphor.

sations connected with Black Consciousness, sent hundreds of activists into exile and scattered our community in King William's Town. The new and varied environments in which each one found herself or himself either helped to nurture our growth into a deeper understanding of ourselves and our social relations, or increased our sense of insecurity to a level where further growth failed to occur.

New social environments facilitated the renegotiation of many personal relationships. The absence of kin, of in-laws in particular, enabled many exiled couples to rethink their marriage commitments, renegotiate domestic responsibilities without the support provided by domestic helpers in South Africa, and in some cases to discuss sexuality in ways they had never thought possible. Exposure to different models of domestic politics in European and other countries also had a significant impact on the personal growth of some exiles. For example, Barney and Dimza Pityana have evolved a lifestyle which is radically different from the one they had prior to their exile in Britain. Thus, for some people exile has provided space for more egalitarian gender relationships to emerge.

For those activists who ended up in exile communities, little space was provided for growth. Exile communities in Tanzania, Zambia and elsewhere in Africa seem to have been constrained by gender and other entrenched stereotypes which the South African exiles brought with them from their home environments. Their dependence on and need to remain within the supportive fold of such communities prevented many from taking risks to break with tradition.

My own 'exile', under a banishment order, in Tzaneen forced me to grow. I had to wean myself from dependency on a warm supportive community, and learn to think and act as an individual. I also had to learn to live without the security of my friendship with Steve Biko, who had become a pillar in my life. Exposure to the hardships of rural women in Tzaneen, fighting a constant battle for the survival of my soul in an intellectually desolate environment, walking the tightrope of breaking my banning order without being caught, coping with security policemen who both hated and feared me, bringing up two beloved sons as a single parent, and exposure to feminist literature, all contributed to my growth into the person I am now. Fear, pain, loneliness and joyful moments were all part of the process of growth.

Continuities: Past and Present

There are important continuities and discontinuities with respect to the issue of gender within the broad South African liberation movement, between the periods before and after 1976. Such changes as have occurred, or failed to occur, have important implications for the dynamics of gender in the present and the future South Africa.

The experiences and the position of women in the Congress movement have been documented in several books (see for example, Walker, 1982;

Kimble, 1972; Qunta, 1987; Joseph, 1986; Russell, 1990). The common theme in all these accounts is the fact that women fought, and continue to fight, 'side by side' with their men in the struggle for liberation. All these studies recognise the multiple oppression suffered by black women, some referring to it as 'the triple oppression' (Kimble, 1972), through Qunta argues that it is 'the quadruple oppression': race, class, gender and national oppression resulting from colonisation (1987:98).

Congress politics was characterised, firstly, by male dominance in the leadership ranks, although a few exceptional women featured at this level, such as Lilian Ngoyi, Dora Tamana and Helen Joseph (see Joseph, 1986; Walker, 1982). Secondly, participation by women was focussed on membership of women's organisations such as the ANC Women's League and the Federation of South African Women (FEDSAW). These organisations saw their role as that of mobilising women for the national struggle against racial discrimination. Little or no energy was directed at concerns about women's rights as persons.

Thirdly, women's participation was seen more in terms of the extension of their role as mothers, wives and 'significant others' of their male colleagues rather than in their capacity as individual citizens. This was in part the result of the respect women themselves had for 'tradition', which acknowledged the primary role of the man in the patriarchal, patrilineal and patrilocal system that underpins most gender relations in South Africa (see Ramphele & Boonzaier, 1988:154).

The only area where women participated as individuals was in the field of trade-union politics (see Walker, 1982). But even here, male dominance in the coordinating structures was the norm rather than the exception. Most women in the trade-union movement were urbanised factory workers in the garment industry, and they were organised under the male-dominated Trade Union Council of South Africa (TUCSA) and the South African Congress of Trade Unions (SACTU).

It would thus appear that the nature of women's oppression and the constraints such oppression placed on them in Congress politics was similar to the position of women within BC organisations. Joseph's account of the role of women within the Congress movement also indicates an ambivalence between accepting women as equals, and falling back on the need to maintain traditional roles for men and women.

Walker's review of the same era is more critical than Joseph's. For example, the debate about the proposed women's march on Pretoria in protest against passes in 1956, although couched in terms of concern for the safety of the women, given the repressive system they were up against, also had sexist undertones (Walker, 1982). There were strong sentiments that women could not possibly succeed where men had failed. Hooper's account of rural resistance to the imposition of passes on women in the late 1950s, also points to the fear men had for the consequences of women being arrested (1989). Men feared they would be left to tackle domestic chores, including taking care of babies, which they were uncomfortable to be seen

doing. There was genuine fear that the women would not survive the brutality of the police and other officials enforcing passes; and there may have
been some fear of women succeeding where males had failed.

The determination of the women in their anti-pass campaign was encapsulated in the slogan: 'Strijdom, now that you have touched women, you
have struck a rock!' This determination was rewarded by greater respect
and acknowledgment of the important role of FEDSAW within the
Congress movement.

The same pattern of gender dynamics seems to be evident in current liberation politics. Men dominate in leadership ranks, both in general political
organisations and in the trade-union movement. Women workers, like
their counterparts in the fifties, face sexism at the workplace from both
employers and male colleagues. For example, at the 1989 COSATU annual
conference there was significant resistance from men to discussion of sexist
practices within the trade-union movement itself. Sexual harassment
within trade unions was the main bone of contention (see July 1989 conference report in WIP, No. 59). These continuities in gender dynamics thus
beg the question: What accounts for the pattern of gender relationships
within the liberation movement in South Africa, and in what ways can
change be brought about?

Issues for Transformation

Most contemporary analysts agree about the need to address the multiple
oppressions suffered by women. The problem seems to be one of according
primacy to one form of oppression over others, which thus affects the
prioritisation of strategies (see Qunta, 1987; Joseph, 1986; *Umtapo Focus*,
11/1987).

The same debate has taken place in liberation movements elsewhere, past
and present. In Algeria, women were asked to waive their demands for
freedom from sexism in the interest of national liberation, on the promise
that their demands would be attended to afterwards. Those women are still
waiting (Seager & Olson, 1986). In Guinea-Bissau, Cabral insisted on an
integrated approach to power relations (Cabral, 1973), but met with resistance from other men within the movement. It is thus not surprising that
after his assassination, some retrogression occurred in this regard (Urdang,
1979). The current position of women in Zimbabwe (Weiss, 1986), Mozambique (Urdang, 1989), and in many other African countries bears witness to
an overwhelming tendency to perpetuate sexism in the post-liberation
period.

Resistance to addressing the issue of the subordination of women is not
confined to Africa. Irish women also face similar predicaments within the
IRA (Ward, 1983). So, too, black American women in the civil rights movement in the 1960s and 1970s found themselves torn by the dilemma posed
by the debate about the primacy of race over gender. Some argued, and still
argue, that there is greater solidarity between black women and men, than

between black women and white women in the feminist movement (Davis, 1981). Others felt, and still feel, that racism articulates with sexism, with detrimental effects on black women in particular, and that both forms of oppression should be addressed vigorously by the feminist movement (Ruether, 1983).

Marxists have also attempted to privilege class as the primary differential in society (see Davis's critique of Marx, 1981:11, and the conflicting views of women in Sargent's review (1981), *The Unhappy Marriage Between Marxism and Feminism*). Analyses of socialist countries do not support the view that sexism is a creation of capitalism, or that it is specifically enhanced by capitalism in contrast to socialism (Woolf, 1957; Randall, 1981).

I would like to suggest that various differentials of power need to be seen as an integral whole. They articulate one with the other in ways that constrain people's lives. Analyses of women's lives in South Africa show how race, class and gender form a mesh around both men and women, and constrain their capacity for transformative action (see Ramphele & Boonzaier, 1988; Ramphele, 1989). Some analysts contend that one form of oppression acts as a paradigm for other forms (Brittan & Maynard, 1984), and that those who are oppressed in one way are likely to replicate unequal power relations among themselves. This argument contrasts with the romantic view which suggests that the oppressed are necessarily endowed with goodwill, if only they could be given freedom.

Sexism in the private sphere also limits women's chances of developing the capacity to participate meaningfully in the political process. Many women lack the power of rhetoric essential for public debate, and lack the self-confidence which comes with practical experience, and thus are given to self-deprecation. This becomes a vicious circle. I am not suggesting that women are hapless victims of patriarchy. On the contrary, I argue in another context that all human beings are active agents of history and thus play a part actively or passively to shape history (Ramphele, 1990).

Men are also scarred by sexism. The macho image that men have to maintain comes at a cost to themselves and to others around them. The need for 'brotherhood' submerges the instinct of the individual in personal and social relationships (see also O'Brien, 1981; Ruether, 1983). The pressures on men to conform to expectations of a patriarchal society have in some cases driven men to family murders and other violent crimes.

Moreover, the unwillingness to discuss sexuality within society in general poses a major problem for the transformation of gender relationships. How can one be expected to exercise the right to control one's body and to choose whom to relate to sexually if sexuality remains a taboo subject?

Finally, there is the issue of 'political sexuality', which concerns the public image of political leaders generated by the conduct of their personal relationships. The message of caring about the liberation of the oppressed is often devalued by the lack of respect some leaders display in their family relationships or in the conduct of their other personal relationships. The saying that the personal is political has relevance in this matter.

Successful transformation of gender relationships will need more than just a theoretical understanding of the problem. It requires courage and the determination to take risks, because there is no possibility of growth without pain. Both men and women will have to confront their own fears of exchanging the known for the unknown, and put tradition at risk before a new pattern of gender relations can emerge.

True transformation in South Africa cannot come about without serious attention to the issue of gender. Central to transformation, I would suggest, ought to be an understanding of power as defined by Giddens (1983, 1984) and Barnes (1988). They argue against the 'zero-sum' notion of power, which posits that power is vested in someone to the extent that it is not vested in someone else. The zero-sum notion of power prevents men from seeing the benefits of relating to women who are free to make choices. Power is inherent in all of us, but it is the capacity to exercise it which is constrained by external forces. These constraints limit the choices that individuals can make regarding their lives.

There is evidence that the liberation movement in the 1990s is more sensitive and responsive to the demands for women's rights and the need to weed out sexism. The rhetoric of most political organisations has shifted significantly away from sexism in both language usage and conceptualisation. It remains to be seen whether such non-sexist rhetoric will be translated into concrete programmes to redress the inequities of the past.

It remains a serious concern that few women from any political organisation feature in the current negotiation process. The muted voice of women has serious implications for their equality in the future South African society.

A government committed to transformation would benefit from the active participation of all the citizens of the country. Such participation can only be fully realised where all people have the space to make informed choices in their lives. Men and women, young and old, rich and poor, black and white, all have a contribution to make to the new South Africa. They need the freedom to choose without the constraints of race, class *and* gender differentials.

14

Black Consciousness and
the Liberal Tradition: Then and Now
GEOFF BUDLENDER

For white people opposed to apartheid, the emergence of Black Coscious-ness was a painful and bewildering development. For years, a major part of their work and efforts had been directed towards challenging the separatist aspects of apartheid. For years, they had argued that it was the common humanity of South Africans, rather than their differences, which was most important. For years, they had asserted that their sympathies lay with black rather than with white South Africans.

Now Black Consciousness emerged. Black people – their putative allies in a shared struggle to defeat apartheid – took up an explicitly separatist posi-tion. These black people said that the differences were of great importance after all. Black people told them that white people remained white people, and that a shared political struggle was not possible.

It is no exaggeration to say that the psychological impact was devas-tating. The feeling of rejection was painful and profound. Part of the pain was caused by the fact that so much of the Black Consciousness rhetoric and argument seemed to be aimed directly at white liberals, rather than at government supporters. The discomfort was aggravated when government propagandists, fondly believing that their racism was now being vindi-cated by a racism articulated by black people, triumphantly said: 'We told you so.'

The purpose of this chapter is to examine the varying white responses to the resultant feelings of bewilderment and rejection. In order to do this, it is necessary first to look again at the main critiques of the liberal tradition.

The *political* critique attacks the notion that because the ideal is a shared society, shared organisations and methods of struggle are the only ways to achieve it. In the context of the 1960s and 1970s, the inevitable consequence of supposedly shared organisations was white domination. This was partic-ularly vivid in student politics, as the history of NUSAS demonstrates, but it was not limited to student politics: the same pattern was evident, for example, in those premier institutions of liberalism, the South African Insti-tute of Race Relations and the Liberal Party. To say this is not to attribute moral blameworthiness to those involved, whether black or white: it is

merely to point to an objective reality. The result was that those organisations inevitably had a white-dominated agenda and method of operation,
however sensitive they might try to be to black demands: black demands
were mediated through white eyes and mouths.

The traditional liberal view was reluctant to acknowledge that because
power relations in South Africa were essentially group relations, group
mobilisation might be necessary in order to counteract existing power relations. It could not deal with the proposition that, in Biko's words, 'The thesis is in fact a strong white racism and, therefore, the antithesis to this must,
ipso facto, be a strong solidarity amongst the blacks on whom this racism
seeks to prey. Out of these two situations we can therefore hope to reach
some kind of balance – a true humanity where power politics will have no
place' (Biko, 1978:90).

The apparent impotence and ineffectiveness of liberalism was repeatedly
highlighted by Black Consciousness leaders. Liberals not only exercised no
political power: they also did not appear to have any strategy for gaining
power. Indeed, power was not really part of their vocabulary. Power is
always a problem for liberals, for liberalism is fundamentally a philosophy
about the limitation and regulation of political power, rather than an analysis of means of attaining political power. In the words of Charles Simkins,
'liberal proposals about the regulation of power might have considerable
merit, but liberals occupy no significant place in the power constellation
and therefore cannot see to the realization of these proposals' (Simkins,
1986:5).

South African liberalism had increasingly found protest as its major
political mode of expression. On the campuses this was symbolised by
annual days of affirmation of academic freedom, which took on a ritual
character. While protest effectively claimed the moral high ground, it was
patently ineffective as a challenge to political power structures.

This impatience with the impotence of protest was not restricted to black
students. On the NUSAS campuses, too, white students were dissatisfied.
The massive students protests of 1968 and 1969 and their 'total failure to
achieve any success resulted in a period of massive disillusion among the
left in NUSAS' (Van der Merwe & Welsh, 1972:114). I come back to this
point later.

The *psychological* and *cultural* critique pointed out that when white people
proposed integration as the ideal, what was really proposed was assimilation: black people should adopt white (liberal) values and attitudes: 'The
concept of integration, whose virtues are often extolled in white liberal
circles, is full of unquestioned assumptions that embrace white values... It
is an integration in which the black man will have to prove himself in terms
of those values before meriting acceptance and ultimate assimilation...'
(Biko, 1978:91).

It is beyond the scope of this chapter (and indeed beyond my own ability) to explore in any depth the nature of the 'white values' in question.
Only one (I think uncontroversial) aspect need be mentioned: classical

liberal values are premised on individualism, with liberal principles stressing the value and protection of individual rights, whereas traditional black values are much more communally orientated.[1] And one other point might be added here: the assumption is always that any 'non-racial' debate and organisation will take place on white linguistic terms, in that it will be conducted in the language in which whites find themselves most comfortable.[2]

The *economic* critique is that liberalism is the philosophical underpinning of capitalism – and in the South African context, in the words of Simkins, that 'liberalism is a first-line defence of a capitalist system marked by great inequality' (Simkins, 1986:4). Whatever the validity of the more general critique, there can be little doubt that in South Africa, it has been mainly the relatively wealthy who have actively promoted the ideology of liberalism. The critique is therefore that those who propagate liberalism do not want any fundamental change in an exploitative system. All they want, it is argued, is a free market which is not distorted by the irrationalities of racism, and a more or less equal opportunity for all to become exploiters. On this subject the early proponents of Black Consciousness had relatively little to say. What was said tended to be fairly vague, with references to black communalism.

Finally, one should also remember the *personal* critique of the white students. The fundamental attack was on white political and economic power. White students were the sons and daughters of the holders of power, and the beneficiaries of that power. How, it was asked, could it be seriously suggested that they should play a major role in challenging that power – and how could they work together with the objects of that power? There was a great deal of cynicism about the good faith of the white students. Black students pointed out that most of the white students, having completed their rebellious university days, fitted very neatly into white society on graduation.

White Liberal Responses

White liberal responses to Black Consciousness were of course varied. In this account I concentrate particularly on the responses in student circles, where the critique was most sharply expressed and where I had most of my personal experience.[3]

1 It is worthy of note that the key elements of the traditional liberal philosophy are well articulated in the classic 'first generation' (political) human rights, as opposed to the 'second generation' (social and economic) human rights.
2 The story is told that at one NUSAS meeting there was a heated debate about Black Consciousness. One after another, white students made eloquent speeches arguing the need to fight racism through non-racial organisations on a basis of full equality and sharing, and denying that this took place on white terms. It is said that Steve Biko then stood up, made a speech in Xhosa, and sat down to silence around him. The story is probably apocryphal, but it is certainly telling.
3 There were, of course, also black liberals: liberalism is not and was not a 'white' philosophy or ideology. In this chapter I do not deal with the response of black liberals, whose position was very different. Many of them would have supported at

A widespread initial response was denial. At the 1969 NUSAS Congress, the Freedom in Society Commission reported that blacks and whites enjoyed different degrees of freedom; that the issues of immediate concern to blacks were different from those which were of concern to whites; and that in the past, because whites dominated NUSAS, the issues on which NUSAS acted were white issues, which were unreal or not immediate to blacks. Despite this, however, recognition of SASO – a black organisation proposing to work on these immediate black concerns – was rejected on the grounds that SASO was racist (Curtis, 1971:3). It is worth remembering that at this stage SASO still accepted 'the principle that in any one country at any time a national union must be open to all students in that country, and in our country NUSAS is the national union and SASO accepts her as such and offers no competition in that direction' (Biko, 1978:5).

For some people, denial remained dominant. Even today, you will find white student leaders of that period who persist in the attitude that SASO was racist and should have been rejected by NUSAS. Others found a more skilful method of denial: if the critique was of liberalism, the obvious response was to deny that one was a liberal. And so new labels abounded: some called themselves radicals; others said that they were liberal radicals. The writer 'A.P.' (presumably Alan Paton) gently satirised this in *Reality* (which from November 1972 called itself a journal of liberal *and radical* opinion) as follows (January 1973):

> Sometimes I was a glad lib
> Sometimes I was a sad lib
> No more I'll be a bad lib
> For now I am a rad lib.
> I never was a mad rad
> I would have made a bad rad
> Although I hate the glib rad
> Myself am now a lib rad.

None of this, however, was terribly convincing to anyone. For a start, the values propagated by those denying their liberalism remained, for the most part, liberal values. Even those who could genuinely be called radicals, adopting methods of class analysis which were just beginning to take root in the universities, retained fundamentally liberal values. And in any event, changing one's name did not resolve any of the practical problems raised by the challenge of SASO and Black Consciousness.

NUSAS was in crisis. Black students, the putative allies, had walked out. On its own campuses, 'a new radicalism began to emerge, anti-organisation, anti-establishment' (Van der Merwe & Welsh, 1972:113). The emergence of SASO, which fundamentally challenged a basic premise of NUSAS

---

least some of the Black Consciousness criticisms of the liberal tradition. It is beyond the scope of this chapter (and my own ability) to attempt to unravel the implications of this, which really go to the question of the meaning of liberalism.

– building a unified and inclusive student organisation – was a critical catalyst in what was to follow.

Against this background, a major reassessment of NUSAS took place, over a period of a year. There had been conflict in NUSAS over the political role of the organisation: was the major political concern of NUSAS to be with issues which concerned 'students as such', or was it to be with issues which concerned 'students in society'? Now NUSAS finally resolved this dispute: a clause was inserted in the new constitution, stating that it was the primary responsibility of students to work for change in South Africa.

The reassessment was more far-reaching than this, however. It led to an ideological shift and structural changes, and a more action-oriented approach was adopted. In the words of Curtis and Keegan:

> Reassessment lessened the rigidity of the liberal ideology and returned it to a broad directional statement, more realistic and more radical; and it reintroduced the tolerance of the realization that many different goals could be right for different people in different circumstances... [There was] a diversification of structure which allowed for specific work in different areas – cultural, educational and social action – by establishing different affiliated organisations within NUSAS's boundaries... At the same time ended the dichotomy of adhering to principle in a ritual and symbolic fashion, and placed the value on *working for the realization of the ideal*. This shift from talk to action is fundamental, as is the shift from seeing oneself as an instrument of change, to seeing oneself as being instrumental to change generated from elsewhere (Van der Merwe & Welsh, 1972:119-120).

The reassessment was to a significant extent triggered by the challenge of the emergence of SASO. By 1970, NUSAS Congress had recognised that SASO was the body best able to represent the interests of black students, and resolved that the role of NUSAS was to be 'supportive of black initiative'. And by 1971 the NUSAS Congress (having noted 'the emergence and growth of SASO over the past two years') had instructed its Executive to involve itself on black campuses only where this was requested by SASO or the centre or individuals concerned, and to give and receive information.

However, these formulae did not resolve the crisis of identity. What precisely was NUSAS to do? How should white students respond to the trenchant critique of liberalism? And what did it mean to be 'supportive of black initiative'?

The state, inevitably, misunderstood what followed. A few years later, four NUSAS leaders and a sympathetic academic were prosecuted under the Suppression of Communism Act for conspiring to further the aims of communism or the ANC or both. One of the acts alleged against them was that in furtherance of this conspiracy, they held a (white) student seminar for 'advocating, advising, defending or encouraging "Black Consciousness" as a means of change towards achieving black domination in South African society and Government'. They were also alleged to have 'actively worked towards the organising and/or the "building up" of black masses', *inter alia* by 'presenting to the black population that they are the oppressed and that the whites are the oppressors' – news which must have come as a great shock to millions of happy black people.

The reality is that at a directly political level, no satisfactory answer was reached. White students had been told to go and work in their own community. But what did this mean? If it meant that they should enter parliamentary politics, this was an uninviting prospect. Parliamentary politics was quite obviously structured in such a way as to perpetuate white power. It certainly did not seem a likely place to start offering radical critiques of white power and privilege.

Some argued for a new 'white consciousness' in response to the challenge to whites to liberate themselves (see Nettleton, 1972). But it all seemed very abstract and intangible: it was difficult to know what this meant in terms of practical programmes and activities.

The result was that many of those who were most challenged by Black Consciousness, and who were most persuaded by the force of this critique, found themselves without a directly political home. The option for most was either to drop out of political engagement or to find indirect methods of engagement which were consistent with the lessons they had learned. Some of these were to be found within the new structure which had emerged from the NUSAS reassessment.

A small but significant number chose to engage the system at the point at which Black Consciousness was weakest, both ideologically and organisationally. The process is well described by Steven Friedman:

> Their rejection wounded many white student activists and forced them to rethink their role. They accepted many of the black students' charges, but refused to watch the battle for change from the sidelines... Their background prevented them from leading the fight, but, they began to argue, it also gave them tools which could help it along: in particular, it gave them knowledge and skills which they could share with blacks and so help them to organise for change ... they saw African workers as the black group which could most use their skills. This view gained most ground in Durban, where a small group of politically aware students were deeply influenced by a political scientist, Richard Turner. It was he who first prodded students to take an interest in worker issues: they formed a Wages and Economics Commission to stimulate student involvement in labour and, in 1971, persuaded NUSAS to set up similar bodies on all its campuses.
>
> At first, the students researched African wages, gave evidence to the Wage Board – which ignored them – and exhorted employers to pay the poverty datum line... But they soon began to look for ways of backing these moral appeals with worker muscle. Again, Durban took the lead. Bolton (a union organiser) contacted Turner, who suggested that she offer Wages Commission students jobs in registered unions,

so giving them a base from which to organise Africans – she agreed and a new alliance was formed which did much to revive worker organisation.

The students brought to the union movement an energy and enthusiasm it had not seen for years: in return, Bolton offered them her experience, access to workers and registered union resources (1987:42).

White students and workers set up advice offices and benefit funds in Durban, Cape Town and Johannesburg. These grew at a tremendous rate. From them emerged fully fledged and powerful trade unions. These unions were a major part of the core of what in time became FOSATU and eventually COSATU.

Cause and effect are always difficult to define: certainly, few people other than the then Minister of Labour can have believed that NUSAS and the Wages Commissions were responsible for the massive strikes which swept Durban during 1973 – and his level of knowledge and expertise did not lend much authority to the claim. But there can be little doubt that the white students who moved into this area of work had a very substantial impact. Many of them were amongst the most able and dedicated of the student political leadership. There can also be little doubt that the lessons they had learned from the Black Consciousness Movement contributed significantly to their ability to do the work effectively – in particular, the lesson of the need to work *with* rather than *for* people.

A similar process can be observed in other areas. Many of the students took a similar approach into their work when they left the universities – whether as journalists, lawyers, academics, doctors or community workers. The idea that whites had skills to offer and could play a supportive role to black-led organisations, became widely accepted as a model for engagement. It would be simplistic and invalid to attribute this solely to the impact of the Black Consciousness Movement on white students. At the end of the day, one can only speak for oneself – and even at an individual level, how can one untangle all the many factors which influence one's development? Having said that, however, I should also say that the psychological impact of Black Consciousness, particularly on the white, English-speaking student generation of the early 1970s, was so great that it is inconceivable that it did not play a significant role in what followed.

Development in the political field had to wait for some time. In the second half of the 1970s, NUSAS ran campaigns aimed at white students around the theme of Africanisation, stressing the African (as opposed to European) future of South Africa. This was a period of rapidly growing political resistance in South Africa. NUSAS leaders tried to relate student activities to black-led campaigns, and increasingly participated in them. These included, in 1980, a campaign for the release of Nelson Mandela and other political prisoners, as part of the commemoration of the twenty-fifth year of the Freedom Charter; and in 1981, a campaign with COSAS and

AZASO against the celebration of Republic Day.

The nature of these campaigns tells part of the story of the changing political context in South Africa. Similar campaigns – against the celebration of Republic Day and for the release of political prisoners – had been run in 1971. The 1971 campaigns were dominated and largely led by NUSAS. At that time, there was little visible political resistance in the country. Indeed, the major co-contributor to the anti-Republic Day campaign was the (Coloured) Labour Party! By 1981, the growing resistance in South Africa meant that these were black-led campaigns in which NUSAS participated.

Each generation of students has to interpret its own history and to re-interpret the history of its predecessors. The new generation suggested that the invitations to participate in these shared political campaigns were the result of the changes NUSAS had undergone since 1976 (see *South African Outlook*, November 1984:166). The reality, I think, is different. What had happened was that viable black political leadership had re-emerged. Trade unions, civic associations, women's organisations, and student and youth organisations mushroomed and flourished. There was a new self-confidence afoot. White students were no threat to this: there was not the remotest possibility that in this new context the whites would again be able to take over and speak 'for' black South Africans, or that they would dominate the agenda. And so (having proved their bona fides) they could be invited to participate, as a minor but welcome ally. The truth is, therefore, that this shared political activity was not the result of changes in NUSAS: it was the result of changes in black political activity.

A new relationship now developed between NUSAS and the black student organisations, COSAS and AZASO. This trend was most publicly demonstrated when in 1981, the AZASO president addressed the NUSAS Congress. He was the first black student leader to participate in a NUSAS meeting since the NUSAS seminar of December 1970.

In 1983, the United Democratic Front was formed. NUSAS was one of the many organisations which affiliated at the inaugural conference. A former NUSAS president and member of the National Executive Committee of the UDF was explicit as to what this meant: 'The UDF tells all students in general, and white students in particular, that theirs is a role of support for, not leadership of, the mass-based people's organisation' (Boraine, 1985:171). The resonance is strong. He also referred, however, to the continued existence of a residual suspicion in some quarters: 'Critics of UDF have often condemned the participation of NUSAS. Fears are expressed that NUSAS could "dominate" the other organisations in UDF and that the organisations of the people would be led by "white liberals".' There is another strong resonance.

In the new student generation's rewriting of history, the long-term impact and significance of Black Consciousness do not seem to receive due recognition. For example, the November 1984 issue of the *South African Outlook*, written mainly by students to mark the sixtieth anniversary of the establishment of NUSAS, largely treats the Black Consciousness Movement as an issue of the 1970s and does not reflect on the lasting impact which it has had. This is now a student of the early 1970s rewriting the history of the late 1980s.

It is unsurprising that the changed political context has altered perceptions of the issue. In addition, there are now very significant numbers of black students at the 'open' universities, which must inevitably lead to alliances and shared political activities. The impact of the changed political context on student politics has been most dramatically affirmed since the amalgamation of SANSCO and NUSAS in 1991. The changed political context is further symbolised by Nelson Mandela's repeated calls to white South Africans to join hands with black South Africans.

Does this suggest that Black Consciousness is played out as a significant political factor in South Africa? In order to assess the current implications for whites opposed to apartheid, it may be helpful to turn back to the three critiques referred to in the first section of this chapter.

The *political* critique pointed to the inevitability of white domination of shared organisations. This can surely no longer be the case, at least as far as mass-based organisations are concerned. There are certainly very significant political tendencies and organisations other than the ANC in South Africa, but it can surely not be denied that the ANC represents a majority viewpoint. I do not think anyone could seriously argue that by opening its membership to all, the ANC has taken any real risk that it will be dominated by white people. However, that does not lay the issue to rest. It needs to be recognised that when they join any organisation, white people sometimes bring with them resources and skills (and habits of domination) which potentially give them a weight and influence out of proportion to their numbers. The remnants of white power remain intact, and all white people carry part of that legacy with them, both as a privilege and as a burden. It must be acknowledged that for good reason, suspicion and reserve have not disappeared. White people who engage politically without being aware of this, do so at great risk.

The *psychological* and *cultural* critique pointed to the dominant character of white culture, and the destruction and denigration (the word is deliberate) of black culture through generations of ideological, legal and economic attack (see Sachs, 1990:66). The changed political context does not automatically address this issue. Unless it is addressed, black South Africans will remain fundamentally disadvantaged and discriminated against: only those who can adapt successfully to the still dominant white culture will be able to succeed in the new, legally non-racial society. The result will be the impoverishment of all South Africans. A truly democratic South Africa will have to embrace the cultural values of all of its citizens.

The *economic* critique was that liberalism was the philosophical underpinning of capitalism and called only for more or less equal opportunity to exploit. As South Africa de-racialises, the significance of this critique is likely to increase. Conversely, the relevance of the colour of an exploitative employer or landowner will surely decrease. Paradoxically, therefore, as the significance of the economic critique of liberalism increases, so the relevance of Black Consciousness as an answer will surely diminish.

The *personal* critique challenged the good faith of the white liberals. That challenge remains valid today. Many students of the early 1970s responded by dropping out, thereby attempting to disengage themselves from the exploitative and oppressive white power structures. Today, the challenge is to find ways of opting *in*, in ways which make a constructive contribution to the building of a new society – and to do so not just during a few years at university, but on a long-term basis.

Conclusion

This has been a very personal account of the impact of Black Consciousness on the liberal tradition. For that I make no apology.

Today we stand on the threshold of a new society. It seems a paradox that although liberalism has been under sustained attack for an extended period, a good many of its fundamental precepts seem about to be realised. A genuinely non-racial society does seem to be a real, inevitable prospect. And almost all of the significant political actors are agreed that in the new society, the power of the state should be limited and basic human freedoms should be protected by a bill of rights. Perhaps the paradox is only apparent. As Albie Sachs has pointed out, it is those people who have been subjected to pass laws who will be most concerned to protect freedom of movement; it is those people who have been discriminated against in the past who will be most concerned to build a non-racial society. Perhaps this is not axiomatic, but it is surely an important legacy of the tradition of political struggle in South Africa. Perhaps it is therefore precisely the negative and destructive elements of the dying society which should give us the greatest hope for a new society that will be genuinely shared by all South Africans.

15

Black Consciousness:
A Reactionary Tendency?
NEVILLE ALEXANDER

An undying love for black people that denies the humanity of other people is doomed. It was an undying love of white people for each other which led them to deny the humanity of coloured people and stripped white people of humanity itself (Eldridge Cleaver, 'Open Letter to Stokely Carmichael', 1969).

Unlike us, our people are still hung up on this thing of believing that it's not the system but it's the white man who is oppressing them. It takes time and effort to teach people that it's not the white man but it is the system that oppresses them (Rafael Viera, Chief Medical Cadre of the Young Lords Organisation, 1970).

I was under house arrest when I wrote this piece in 1974. As a result, I had limited access to both people and documents. This was doubly the case since so many of the relevant people were themselves banned or restricted in some or other way. Many of the documents, such as *Black Review*, were banned or inaccessible so that I was dependent on a small circle of people who were in the Black Consciousness milieu, either as members of organisations or as sympathisers, for most of my first-hand information. Paucity of sources was without doubt an important reason for a narrowing of my personal perspective. The fact that what I was doing was 'illegal' at the time and the need to bear in mind that the articles would be published in a 'legal' journal also restricted the scope of my analysis. I have no doubt that my approach was coloured, although not unduly, by the fact that the series of articles was going to appear in a Unity Movement publication, since I could not but be aware of the myopic character of that tendency's opposition to the Black Consciousness Movement. However, in fairness to myself, I should stress that I did not write anything in which I did not actually believe at the time. In view of the sequel to this story (see below), it is important that this be stated quite clearly.

It should be noted that I have not made any changes to the content of the original paper in the interests of historical veracity. Some editing and vocabulary changes have been made here and there in order to make clear thoughts which in the idiom of today might not be immediately comprehensible. Otherwise, the original is reproduced warts and all, including incidentally the male chauvinist language which I continued to use unproblematically at the time.

In the original paper, of which this is approximately the second half, a lengthy analysis of the Black Consciousness Movement in the United States of America preceded the section that is reproduced here. The section that is omitted traced the genesis of BC in the USA in the context of the oscillation between 'inclusionism' and 'separatism' in the political movement of African-Americans since the emancipation of slaves. For the purposes of this book, I consider the treatment of the subject to be much too detailed and not directly relevant. What follows, then, is an edited version of the last section of the paper dealing with the developments in the USA and most of the second half of the original paper, dealing with what I considered to be the transplantation of the BC discourse to the soil of South Africa.

Were I to write a similar series today, I would definitely put less emphasis on the US influences on the genesis of BC in South Africa. Instead, I would emphasise much more the indigenous – especially Africanist and, paradoxically, Unity Movement – influences on the evolution of the ideology and the political practices of the BCM. This is something that became clearer to me only in later years as I met more of the people who actually structured the politics of the movement. Thus, for example, I discovered that some of the more famous ideas and passages in the writings of some of the BC publicists were drawn directly or indirectly from PAC, ANC and NEUM sources. Only very few of the more fashionable ideas ('Black is Beautiful') can be traced back to their US origins. I also think that there was much more clarity in leadership circles about the real nature of the Bantustans than I credit them with in this essay. I do not believe, however, that there was much more than the dawning of the need for a class analysis, despite claims to the contrary by many present-day BC propagandists.

Were I to write a *critique* of the Black Consciousness Movement in South Africa today, I would undoubtedly treat its origins quite differently. I have therefore drawn attention to what I consider to be the main shortcomings of the paper as it stands here. It might also be useful to restate my position on the question of the writing of contemporary history: we need to remember that Biko was murdered in 1977, barely 14 years ago, and that we are trying to situate him and the movement of which he was the most prominent member at the time, in the broad stream of South African history. This is an exceptionally difficult enterprise under the best of conditions, but in the South African context it is often a task that ought not even to be considered in view of all the constraints on research and scholarship. In the case of my paper, written before the 1976 uprising – before BC had manifested itself in this country as a mass phenomenon in the political arena – these constraints are even more crippling. It is, as I must stress again, a *contemporary* assessment of BC as it was happening, so to speak. However, the thrust of my critique of the concept of a 'black culture' would remain, although from a conceptual and methodological point of view, I would approach the matter very differently today. (I have dealt with these questions in some detail in my essays on education and culture. See, for example, *Sow the Wind, Language Policy and National Unity in South Africa/Azania,* and *Education and the Struggle for National Liberation in South Africa.*)

By way of concluding this short note, it is only necessary to add that my own political practice has demonstrated that over the years I have continued to respect the consistency and militancy of those activists in South Africa whose world-view is inspired by the philosophical and political points of departure of Black Consciousness. While I believe that the general direction of our contemporary critique of BC, as represented in the following essay, has stood the test of time, I am happy to confirm once again that the ideology and practices of BC were among the most creative phenomena of the 1970s, to which period this chapter relates.

Postscript. I had been asked by a friend[1] associated with the Teachers' League of South Africa to undertake research and to write the series of articles on the evolution of the Black Consciousness Movement in South Africa. I did this gladly, especially since there was a clear understanding between the two of us that no major editorial interventions would be undertaken without referring them back to me. This was important since I was under house arrest and the series would in any case appear under a pseudonym. It is with great regret, therefore, that I have to record that this trust was breached. The article was turned inside-out and upside-down in such a way that the sympathetic but nonetheless thorough and honest critique became a strident, name-calling indictment of the BCM. This transformation is best captured in what was done to the title of my piece. Whereas I had labelled it – as here – *Black Consciousness: A Reactionary Tendency?* with the unmistakable question mark at the end of the line, the article as published eventually left out the question mark and substituted a full stop for it! I need only add that I was so incensed by this that I had the original published in a *samizdat* version as a research essay allegedly read in a seminar at London University as a *critique* of 'my' articles in the Teachers' League journal! Such are the ways of a repressive society. We had numerous copies of this 'new' article sent to known BC activists throughout the country in the hope that the damage that might arise from the series in the *Educational Journal* would thereby be reduced to the minimum. I have no idea whether this ploy worked, but it is important that the story be told at least.

1 Because I do not wish to besmirch the name of a comrade and a fighter, who has in the meantime passed on and is, therefore, in no position to explain his version of what follows, I shall, contrary to my normal practice in a polemical situation, refrain from mentioning any names.

Black Consciousness in the USA

Inclusionists and Separatists

In my analysis of the evolution of Black Consciousness in the USA, two groups – the 'inclusionists' and the 'separatists' – are in fact articulating different aspects of the caste status of blacks taken as a whole. Rather than there being a contradiction between the two groups, the common aim is to remove the subordinate caste status of African-Americans *within* the framework of US society. There are three assumptions of inclusionist strategies. First, they assume that moral suasion is enough to bring about a change in what is termed the 'wrong' attitude of the governing classes towards black people. Secondly, they assume that racism can be eliminated from US society without a radical transformation of the polity and economy. Thirdly, they assume that it is vital to prevent a specifically black identity from emerging.

The 'separatists' have succeeded in getting beyond some of the illusions of inclusionists. In particular, many have realised that racism in the USA, as elsewhere, is an institutionalised aspect of the culture of present American society. Some of the more insightful theorists worked out, in cruel detail, the implications of this. Here the theories of Frantz Fanon have been especially important. This is the reason the separatists insist that blacks should organise themselves in every sphere as though they were an independent group, even at the risk of making many mistakes of a political and cultural nature. Indeed, the progressives among them have seen it as the major task of leadership to isolate these mistakes and to steer the movement as a whole away from them.

The separatists deny that US society is a basically healthy social order from which the local disease of racism must be extruded. They realise that radical socio-political and economic change is essential if the racist attitudes of Americans are to be transformed and humanity is to assert itself. Blacks must organise themselves as a group to accumulate sufficient power with which to bargain their way into the body politic. Some, indeed, believe that blacks must *force* their way into the body politic. In their book on Black Power, Carmichael and Hamilton are of the opinion that it 'presents a political framework and an ideology which represents the last reasonable opportunity for this society to work out its racial problems short of prolonged destructive guerilla warfare' (1967:vi). That such violent warfare may be unavoidable is not herein denied.

While all Black Consciousness tendencies agree that some measure of 'separatism' has become a political necessity, most of them are equally clear that the restructuring of the social order should be such that colour will become really irrelevant. The goal (in particular, that of the Black Panther Party) is to mobilise the most oppressed and exploited group and link it up with oppressed groups interested in the transformation of the society and ethos. They are not opposed to 'coalition politics' with progressive white or non-racial organisations, seeing such coalitions as the guarantee that the movement will not be sidetracked into the swamps of black racialism. They insist, however, that until the slave mentality has been eradicated blacks must organise as blacks.

It is clear, therefore, that the separatists are not opting out of American society, but there is an important difference between them and the inclusionists. The separatists see black people taking their place in the new order as an organised body, an 'ethnic minority', whereas the inclusionists conceive of the absorption of blacks as individuals by the larger body. This is a peculiarly American question. If the economic restructuring of the USA eventually eliminates the base of all ethnic thinking and the exploitation of it for private gain, it may well be possible to suppress the instinctive shudder caused by talk of a 'black ethnic group'. Although one may question the dialectics of some of them – as I do – one cannot deny them a startlingly penetrating historical gaze. If the movement can at all stages recognise and avoid the dangers of communalism and the bloody, futile strife that it occasions, Black Consciousness, in association with long-term, relevant strategies, represents for the people of the USA a viable political tactic. Because of the class character of the black people of the USA, their struggle – unless control of it is captured by the reactionary tendencies – must inevitably merge with the attempts of all those forces that are intent on disestablishment. In the course of these struggles, that which is not genuine will be weeded out by polemics and because it has not taken real root among the people.

Only if the struggle of the black people of the USA merges into the general struggle against the oligarchic order in that country, which also controls the rest of the 'Free World', can that struggle make a positive contribution to humanity. If the present crop of leaders is bought off by the powerful and all-pervasive oligarchy to become satellite 'capitalists' or the apologists for these, the Black Consciousness Movement will become another conformist attempt: it will become a consumerist movement, providing the ideological basis of firms catering for 'Afro-styles'. It will give the appearance of militant opposition while in reality constituting a necessary and even a vital aspect of the Establishment.

Négritude as a Phenomenon of Black Consciousness

'Black' Culture. A 'black' culture, either as a fact or as an aspiration, is non-existent and incapable of existing. Fanon has analysed acutely this problem of what he calls the 'racialisation of culture' (1968:206-248). Once it is clear that there can be no 'culture' outside the limits of the nation, it follows that there can be no such thing as an 'African culture', much less a 'black culture'. Black intellectuals throughout the world have tended to react to the domination by European ruling classes and the concomitant degradation of their respective heritages by wishing to transcend boundaries of nationality. In fact, this is an impossible dream. The products of every artist are willy-nilly stamped with the imprint of his nation because his own personality is moulded in a particular national context. In short, a

'black culture' is a blind alley. It leads into the cul-de-sac called 'exhibition-ism' because it is perpetually concerned to demonstrate to 'white' people that there is such a thing as a 'black culture'. Perhaps the most poignant demonstration of this thesis is the historical fact that the African Cultural Society (founded in the USA in 1956), from its inception, almost served to negate African-American intellectuals' dreams of cultural homogeneity between themselves and Africans.

> Négritude therefore finds its first limitation in the phenomena which take account of the formation of the historical character of men. Negro and African-Negro culture broke up into different entities because the men who wished to incarnate these cultures realized that every cul-ture is first and foremost national, and that the problems which kept Richard Wright or Langston Hughes on the alert were fundamentally different from those which might confront Leopold Senghor or Jomo Kenyatta (Fanon, 1968:216).

Humanism. Humanism, defined in terms of subverting exploitation and facilitating cooperation (with all its implications for the emotional and psychic dimensions of life), is the sole ideological criterion of art. A critic who merely condemns a work of art because its author happens to sub-scribe to a certain political ideology has not begun to understand his critical task. This task is to indicate whether and how the artist has through his vision of reality compelled others to see the reality afresh, with a new per-spective, one which draws people together as human beings rather than as instruments. It should be clear, then, that the objections of aspirant whites to a cultural product which emphasises that 'Black is Beautiful' (without implying that anything else is not beautiful merely because of chromatic differences) are mischievous and misleading. Any cultural product that enhances humanity by weakening the perpetuation of the system which enables men to exploit others, is beautiful. Anything, whether black, blue or red, which does the opposite or tends to do so, is ugly. The Black Con-sciousness Movement has undoubtedly made important cultural contribu-tions in the USA.

In the same way as the progressive women's movement has compelled the re-examination of attitudes and vocabulary – themselves the deposit of ruling-class conventions – so the Black Consciousness Movement has forced people to change their terminology (though probably the majority have not concomitantly changed their attitudes!).

Exoticism. We must not be repelled or even overly amused by the harm-less exoticism that the Black Consciousness Movement has spawned on the cultural level. Needless to say, those features which are not so harmless have to be subjected to rigorous criticism and condemnation where neces-sary. The critic ought to guide the artist by criticising his false perception and showing him its origins. Moreover, the critics must criticise the critics.

Any static conception of culture leads to ritual, repetitive hocus-pocus. Anyone who has read Fanon's work on the embarrassing illusions harboured by native colonial intellectuals about the value of recreating the past instead of interpreting the present, developing reality and illuminating the future struggles of the nation, cannot doubt that this is the model of constructive culture criticism: 'In an underdeveloped country during the period of struggle, traditions are fundamentally unstable and are shot through by centrifugal tendencies. This is why the intellectual runs the risk of being out of date. The people who have carried on the struggle are more and more impervious to demagogy; and those who wish to follow them reveal themselves as nothing more than common opportunists, in other words, latecomers' (Fanon, 1968:224).

The leaders of the Black Panther Party and others condemn 'cultural nationalism' as mystifying, obscurantist, and profitable to individuals who have accumulated wealth. They are careful, however, not to tar all and sundry with the same brush. One has perforce to refer to Fanon again: 'The passion with which native intellectuals defend the existence of their national culture may be a source of amazement; but those who condemn this exaggerated passion are strangely apt to forget that their own psyche and their own selves are conveniently sheltered behind a French or German culture which has given full proof of its existence and which is uncontested' (1968:209).

In matters of culture the serious critic does not state that a work of art, for instance, must be like this or like that; he insists only that it shall not facilitate dehumanisation and that it must be art, not something else.

Assessment

It should not be too difficult to understand why it is that the contradictory phenomenon of 'Black Consciousness' in the USA has given rise to so much soul-searching and so many agonising reappraisals; why the American oligarchy – especially its so-called Liberal wing – has done everything in its power to bring the whole of this movement under its sway. In this it has succeeded in a large number of cases and, as a result, the Black Consciousness Movement itself has been polarised. There is a clear division between progressives and reactionaries: people like Cleaver and Davis represent a totally different direction from others such as Carmichael, and are the deadly enemies of the 'Black Caucus'. They have developed far beyond their original premises. But there is a question mark over the future of what they represent. For unless they join forces with all other groups striving to restructure the social order in the USA, unless their self-chosen catalytic role materialises soon, the very weight of inertia will submerge them, and their tendency too will pass into history. They certainly are aware that the victory of what they call Black Consciousness depends on its disappearance and its replacement by a consciousness which transcends caste to include all those who are enslaved by the wage system.

Black Consciousness in South Africa

Black Consciousness was inserted into a particular soil. It must either die because of lack of nurture or adapt itself to the environment through certain necessary mutations if it is to enrich the liberation movement. Superficially, South African society consists of two colour castes – namely, a superordinate white and subordinate black caste. The latter is subdivided further through the unequal castes of Coloureds and Indians and the lowest, most oppressed caste of Africans. The white sector is itself divided along lines of language between Afrikaners and English-speaking. At a deeper level there is the class division between the white employers and the white workers. We can safely disregard the intermediate class divisions for our present purposes. The oppressed black majority consists overwhelmingly of the class of urban and rural workers and a significant percentage of landless peasants (commonly called 'migrant workers') who perforce earn their means of subsistence in the capitalist sector. (The true peasantry in South Africa is an extremely small group of people, though this should not cause us to misunderstand the importance of the land question in the struggle for liberty.)

A self-perpetuating mechanism of colour-caste oppression was evolved in order to keep the labour of the blacks exploitable. By reserving most skilled, supervisory, and well-remunerated employment for workers of European descent, while all the unskilled and semi-skilled work was allotted to the blacks, economic competition and the white labour aristocracy's fear of being displaced were created and perpetuated. Racism and racial thinking became the life-blood of this system at the ideological level. As long as this caste barrier could be maintained for so long, a low standard of living for black people could be justified and the wage bill of the employing class could be pegged at a relatively constant percentage of the value of the national product.

Except for a small class of merchants (located mainly in the Indian sector), there was no class of employers among the blacks, and only very few blacks actually exploited the labour of others. However, there were those who aspired to do this as the result of their absorbing the ethos and the values of the system of private accumulation of wealth. These people, together with the traditionalistic, backward-looking group of chiefs, formed the social base from which came initially that leadership which was prepared to collaborate with the rulers in ensuring the smooth functioning of the system described above.

These are the basic reasons why caste consciousness (misnamed 'racial consciousness') has hitherto always superseded class consciousness, why black and white workers (and even African, Coloured and Indian workers) in South Africa have not been able to forge the unity which workers in other parts of the world have used so effectively to create a new society. It is also clear, on the other hand, that the system of racial oppression is umbilically linked to the system of property relations in this country and that, therefore, the consistent prosecution of the struggle against the former must needs put the latter in jeopardy. It should also be clear that any attempt to unite the oppressed castes is, in essence, an attempt to forge an alliance between the most exploited workers and the landless peasants. And this is the real reason why the unity of the oppressed is anathema to the rulers, whatever party they belong to. But this is also the reason why it has been all-important to understand that the nation-to-be-born in this country cannot exclude any section of the people. All ruling parties have hitherto systematically aborted the birth of the nation of South Africa in the interest of perpetuating the system of super-profits based on the exploitation of cheap black labour. And this is why the basic assumptions of the Black Consciousness Movement about the nature and the dynamics of South African society represent a retrogression.

Growth and Acceptance of BC

There is no need to discuss the formal importation of Black Consciousness from the United States into South Africa. Its gestation in the University Christian Movement and in NUSAS is well known. More important to understand are the following factors:

1. The ideas of Black Consciousness were first advocated by students of the oppressed at the 'tribal' university colleges. They were attracted to these ideas because they seemed to hold the promise of a dignity which these institutions had until then by definition been incapable of imparting to the students. They also believed that the ideas of Black Consciousness could negate the arbitrary attempt to retribalise the oppressed communities and cut off the struggle of the oppressed from the liberal leadership under which it had once again come as the result of the decapitation of the liberatory movement in the early 1960s.

2. None of the students concerned saw, at the beginning, that an uncritical acceptance of the ideas of Black Consciousness could mean the blunting of the tools of political analysis and action which had been forged and sharpened in decades of bitter and desperate struggle. The transplantation of the Black Consciousness Movement to South Africa represented a decided retrogression from the point where politically conscious people well understood the inevitability of caste solidarity in the South African context, while nonetheless laying bare in their analysis (and in the action which flowed from this) the real sources of political and historical motion in this country.

3. The Moeranes[2] and their ilk helped to father the movement, thus limiting it *ab ovo* within the confines of reformist politics well suited to the present period of 'dialogue' and 'détente'. If, as I shall show, Black Consciousness has in certain respects and in certain instances been forced beyond these limits, this has occurred because of the dynamics of the present situa-

2 M. T. Moerane was editor of the *World* and president of ASSECA (the Association for the Educational and Cultural Advancement of the African People).

tion in southern Africa and not because of a clear-sighted strategy on the part of its leadership.

We need not dispute the fact that the Black Consciousness Movement in South Africa has made a considerable, if temporary, impact on black students and, to a lesser extent, on the urban youth in certain cities. It has been able to impinge episodically on the day-to-day struggles of black workers in certain parts of the country. There are several reasons for this relative success of the tendency. Firstly, the political vacuum created by the cataclysm of the early sixties made it possible for any group which was apparently opposed to the colour bar and which demanded full citizenship rights, to assume a musculature for which it lacked the appropriate skeleton. Because the Black Consciousness Movement stressed at the outset that it intended to work outside the institutional framework of the Bantustans, it appealed to the dormant consciousness of an intimidated people.

Secondly, from the very beginning the more discerning liberals (read 'Imperialists') at home tried to inspan the Black Consciousness Movement in their family quarrel with the National Party and the Broederbond. One of the unfailing regularities of South African history in the twentieth century has been the depressing sight of incipient protest movements being dissipated by the fact that their 'leaders', instead of waging a consistent struggle against the colour bar and the sources of racial oppression and exploitation, tie such movements to the apron-strings of liberals. Some of the most heroic struggles of the oppressed and some of their most upright leaders have been prostituted in this way.

Thirdly, the National Party attempted at the beginning to harness the Black Consciousness Movement to the oxwagon of separate, multinational development. It felt entitled to do so on both formal and historical grounds. Superficially – if one ignored certain non-tribal and anti-tribal flourishes and extravagances – the exponents of Black Consciousness were saying the same thing as the ruling party was saying. Historically, these very exponents had been incubated in the broiler-houses of apartheid education. Vorster's grand strategy for southern Africa consists of the attempt to create a class of satellite black capitalists ruling over client 'nation-states' and exploiting, as junior partners to southern African and foreign imperialist capital, the landless peasantry and the ghettoised black workers of the country. If, therefore, his stooge-chiefs could place themselves at the head of this movement, it could well serve to persuade the recalcitrant urban oppressed to make their peace with the system, which they had been taught to reject and to abhor for more than a quarter-century. Tyrants have ever mistaken power for the understanding of the driving forces of history. The Broederbond failed to understand that the apparent erasure of the liberatory movement did not mean that they had before them a clean sheet. The direction in which the consciousness of the oppressed majority had tended to develop was not to be deflected so easily.

Against the background of what I have said about Black Consciousness in the USA, I want to stress the following points.

1. The liberation struggle in South Africa has not failed. Despite heavy blows it has grown to such an extent that only the most obtuse collaborators today speak as though the slave mentality is still with us. By 1960 the role of the liberals had been so thoroughly exposed for what it was that they had desperately to seek any possible forces in the liberation movement that they could use. Changes in the calibre and determination of the politically conscious and active youth have occurred, changes which have forced the liberals themselves to use the language of the liberation movement if they wish to be heard. The 'evolution' of the programme of the defunct Liberal Party is perhaps the best evidence of this point.

2. A 'Black Consciousness' – in the sense of the assertion of the right to equality of opportunity on grounds of a common humanity and of one developing world civilisation – has long existed in South Africa. Indeed, I make bold to say that, with the exception of those trained by Liberalism, the black intelligentsia of South Africa had for decades been in the lead in Africa as far as this is concerned.[3] The progressive wing of the national liberation movement had for decades stressed to the oppressed that they are not inherently inferior, that they have a history of struggle and of achievement of which any people can be proud, that they and they alone can lift all the people of this country higher into the mainstream of world civilisation; in short, that they must rid themselves of the slave mentality. This ethos was never enunciated in terms of a 'Black Consciousness' for the simple reason – as the epigraph from Cleaver's Open Letter to Carmichael indicates – that they believe, on the basis of the historical experience of people throughout the world, that any exclusivism is self-devouring and reactionary in the final analysis. The classic exposition of this point of view is B. M. Kies's *The Contribution of Non-European Peoples to World Civilisation*, in which he shows clearly the dignity of all men irrespective of colour and trenchantly negates the Herrenvolk myth.

3. In South African politics, there is no pluralist, ethnic-group tradition. The oppressed as a whole have for most of this century been cast out of the body politic. There has, therefore, never been any system of bargaining and negotiating as between 'ethnic groups'. Oppression has been total and absolute in principle. What there has been, what there still is, is a clear dividing line between collaboration and non-collaboration. Opportunists, interested in private gain, prestige, status and vicarious power, have at all times been found to collaborate in the running of the oppressive system, and it has been the hallmark of the liberation struggle in South Africa that its progress could be measured by the degree of participation of the oppressed in the instruments of their own oppression, by whether they followed the collaborators or the non-collaborators.

4. For economic reasons the rulers now find it necessary to broaden the

---

3 See historical works such as *The Role of the Missionaries in Conquest* by Nosipho Majeke, *300 Years, A History of South Africa* by 'Mnguni', *Background to Segregation* by W. P. van Schoor, and *Time Longer than Rope* by Edward Roux.

base of the state by allowing black entrepreneurs a negligible slice of the national profits. There is a systematic attempt to create a class of capitalists, even though these men and women will remain junior to the real controllers and owners of wealth in South Africa. Hence, in accordance with the logic of the accumulation of wealth, these entrepreneurs and their political mouthpieces in 'homeland' and other 'tribal' councils have come to see themselves as centres of actual and potential economic and political power. They imagine themselves as bargaining with the whites eventually for a greater say in the running of the state. And, whether intentionally or not, even if they actually criticise these men – the Buthelezis, Matanzimas, Motsuenyanes – the exponents of Black Consciousness who have imported this philosophy without considering the contradictions in South African society or, for that matter, in the USA, are doing yeoman service to the very men they abuse so vociferously. For it follows that by spreading undisguised anti-white ideas and failing to stress that black faces can exploit and oppress, by supporting 'Buy Black' campaigns organised for private gain, they are actually creating the climate in which these tendencies can thrive; they are enlarging the captive ghetto market for people who have no interest in any real unity of the oppressed. This is the 'cunning of reason', the dialectic of history whereby the naive, well-meant intentions of honest people are turned into their opposite if they are implemented in a practical context conducive to the materialisation of that opposite.

Those exponents of Black Consciousness who, it is clear, have become aware of the complexity and the contradictions inherent in our society and who genuinely want to prevent their tendency from becoming the means whereby oppression and exploitation will be perpetuated under new names, certainly do not intend to create a communalist set-up in South Africa. The rulers, however, with different yet converging strategies, have created the material and legislative base for such a situation. So that the oppressed can, in the absence of a clear vision of who their friends are, easily be led into the abyss once they are made to believe that black is beautiful, even if it is out of personal gain.

5. Self-help and other community projects for their own sake are basically reformist conceptions. They merely beautify the ghetto and become thus an essential part of the established order of racial oppression and exploitation. Like trade unions, ratepayers' associations, and other civic bodies which try to alleviate in the short term the misery of life for the oppressed, they can only be meaningful if they become the vehicles whereby the political understanding of the people can be raised and their readiness to act for the attainment of their political rights can be stimulated and maintained. It is therefore short-sighted in the extreme to think of such projects merely as a demonstration of the ability of the black people to organise themselves in spite of the depressing conditions of their environment or as a means of deceiving themselves that they are really independent of the 'white man'. It is certainly easy for relatively comfortable authors of articles such as this to say that we do not want 'more beautiful Sowetos' or 'happier Hanover

Parks' and so forth. And they should be reminded of this fact. But I say nonetheless that if the matter ends there, then we do not want these things because we want to eradicate the ghetto and the ghetto mentality just as we want to eradicate suburbia and its mentality.

6. Franchise rights are not going to be bargained for in South Africa. The people will eventually take what is their right. Pressure tactics based on implicit threats in the normal course of political action can only lead to an accommodation between the 'leaders' (representing the interests of those among the oppressed who want more, not really equal, rights) and the rulers. There is great danger that the Black Consciousness Movement, or important tendencies in it, could become the national organ for such a strategy. The resilience of the liberation movement and the deeply rooted tradition of principled struggle, which has influenced many of the protagonists of Black Consciousness themselves, have hitherto prevented especially the younger section from running blindly into these traps.

Balance Sheet

I now wish to draw up the balance sheet of Black Consciousness in South Africa in a spirit of frankness and without implying that the people who genuinely think that in Black Consciousness the oppressed have found a 'final solution' are incapable of viewing their own beliefs and actions in historical perspective. My aim is to stimulate discussion on a matter which is of great importance to the youth in particular so that nobody may say that there was no opportunity to reflect on the possible errors of his or her actions.

The Black Consciousness Movement correctly stresses the unity of the oppressed people of South Africa. In this it is following and furthering the most vital strand in the tradition of struggle here. It is wrong in so far as it projects the need for unity as arising from the fact of blackness. Of course, the people who are oppressed are identifiable in the majority of cases by the criterion of colour because the rulers use this historical accident, as I pointed out. But unity arises from the fact that oppression is common to all who are oppressed. It is designed to eradicate the belief that, for instance, those classified 'Bantu' are oppressed whereas those classified 'white', 'Coloured' or 'Indian' are not. And so forth.

The Black Consciousness Movement correctly rejects the Bantustan strategy. It is not consistent in this precisely because it cherishes unwarranted illusions about the 'virtues' of blackness. The very idea of wanting to dignify the 'bush colleges' (or ethnic universities) by transforming them into 'black campuses' betrays a complete lack of understanding of what a university is supposed to be. Let us not delude ourselves about the fact that the so-called white campuses are just as much bush colleges today. There must be no soft-pedalling on this score. In pursuit of this attempt to dignify sectarian institutions of education the students, inspired by SASO teachings, called for a black rector at the University College of the Western Cape. But none of them seems to have realised that in doing so they were accepting the idea of working the administrative apparatus of apartheid. There is no difference at all between administering a 'Coloured University' and administering a 'Coloured Persons Representative Council'. Thanks to Professor R. van der Ross, the 'black rector' of UWC, the students now understand this point. The Black Consciousness Movement has to draw a clear line in theory and in practice between itself and the Bantustan strategy. It can only do so if it casts off all illusions about some innate, mystical and virtuous quality attached to the fact of 'being black'. Otherwise it serves in the capacity of opinion-maker, preparing the soil for the Bantustan reapers.

The Black Consciousness Movement correctly rejects the 'system'. But what is the 'system'? Some think of it simply as the plethora of apartheid signs and institutions. They will end up with the Progressive Party eventually. Only if the movement's analysis penetrates to the socio-economic roots of the apartheid structures – as I have indicated all too briefly above – can it hope to play a positive, unambiguous role in furthering the struggle for liberty. The war on 'whitey', even if defined theoretically in terms of Herrenvolkism, will reintroduce the cancer of racist thinking into the liberatory movement.

I repeat, it is not the 'white' man, it is the system that oppresses us. If it is predominantly white-skinned people who are defending the system against predominantly black-skinned people, they do so not because they are fair-complexioned but because they are the privileged captives of this system. After all, black-skinned people like Matanzima defend the system for the same reason even though, slaves that they are, they enjoy only the privilege of exploiting to a certain degree other black-skinned people.

The Black Consciousness Movement correctly rejects 'white liberals'. But it is mistaken in so far as it believes that all liberals are white. We have recently acquired a whole litter of black liberals in 'Democratic' and in 'Labour' parties, in 'Inkatha' and in other 'opposition' parties. Liberalism knows no colour and it is futile to argue – as some will do – that even a 'black' liberal is in reality 'white'. Liberalism is a greater danger in the long run to the struggle of the oppressed than Fascism, for the very reason that it seems to speak with the tongue of the people. Yet there are grave doubts in my mind about the candidness of many exponents of Black Consciousness in this regard. It is an open secret that there are close links between the liberals and the Black Consciousness Movement in South Africa. I need not spell out the details. Only if these links are severed will Black Consciousness become an independent movement, a refuge of the oppressed.

The Black Consciousness Movement correctly upholds the dignity and the inalienable right to equality of opportunity of black people, but they are wrong to assert this dignity and this right on the grounds that these people are black. Blacks have these rights because they are people, a link in the great chain of humanity. Those authors who do so are treacherous when they try to denigrate the contributions of Europe (or of 'white' people) to world civilisation in the belief that they thereby enhance the contributions of blacks.

A movement, in educating and dignifying an oppressed people, will readily and unambiguously condemn what is anti-human in any cultural tradition, be it located among black people or among whites. It will not distort history in order to arrive at a so-called black truth. There is no need – even though it is the easiest thing in the world, as the history of Fascism proves – to racialise culture in order to make a people feel confident in its future or to give it a sense of mission. The oppressed are bearers of culture and of historic development because they alone can ultimately defend those truths which may shatter society as constituted at present.

The oppressed have an historic mission not because they are black but precisely because they are oppressed and have, therefore, a vital interest in the restructuring of a society which is rotten to the core. 'White' soldiers in the USA and in Portugal realised after decades of delusion that their governing classes misled them to believe that the structure of society in Indochina and in Africa was vital to their own future. And they threw in their lot with the oppressed colonial peoples. It was not whites who were defeated in Vietnam, in Guinea-Bissau, Mozambique, Angola; it was Imperialism. And it was defeated through the joint efforts of black people and white people.

By all means, let us encourage cultural creativity among the oppressed – in art, drama, poetry, dancing, in every sphere. But let us not think that artistic works inspired by an anti-humanist philosophy can ever produce great work. Only where the common humanity of all – like a pair of spectacles on a child – rectifies the racist squint, can art begin to live. There are no sacred canons of art, but let us accept that there is one great developing tradition in all spheres of culture and that nations through cross-fertilisation bring forth new products and forms that in turn enrich the rest of mankind. Let us 'conscientise' by all means, but let us not create the kind of illusions which ultimately may lead to that social schizophrenia that throws the patient back into the depths of depression worse than the one out of which he or she was hypnotised. Liberation *is* a psychological process but it is not only that.

Three things are urgently required: the militant youth in the Black Consciousness Movement should reflect on the nature and the origins of the ideas and the movement they espouse; they should consider their movement in the context of the *whole* history of struggle in South Africa; and they must open a real, meaningful debate with the rest of the tradition of the struggle and in order that the movement itself can find a proper place for them.

I have tried in this chapter to sketch what I consider to be the correct approach to the solution of this problem. If such a debate – based on non-antagonistic contradictions among the people – were to ensue, the effort involved in rethinking my own position and trying to understand the genuine agony of our youth would have been well worthwhile, and the result can only serve the determination to prosecute the struggle for the liberation of the oppressed and the emancipation of all.

PART FIVE

16

The Legacy of Steve Biko*
N. BARNEY PITYANA

Bantu Stephen Biko was part of a movement that, after a long and dispirit-
ing hiatus, took effective charge of the people's struggle in the 1970s, thereby opening the way to higher stages of resistance. The irony about this
book is that it may serve to elevate someone who would be most embarrassed by that, for he would not want to be seen outside the context of that
struggle alongside the people. Biko was no saint. He would not wish to be
considered as set apart from the people. If hero he was, then it was not by
his ambition but by force of circumstance whose only virtue was that he
willed the people to stand up and to bring an end to the rule of the oppressor. Biko can only be understood as a martyr – a witness to the will and
inner resolve of so many of our people to give everything to bring about
justice and liberation. It was necessary to animate them with the values of
humanity so that they become more spirit-filled and godlike.

Biko built his political system on spiritual foundations. For him 'spiritual'
owes less to Plato and the rationalist movement than to Tillich and the existential school; spiritual is not being discrete but concrete, holistic, bringing
the fullness of humanity to bear on the material and objective world. If
blacks were to resist oppression and thereby assert their human dignity –
in Biko's words, when speaking of the black man, 'pump back life into his
empty shell; to infuse him with pride and dignity' – then Black Consciousness was unquestionably a liberation ideology, 'for we cannot be conscious
of ourselves and yet remain in bondage'. In his celebrated essay, 'Black
Consciousness and the Quest for True Humanity', he spells out what this
commitment to liberation must mean: 'Freedom is the ability to define oneself with one's possibilities held back not by power of other people ... but
only by one's relationship to God'. 'Consciousness' must not be understood
as a rarefied abstraction but as a concrete materialism that leads people by
their full participation from bondage to liberation. People 'can become
agents of qualitative change', writes Rudolf J. Siebert. 'They can put their

* Adapted from a memorial sermon given on 13 September 1987 in the Nottinghill
Methodist Church.

whole existential weight passionately into each world-changing deed for which time is ripe. They can truly change the face of the earth.'

What, then, is the legacy of Steve Biko and Black Consciousness? Understandably its greatest or deepest manifestation has been best expressed in those hidden and unquantifiable virtues that make people human. It infused blacks with a spiritual fibre, a mettle and a fighting spirit. It is the inner soul-force seen to be invincible and without which we could never withstand the psychological onslaught that apartheid so ruthlessly inflicted upon us. The oppressed people of South Africa have shown that they are not vanquished people; they are struggling and fighting people. Witness, for example, the mineworkers: those who are marginalised and maintain a precarious existence far from their own families and other support systems; who are weak and vulnerable as against the powerful mine bosses; who have no law to defend them and can only look to the support and solidarity of their union to defend their interests. With odds stacked against them they have taken militant action, and today the stature and esteem of the workers and their union have never been higher. Tested to the limit there is a way in which even people placed in impossible situations can act in defence of their rights.

It is my considered opinion that Biko would have found the prevailing mood of discord among black people most unfortunate. Black Consciousness prides itself on its capacity to bring people into active participation in struggle regardless of their ideological positions. To do so requires sensitivity and an overriding commitment to the absolutes of liberation to the extent that strategically we could appreciate our need of allies. In Black Consciousness, the struggle could be lifted above the particularities of the moment or of organisations or personalities. It is not without significance that Black Consciousness was again and again defined as 'a way of life; an attitude of mind'. It is the fibre or material that we take with us into battle. The danger, indeed the obscenity, can be seen in the extent to which the system has been able to drive wedges through the forces of change. It is still our task to discover our unity in struggle. It is not for nothing that Biko was detained on his way back from a risky mission that sought to bring together elements that had become entrenched in ideological divisions in the Western Cape. It is now common knowledge as well that he was anxious to bring Black Consciousness as a catalyst of unity by initiating dialogue with the African National Congress, the Pan-Africanist Congress, the Unity Movement and other defined political movements.

Black Consciousness has made sure that black South Africa is never without its own leadership. During Biko's time many black people were trained and had experience of leadership, planning, strategising and mobilising, and yet drew closer to the broad masses of people in their suffering and pain and frustrations. Arguably, one can hardly find a notable leader in South Africa today who was in his or her twenties in the early 1970s, who has not been through the Black Consciousness mill, whether in church, the trade-union movement, progressive professional organisations and other community associations: people like Cyril Ramaphosa, Patrick Lekota, Frank Chikane, Zwelakhe Sisulu, to name only a few. One must not underestimate the psychological value of this. When Black Consciousness emerged, leadership had become remote and ideas seemed to owe more to the guilty conscience of the white liberal establishment than to the concrete experience of the oppressed people themselves. Prior to that there had been leadership of a more traditional, one-man, individualistic kind. Biko spread the net so that leadership could come from many sources.

Personally, Biko held high for our people the hope in human values and the triumph of the human spirit; he encouraged us not only to rise above our limitations but so that through his life and death we would never collude in our own suffering. It is very rare that one lives prophetically what one teaches. He did. 'You are either alive and proud or you are dead; and when you are dead, you can't care anyway. And your method of death can itself be a politicising thing. So you die in riots... So if you can overcome the personal fear of death, which is a highly irrational thing, you know then you are on your way.' Dying, as he lived, he thereby expressed to many young blacks a fearlessness that helped change the face of the country. It is that youth who confronted the might of the apartheid forces and often died, who took up arms or used their own bare hands in the townships, whom Biko's legacy now challenges and addresses. What is the new consciousness of the 1990s, now that one particular aspect of the struggle has begun to be overcome?

Bibliography

Interviews conducted by Lindy Wilson

NA	Neville Alexander (Hogsback, 1991)	TM	Thenjiwe Mtintso (Harare, 1990)
MB	'Mamcete' Biko (Ginsberg, 1989)	BP	N. Barney Pityana (Geneva, 1989)
NB	Nobandile Biko (Mdantsane, 1990)	DP	Dimza Pityana (Geneva, 1989)
NtB	'Ntsiki' Biko (Ginsberg, 1990)	MR	Mamphela Ramphele (Cape Town
NC	Neville Curtis (Harare, 1990)		1989)
MG	Mafika Gwala (Lodon, 1989)	DR	David Russell (Grahamstown,
AH	Anne Hope (Cape Town, 1991)		1990)
BK	Bennie A. Khoapa (Roma, 1990)	MWS	Mongane Wally Serote (Harare,
ML	Mandla Langa (London, 1989)		1990)
BM	Bokwe Mafuna (Paris, 1989)	AS	Aelred Stubbs (Sunderland, 1989)
MM	Malusi Mpumlwana (Grahams-	FW	Francis Wilson (Cape Town, 1991)
	town, 1990)		

Gail Gerhart (GG) interviewed Steve Biko (SB) in 1972 and Neville Curtis in 1990
Aelred Stubbs (AS) interviewed Barney Pityana in 1978

Books, Articles, Theses and Papers

Abrahams, L. 1980. The Purple Rhenoster: An Adolescence. *English in Africa*, 7, 2

Adam, H. 1973. The Rise of Black Consciousness in South Africa. *Race*, 15, 2

Arnold, M. (ed.) 1978. *Black Consciousness in South Africa/Steve Biko*. New York: Random House

Barnes, B. 1988. *The Nature of Power*. Urbana & Chicago: University of Illinois Press

Biko, S. 1969. SASO: Its Role, Its Significance and Its Future. Address to the First National Formation School. Mimeo

Biko, S. 1970. Letter Addressed to SRC Presidents, National Students' Organisations, Other Organisations, Overseas Organisations. Issued by SASO

Biko, S. 1971. Understanding SASO. Paper presented to a SASO formation school held at Edendale. Mimeo

Biko, S. 1971a. White Racism and Black Consciousness. Paper presented at a symposium sponsored by the Abe Bailey Institute for Inter-Racial Studies, Cape Town, January 1971. Mimeo

Biko, S. 1977. Definition of Black Consciousness. Paper presented at a SASO leadership training seminar, Edendale, December 1977. Mimeo

Biko, S. 1978. *I Write What I Like*, ed. A. Stubbs. London: Bowerdean Press

Biko, S. 1979. *I Write What I Like*, ed. A. Stubbs. London: Heinemann

Biko, S. 1986. *I Write What I Like*, ed. A. Stubbs. San Francisco: Harper & Row

Biko, S. 1988. *I Write What I Like*, ed. A. Stubbs. Harmondsworth: Penguin

Boraine, A. 1984. NUSAS and the UDF: Some Implications. *South African Outlook*, November 1984

Boston Women's Collective. 1984. *Our Bodies by Ourselves*. New York: Simon and Schuster

Bouchier, D. 1977. Radical Ideologies and the Sociology of Knowledge. *Sociology*, 11, 1

Brittan, A. and M. Maynard. 1984. *Sexism, Racism and Oppression*. Oxford: Basil Blackwell

Cabral, A. 1973. *Return to the Source: Selected Speeches*. New York: Monthly Review Press

Carmichael, S. and C. Hamilton. 1967. *Black Power: The Politics of Liberation in America*. New York: Vintage Books

Carson, C. 1981. *In Struggle: SNCC and the Black Awakening of the 1960s*. Cambridge, Mass.: Harvard University Press

Chambers, R. 1983. *Rural Development: Putting the Last First*. New York: Longman Inc.

Couve, C. 1984. The Psychologist and Black Consciousness in South Africa: The Work of N. C. Manganyi. Paper presented at a Centre for African Studies seminar, University of Cape Town

Cruse, H. 1962. Revolutionary Nationalism and the Afro-American. *Studies on the Left*, 2, 3

Curtis, N. 1971. Position Paper on Student Action. Mimeo

Damana, S. 1984. Rendering Welfare and Development Services with Special Reference to Grahamstown. Carnegie Conference Paper no. 40. Cape Town: SALDRU

Davis, A. 1981. *Women, Race and Class*. London: Women's Press

De Gruchy, J. W.. 1979. *The Church Struggle in South Africa*. Grand Rapids: Eerdmans

Degenaar, J. 1990. The Concept of Violence. In *Political Violence and the Struggle in South Africa*, ed. C. Manganyi and A. du Toit. Johannesburg: Southern Books

Dictionary of Christian Ethics, ed. J. Macquarrie. 1967. London: SCM

Dictionary of Medical Ethics, ed. A. S. Duncan, Dunstan and Welbourn. 1977. London: Darton, Longman & Todd

Driver, D. 1990. Women, Black Consciousness and the Discovery of Self. Unpublished paper.

Erikson, E. H. 1968. *Identity: Youth and Crisis*. London: Faber and Faber

Fanon, F. 1968. *The Wretched of the Earth*. New York: Grove Press; and Harmondsworth: Penguin

Farisani, T. S. 1987. *Diary from a South African Prison*. Philadelphia: Fortress Press

Farisani, T. S. 1988. *Justice in my Tears*. New Jersey: Africa World Press.

Fatton, R. 1986. *Black Consciousness in South Africa*. New York: State University of New York

Finnis, J. 1980. *Natural Law and Human Rights*. Oxford: Clarendon Press

Fiori, G. 1990. *Antonio Gramsci: Life of a Revolutionary*. London: Verso

Foster, D., D. Davis and D. Sandler. 1987. *Detention and Torture in South Africa*. Cape Town: David Philip.

Fredrickson, G. M. 1990. The Making of Mandela. *New York Review of Books*, 27 September

Freire, P. 1970. *Cultural Action for Freedom*. Harmondsworth: Penguin

Freire, P. 1972. *Pedagogy of the Oppressed*. Harmondsworth: Penguin

Freire, P. 1978. *Pedagogy in Process: The Letters to Guinea-Bissau*. New York: Seabury Press

Gendzier, I. 1985. *Managing Political Change*. Boulder: Westview Press

Gerhart, G. 1979. *Black Power in South Africa: The Evolution of an Ideology*. Berkeley: The University of California Press

Gerwel, G. J. 1975. Coloured Nationalism. In *Church and Nationalism*, ed. T. Sundermeier. Johannesburg: Ravan Press

Giddens, A. 1982. *Profiles and Gritiques in Social Theory*. Berkeley: The University of California Press

Giddens, A. 1983. *The Nation-State and Violence*. London: Hutchinson

Giddens, A. 1984. *The Constitution of Society*. Cambridge: Polity Press

Gordimer, N. 1968. Towards a Desk Drawer Literature. *Classic*, 2, 4

Gordimer, N. 1973. New Black Poetry in South Africa. In *The Black Interpreters: Notes on African Writing*. Johannesburg: SPROCAS – Ravan

Haigh, H. D. Record of a Conversation with B. S. Biko, 13 January 1977

Halisi, C. R. D. 1990. Intellectual and Black Political Thought in South Africa. Paper presented at a South African Research Program seminar, Yale University

Harding, V. 1983. *There Is a River*. New York: Vintage Books

Heller, M. and A. Nekrich. 1988. *Utopia in Power*. New York: Summit Books

Herbstein, D. 1978. *White Man, We Want to Talk to You*. London: Deutsch

Hirsch, A. 1981. *The French New Left: An Intellectual History from Sartre to Gorz*. Boston: South End Press

Hodge, N. (ed.) 1984. *To Kill a Man's Pride*. Johannesburg: Ravan Press

Hooper, C. 1989. *Brief Authority*. Cape Town: David Philip

Hope, A., S. Timmel and Hodzi. 1987. *Transformation Work Books 1, 2, 3*. Gweru: Mambo Press

Howard, R. and K. E. Klare. *The Unknown Dimension: European Marxism since Lenin*. New York: Basic Books

Hyden, G. 1980. *Beyond Ujamaa in Tanzania*. Berkeley: The University of California Press

Hyden, G. 1983. *No Short-Cuts to Progress*. Berkeley: The University of California Press

Jones, S. 1990. Assaulting Childhood. Unpublished M.A. thesis, University of Cape Town

Joseph, H. 1986. *Side by Side*. London: Zed Books

Kavanagh, R. M. (ed.) 1981. *South African People's Plays*. London: Heinemann

Kimble, J. 1982. 'We Opened the Road for You. You Must Go Forward'. ANC Women's Struggles, 1912—1982. Mimeo

Kuper, L. 1965. *An African Bourgeoisie: Race, Class and Politics in South Africa*. New Haven: Yale University Press

Lodge, T. 1983. *Black Politics in South Africa since 1945*. Johannesburg: Ravan Press

Mannheim, K. 1974. What is a Social Generation? In *Conflict of Generations in Modern History*, ed. A. Esler. Lexington: D. C. Heath

Marx, A. W. Forthcoming. *Lessons of Struggle: South African Internal Opposition*. New York: Oxford University Press

MASA. n.d. *Consequences of the Death in Custody of Mr S. B. Biko: Involvement of the Medical Association of South Africa*. Johannesburg: MASA

Miles, R. 1989. *Racism*. London: Routledge

Mitchell, B. 1970. *Law, Morality and Religion in a Secular Society*. Oxford: OUP

Morley, D. 1983. *Practising Health for All*. Oxford: Medical Publications

Motlhabi, M. 1984. *Black Resistance to Apartheid*. Johannesburg: Skotaville

Mutloatse, M. (ed.) 1981. *Reconstruction. 90 Years of Black Historical Literature*. Johannesburg: Skotaville

NELM. 1987. From Imbongi to Worker Poet. *NELM News 11*. Grahamstown: NELM

Nettleton, C. 1972. The White Problem. In *White Liberation*, ed. H. Kleinschmidt. Johannesburg: SPROCAS

Nolutshungu, S. 1982. *Changing South Africa*. Cape Town: David Philip

O'Brien, M. 1981. *African Women: Their Struggle for Economic Independence*. Johannesburg: Ravan Press

O'Donnell, G. and P.C. Schmitter. 1986. *Transition from Authoritarian Rule*. Baltimore: Johns Hopkins University Press

Pityana, N. B. 1979. Afro-American Influences on the Black Consciousness Movement. Paper delivered at a conference sponsored by the African Studies Center, Howard University, Washington D.C.

Platzky, L. and C. Walker. 1987. *The Surplus People: Forced Removals in South Africa*. Johannesburg: Ravan Press

Popper, K. 1959. *The Logic of Scientific Discovery*. London: Hutchinson

Qunta, C. 1987. *Women in Southern Africa*. Johannesburg: Skotaville

Ramphele, M. and E. Boonzaier. 1988. The Position of African Women. In *South African Keywords*, ed. E. Boonzaier and J. Sharp. Cape Town: David Philip

Ramphele, M. 1989. The Dynamics of Gender Politics in the Migrant Labour Hostels of Cape Town. *Journal of Southern African Studies*, 15, 3

Ramphele M. 1990. Participatory Research: Myths and Realities. *Social Dynamics*, 16, 2

Ramphele, M. 1991. The Politics of Space: Life in the Migrant Labour Hostels of the Western Cape. Unpublished Ph.D. thesis, UCT

Randall, M. 1981. *Women in Cuba Twenty-five Years Later.* New York: Smyrna Press

Reason, P. and J. Rowan. 1981. *Human Inquiry.* London: John Wiley

Rive, R. 1980. Interview with Bernth Lindfors. *Geneva Africa: Journal of the Swiss Society of African Studies*, 18, 2

Roger, S. 1981. Women's Space in a Man's House: The British House of Commons. In *Women and Space: Ground Rules and Social Maps*, ed. S. Ardener. London: Croom Helm

Ruether, R. 1983. *Sexism and God-Talk. Towards a Feminist Theology.* Boston: Beacon Press

Russell, D. 1990. *Lives of Courage.* New York: Basic Books

Sachs, A. 1990. *Protecting Human Rights in a New South Africa.* Cape Town: OUP

Sargent, L. 1981. *The Unhappy Marriage of Marxism and Feminism.* London: Pluto Press

SASO. 1969. SASO Communiqué. Drawn up at SASO conference, Turfloop, July 1969

SASO. 1970. Report on the 1970 SASO Conference (Durban). Mimeo

Seager, J. and A. Olson. 1986. *Women in the World.* London: Pan Books

Seleoane, M. 1989. The Black Consciousness Movement. *South African Foundation Review*

Sepamla, S. 1977. Interview with Stephen Gray. *Contrast*, 11, 3

Serote, M. W. 1990. The Impact of Black Consciousness on Culture and Freedom. Paper delivered to Harare conference

Shils, E. 1969. Dreams of Plenitude, Nightmares of Scarcity. In *Student Revolt*, ed. S. M. Lipset and P. G. Altbach. Boston: Houghton Mifflin

Simkins, C. 1986. *Reconstructing South African Liberalism.* Johannesburg: SAIRR

Sklar, M. J. and J. Weinstein. 1966. Socialism and the New Left. *Studies on the Left*, 6, 2

Sole, K. 1979. Class, Continuity and Change in Black South African Literature. In *Labour, Townships and Protest*, ed. B. Bozzoli. Johannesburg: Ravan Press

Solzhenitsyn, Alexander. 1974. *The Gulag Archipelago.* London: Collins Fontana

Terreblanche, D. 1989. The South African Drama. From Union and High Hope in 1910 towards Disintegration and Despair in 1990? Paper presented to the annual meeting of the Social Welfare Association, Johannesburg

Thornton, R. and M. Ramphele. 1988. The Quest for Community. In *South African Keywords*, ed. E. Boonzaier and J. Sharp. Cape Town: David Philip

Turner, R. 1972. *The Eye of the Needle.* Johannesburg: Ravan Press

Turner, R. 1978. *The Eye of the Needle.* Maryknoll: Orbis Books

Turok, B. 1974. South Africa: The Search for a Strategy. In *The Socialist Register, 1973*, ed. R. Miliband and J. Saville. London: Merlin Press

Urdang, S. 1979. *Fighting Two Colonialisms: Women in Guinea-Bissau.* New York: Monthly Review Press

Urdang, S. 1989. *And Still They Dance.* New York: Monthly Review Press

Van der Merwe, H. W. and D. Welsh. 1972. *Student Perspectives on South Africa.* Cape Town: David Philip

Villa-Vicencio, C. 1983. An All-Pervading Heresy; Racism and the English-speaking Churches. In *Apartheid Is a Heresy*, ed. J. W. de Gruchy and C. Villa-Vicencio. Grand Rapids: Eerdmans

Walker, C. 1982. *Women and Resistance in South Africa.* London: Onyx Press

Ward, K. 1976. *The Divine Image.* London: SPCK

Ward, M. 1983. *Unmanageable Revolutionaries.* London: Pluto Press

Weiss, R. 1986. *The Women of Zimbabwe.* London: Kesho Publishers

Wilson, F. and M. Ramphele. 1987. *Children on the Front Line.* New York: UNICEF

Wilson, F. and M. Ramphele. 1989. *Uprooting Poverty: The South African Challenge.* London and New York: W. W. Norton; Cape Town: David Philip

Wilson, M. and L. Thompson. 1971. *The Oxford History of South Africa*, vol. II. Oxford: Clarendon Press

Wolfenstein, E. V. 1981. *The Victims of Democracy: Malcolm X and the Black Revolution*. Los Angeles: The University of California Press

Woods, D. 1978. *Biko*. New York: Paddington Press

Woods, D. 1979. *Biko*. New York: Vintage Books

Woods, D. 1980. *Asking for Trouble: Autobiography of a Banned Journalist*. London: Victor Gollancz

Woods, D. 1987. *Biko*. New York: Henry Holt

Woolf, V. 1957. *A Room of One's Own*. London: Harcourt Press

Index